ENDORSEMENTS

I just finished reading Alan DiDio's book *They Lied to You About Prosperity*. It is my joy to write an endorsement for this remarkable book that takes one of the most unique approaches to this subject that I have ever read. I find it to be perhaps the most comprehensive book I've ever read on this subject, and I am confident it will spark fresh thinking in you about this important Bible topic that dramatically affects all of our lives.

Many have written on the subject of biblical prosperity, but in this book, Alan undoes many unfounded teachings, even lies, that have been perpetuated over the ages about God's desire to prosper His people. Of course, the devil doesn't want God's people's minds to be renewed in this area, because if he can keep abundance out of their hands, it means they won't fund the Gospel. But God wants His people to be blessed and to use their financial resources for the funding of the worldwide proclamation of the Good News, the message of Jesus Christ.

But in addition to dealing with basic Bible principles of prosperity, Alan dives headlong into capitalism versus socialism. Having lived in the former Soviet Union for soon to be four decades, I can testify to the destruction that socialism produces in a society. Not only is it financially impossible to facilitate, but it steals dreams and the initiative that God has placed in the heart of every human being. Instead, God wants the ceiling of our thinking in terms of dreams, finances, and prosperity to be removed so we can flourish as His people.

Indeed, when God's people are financially secure, their families are secure; their children are fed, clothed, and educated; anxiety about survival subsides; they have more time to serve others; they give more generously; the work of churches and ministries is funded; the poor are fed and clothed and become living testimonies of God's goodness in their lives. When God's people prosper, it gives glory to God!

Some say money is evil, but Alan writes so well that the problem is not money but, rather, who controls it. When resources are in the hands of the wicked, they fund wickedness, exploitation, idolatry, perversion, and the advancement of darkness. But when those same resources are transferred into the hands of the righteous, they fund the Kingdom — evangelism, discipleship, mercy, justice, and the building of God's House.

My favorite part is Alan's writings on the principles of sowing and reaping, which I deem to be one of the most important spiritual laws, as it affects every single part of our lives on so many levels. I could go on and on about the value of this book, but instead of writing more, I encourage you to read through its pages, devour its contents, and ask the Holy Spirit to show you how to implement in your life what you've read.

God wants our minds to be renewed on this important subject — and for mind renewal to happen, we must submit our minds to what God has to say on this matter and then amend our thinking accordingly. Please know that God's will is far higher than any of us has imagined — this book will help you practically walk from where you are into the freedom He longs for you to possess!

Rick Renner
Minister, Author, Broadcaster
Moscow, Russia

Most believers I know carry quiet shame around the subject of money, not because they love it too much, but because the conversation has been so badly handled for so long that many have never actually heard what Scripture says. Bishop Alan DiDio addresses that gap with theological seriousness and pastoral courage, and the result is a book the

Church genuinely needs right now. This is not a book about getting rich. It is a book about getting free.

Mike Signorelli
Lead Pastor, V1 Church

My friend Alan DiDio is one of the leading teachers and expositors of the scripture in our generation. His books powerfully shed light on each subject he addresses. In *They Lied to You About Prosperity*, he has done it again, only now he is offering a spiritual intervention for the Church. This book unmasks the religious lie that poverty is piety while reclaiming God's blueprint for covenant abundance. A powerful revelation put forward by Alan—that "FISH COME FIRST"—is a divine strategy, brilliantly proving from Genesis to Pentecost that provision must precede revival. He lays out the strategic biblical pattern of financial breakthrough, which demolishes containment and sets believers free not only to rise into their spiritual destiny but ultimately to help ignite God's economic engine to advance the kingdom around the world.

This book is direct, uncompromising, and absolutely essential for anyone tired of being held back by financial stress. It doesn't just defend biblical prosperity; it defines it, equipping you to break agreement with the poverty mindset and begin stewarding the overflow God intended for you. It's time to stop apologizing for the blessing and start making "The LORD takes pleasure in the prosperity of his servant" your daily reality!

Alan, you nailed it with this one, my friend!

Joseph Z
Author, Broadcaster, Prophetic Voice
JosephZ.com

Prosperity is something I'm very familiar with because it changed my life at a young age. However, I have never read a book as rich and comprehensive on the subject as this one—and believe me, I've read many. This one stands out.

They Lied to You About Prosperity confronts the hard questions with boldness, clarity, and a deep commitment to Scripture. Alan has written a book that biblically proves God's will for prosperity while addressing the arguments that have kept many people believing lies about it for years. He clearly shows how history and culture have perverted this subject and created long-standing misconceptions.

This book will help anyone who has struggled to believe, as well as anyone who has ever doubted God's desire to prosper His children.

This is a timely and necessary message for every believer who wants to live fully in the promises of God and walk in the freedom Christ has already provided.

Ben Díaz
Author of *Radical Healing*
Senior pastor, Vida Church, Mesa, Arizona

In a time when attacking Biblical prosperity has become popularized, Alan DiDio boldly presents the balanced, Scriptural case for stewardship, generosity, and prosperity. Many well-meaning Christians today have been guilted into rejecting God's blessing upon their finances because of common misconceptions and virtuous-sounding deceptions. DiDio skillfully debunks the religious lies that have convinced far too many that biblical prosperity is at odds with the pure and simple gospel. This work exposes the overcorrections that the modern church has embraced and contributes to what will inevitably become a much-needed generational revelation of generosity and supernatural prosperity.

David Diga Hernandez
Evangelist & President, Encounter Church Network

I do not believe in the prosperity gospel! I believe in a gospel that has prosperity in it! This comprehensive study helps redefine this unlimited

God we serve that has unlimited resources, even in our marginal worldview. GOD WANTS HIS PEOPLE BLESSED!

Pastor Myles Rutherford
Worship with Wonders Church

Bishop DiDio exposes the logical fallacies, theological double standards, and cultural lies that have kept believers broke, missions underfunded, and the Great Commission crippled with precision and Holy Spirit fire.

This is a comprehensive, Scripture-saturated defense of God's heart toward his children's abundance, provision, and Kingdom wealth.

If you're tired of watching sincere believers struggle while critics weaponize twisted Scripture, this book will set you free.

Every pastor, leader, and believer who longs to see the Church fully resourced for the harvest must read this book. It's a divine reset and an invitation for believers to move into God's best.

Jason Avanzini

THEY LIED TO YOU ABOUT PROSPERITY

Destiny Image Books by Alan DiDio

Erasing Israel: Seven Deadly Lies That Rewrite God's Promises and Fuel False Prophecy

They Lied to You About Prosperity: The Shocking Truth About God's Plan for Wealth and Abundance

They Lied to You About the Rapture: How to Prepare for What's Coming

Summoning the Demon: AI, Aliens, and the Antichrist

Armed for Victory: Prayer Strategies That Unlock the End-Time Armory of God

THEY LIED TO YOU ABOUT PROSPERITY

THE SHOCKING TRUTH ABOUT GOD'S PLAN FOR WEALTH AND ABUNDANCE

ALAN DIDIO

All emphasis within Scripture quotations is the author's own. Take note that the name satan and related names are not capitalized. We choose not to acknowledge him, even to the point of violating grammatical rules.

DESTINY IMAGE® PUBLISHERS, INC.
P.O. Box 310, Shippensburg, PA 17257-0310
"Publishing cutting-edge prophetic resources to supernaturally empower the body of Christ"

This book and all other Destiny Image and Destiny Image Fiction books are available at Christian bookstores and distributors worldwide.

For more information on foreign distributors, call 717-532-3040.
Reach us on the Internet: www.destinyimage.com.

ISBN 13 TP: 9798881508197
ISBN 13 eBook: 9798881508203

For Worldwide Distribution, Printed in the U.S.A.
1 2 3 4 5 6 7 8 / 30 29 28 27 26

CONTENTS

FOREWORD

This book is the best volume on the subject of prosperity that I have read. Not only is it well written and extremely well researched, Alan gets to the heart of the matter: the substitutionary work of Jesus Christ, the effect that both prosperity and lack have upon human beings, and the advancement of God's purpose upon the earth.

Having been on the inside of the "Word of Faith" movement from its beginning and ministering alongside my father, Charles Capps, I have seen the absolute craziness that has arisen around this subject. The severe criticism against "prosperity preachers" was not unwarranted in many cases, as was also noted by my dad. Desiring to maintain his integrity and not bring a reproach upon the ministry, he purposefully distanced himself from the "prosperity gospel" that was popular at the time, although he taught people the principles of giving and receiving and how to apply the Word to their financial needs.

Upon reading this book, I realize just how sad that is. Of all the ministers I know, my dad would have been one who could have taught the scriptural based reality of prosperity without the obnoxious bragging, and without the ego driven competition. The climate at the time, however, was such that many people would not have listened to anything he said if he had taught in-depth on financial supply. One person wrote me, "Your father is the best teacher on end-times that I have ever heard. Too bad he is one of those "prosperity preachers."

It was the revelation of redemption from poverty and sickness that changed the course of the entire Charles Capps family.

My dad was physically sick from stress and worry because of financial lack and debt. A couple of bad investments and untimely weather events, along with low grain prices in the farming industry, left him with severe debt and an inability to meet his financial obligations.

He worried himself sick.

Financial disaster was looming and sickness had taken hold. These were the OUTWARD physical manifestations of poverty and lack, but the ultimate damage was on the inside, in his mind and beliefs.

A once successful farmer, through these events, he became convinced he was a failure. He declared, "Nothing I do ever works out right. Everything I do falls apart."

In desperation, he read the book of Job and decided that God was taking away His blessings, and that it was God's will for him to suffer and lose everything.

At that point, his mind was firmly held in the grip of tradition and a false interpretation of scripture. A submission to an unscriptural ideology dominated his thinking. Then someone shared the truth with him, and revelation came: *"For you know the grace of our Lord Jesus Christ, that though he was rich, yet for your sake he became poor, so that you by his poverty might become rich"* (2 Corinthians 8:9 esv).

Someone shared the truth as revealed in this scripture. Revelation came. His thinking was radically altered. Then the transition began from poverty, sickness, and despair to hope, faith, and a change of thinking and speaking. What followed was wiser decisions, healthier crops sold when prices were higher, and debts being paid off. God's wisdom began to flow to him. Within 2 years, great changes took place. God's Word works when you apply it!

I urge you to read this book with an open mind. Pay attention to the evidence Alan presents as a defender of the truth of God's Word on prosperity. This book is truly an apologetic work on prosperity as taught in the Bible. I made many notes as I read for "quotes to remember" until I realized I was copying most of the words of this book.

Here are a few of my favorite quotes:

"Seed-faith is not a modern invention or a manipulation technique."

"God gives you more than enough so that you can be the answer to someone else's prayer."

"Some will attempt to excuse their vicious maligning of this biblical concept by pointing to the errors out there. But two wrongs don't make a right and the solution to bad teaching isn't more bad teaching—it's good teaching."

Thank you, Alan DiDio, for good teaching! You are a man of courage and faith, and I am grateful for your solid biblically based research and obedience to the Holy Spirit.

And for you, the reader, I pray that you will come to fully understand the substitutionary work of Jesus Christ for sin, sickness, AND poverty and access the generosity of the Father God in your own life.

Annette Capps

INTRODUCTION

Before you read another word, it would be helpful if you made a decision: one you cannot avoid, one you cannot defer, one that will determine whether this book becomes a catalyst for transformation or merely another item gathering dust on your shelf.

You must choose whether the authority of Scripture will be the compass by which you navigate your life, surpassing the weight of personal experience, denominational traditions, and the ever-shifting circumstances of this world. In this exploration, we are not merely discussing prosperity; we are examining whether we are willing to let the Bible's truths reign supreme over every other voice.

This is not a small matter, nor is it a question to be treated lightly or postponed for later consideration. What stands before us in these pages is nothing less than the ancient challenge posed to humanity since the Garden: *Will we trust what God has said, or will we allow other voices, however sincere, however established, however numerous, to interpret, dilute, or override His Word?*

Do you remember what happened in Eden? The serpent didn't approach Eve with a frontal assault on God's character. He was far too clever for that. Instead, he whispered a question, innocent enough on its surface: "Did God really say…?" That subtle insertion of doubt, that gentle suggestion that perhaps God's words required reinterpretation, maybe the Creator's instructions weren't quite as clear or as generous as they appeared, was the original sin of hermeneutics.

And the same serpent who whispered, "Did God really say?" in Eden now whispers through religious voices, academic corridors, social media, and denominational statements: "Surely God didn't mean prosperity *literally*. Certainly He was speaking metaphorically. Obviously, those promises were only for Israel, or only for the apostolic age, or only for people more spiritual than you…." The list of reasons that we shouldn't take God at His Word goes on and on.

How convenient. How very, very convenient. The question of biblical prosperity has become a battleground precisely because it forces this confrontation. It is one thing to affirm Scripture's authority in matters safely distant from our material existence; in doctrines of Heaven, in theological abstractions, in spiritual platitudes that cost us nothing and require nothing. It is quite another to submit to Scripture when it speaks to the very substance of our daily lives: our finances, our health, our expectations of God's character and provision, our bank accounts, our business ventures, our actual lived reality in the here and now.

Here lies the uncomfortable truth that many would prefer to avoid: our resistance to biblical prosperity often reveals not a higher spirituality, but a deeper idolatry. As the objections to God's Word grow stronger, I hear the whisper of God growing louder, echoing the proclamation of the prophet Samuel to King Saul:

> *For rebellion is as the sin of witchcraft, and stubbornness is as iniquity and idolatry. Because you have rejected the word of the Lord, He also has rejected you from being king* (1 Samuel 15:23 NKJV).

Some have even made poverty, or at least financial struggle, into a badge of authenticity, as if hardship itself sanctifies, as if lack proves devotion, as if God is more pleased with His children when they can barely pay their bills. We have constructed elaborate theological frameworks to explain why God's promises of abundance must mean something other than what they say, why His declarations of blessing must be spiritualized into irrelevance, and why the testimony of Scripture must bow before the altar of our experience.

The mental gymnastics required to maintain this position would qualify for Olympic competition. But if we are honest, we must ask ourselves: *Who gave us permission to reinterpret God's Word through the lens of our disappointments?* Who authorized us to create a canon within the canon, accepting some promises as literal while dismissing others as metaphorical, whenever the Word challenges our preconceptions?

When did our traditions, shaped by centuries of religious asceticism and medieval mysticism (from monks who took vows of poverty and apparently decided everyone else should, too) become more authoritative than the inspired text itself? When did the tenets of well-intentioned but misguided poverty theology become the touchstone of the day?

History has a way of repeating itself, particularly when the Church drifts from its foundation. On October 31, 1517, an Augustinian monk named Martin Luther approached the door of the Castle Church in Wittenberg, Germany, and nailed a document to its wooden frame. The 95 theses would fracture the religious establishment and ignite a reformation that would reshape Christianity forever. Luther was issuing a theological challenge, demanding that the Church return to biblical authority and forsake the idolatrous traditions and pronouncements of men.

The Catholic Church of Luther's day had accumulated centuries of traditions, practices, and doctrines that had no basis in Scripture. They sold indulgences, literally charging people money to reduce their time in purgatory, a concept the Bible never teaches. They positioned the Pope as an infallible authority whose declarations carried equal weight with Scripture itself. They created an entire economy of salvation built on human works, priestly mediation, and institutional control. And they defended it all by appealing to tradition, to church authority, to "what we've always believed," to the pronouncements of councils and the interpretations of church fathers.

Luther's response was radical in its simplicity: *Sola Scriptura*: Scripture alone. Not Scripture plus tradition. Not Scripture plus the Pope's interpretation. Not Scripture filtered through centuries of church councils. Scripture. Alone. But Luther didn't stop there. He gave us two companion declarations that flowed directly from a commitment to biblical authority: *Sola Fide*: faith alone, not faith plus works, not faith plus indulgences, not faith plus religious performance. And *Sola Gratia*: grace alone, not grace plus human merit, not grace that must be earned or purchased, but grace freely given by the God who loves to give.

Do you see the word that appears in all three? *Alone*. Alone. Alone. Alone. That word is not diplomatic. It is not inclusive. It is not designed to make room for other voices or to accommodate alternative perspectives. It is a line in the sand. It is a declaration of war against every competing authority. It says, "This one thing is supreme, and everything else must bow before it."

Luther understood that you cannot have two ultimate authorities. Either Scripture is the final word, or it isn't. Either faith is sufficient for salvation, or it isn't. Either grace is freely given, or it isn't. There is no middle ground. There is no compromise position. There is no way to satisfy both Scripture and tradition when they conflict, no way to honor both God's Word and man's religious systems when they contradict each other.

The Church of Luther's day had a choice: submit to the authority of Scripture and abandon centuries of lucrative, politically convenient, religiously comfortable traditions, or maintain those traditions and, in doing so, demonstrate that their ultimate authority was not the Word of God but the institutions of men. We face the same choice today.

The religious establishment has once again accumulated traditions that contradict Scripture. They may not be selling indulgences, but they are selling a theology of lack disguised as humility, a doctrine of poverty baptized as spirituality, a worldview that systematically explains away every promise of God's material blessing as either metaphorical, obsolete, or intended for someone else. And they defend it with the same arguments the medieval Church used: "This is what we've always believed. This is what the scholars say. This is what our denomination teaches. This is what tradition demands."

But here we stand, document in hand, ready to nail our thesis to the door: *Sola Scriptura*. Scripture alone will be our authority on prosperity, not the poverty theology inherited from medieval mystics. *Sola Fide*. Faith alone in God's promises will be our foundation, not skepticism dressed up as discernment. *Sola Gratia*. Grace alone, the unmerited favor of our generous God who delights in blessing His children, will be our theology, not a works-based system that measures spirituality by financial struggle or judges someone based on their success.

The question is not whether you agree with prosperity teaching as you currently understand it. The question is whether you will allow Scripture alone to define what prosperity teaching should be. The question is whether that word—*alone*—means anything to you, or whether it's just a nice Reformation slogan we repeat without letting it actually reform anything.

Luther didn't nail those theses to the church door because he enjoyed controversy. He did it because the truth of the gospel was at stake, because people were being held in bondage to lies, because the character of God was being misrepresented, and because someone had to say, "Enough. We return to the Word."

That same moment has come for the doctrine of prosperity. Will we stand on the Word alone, or will we continue to allow tradition, experience, and religious sentiment to override what Scripture clearly teaches? This is a Reformation-level crisis of authority. And like Luther, we must choose: the Word of God, or the doctrines of men. There is no third option.

This point will be repeated throughout this book. Knowing some will ignorantly skip large portions of this work to find a particular section, we will revisit this truth again and again so that no one misses it: What does the Bible say?

The stakes here are eternal, and the cost of getting this wrong is catastrophic. For if we cannot trust God's Word on prosperity, how can we trust it on salvation? If we must reinterpret His promises of provision, why should we accept His promises of redemption? The hermeneutics we employ in one area will inevitably color our approach to all areas. Those who teach that God's blessing should not be expected in this life have inadvertently trained believers to doubt God's faithfulness in every arena.

Consider what happens to believers who embrace poverty theology: They live beneath their covenant privileges, never accessing what Christ died to provide. They misrepresent God's character to a watching world, portraying Him as stingy, reluctant, and withholding rather than as the generous Father He declares Himself to be.

They raise children who view Christianity as a religion of perpetual lack rather than one of covenant abundance, who grow up associating faith with limitations rather than with possibilities. They become walking contradictions, preaching that God owns the cattle on a thousand hills while living as though He's filing for bankruptcy. They become advertisements for a gospel that doesn't work, billboards for a God who makes grand promises He never intends to keep. Is this really the testimony we want to leave?

This book, then, is not merely a defense of prosperity teaching; it is a clarion call back to biblical authority itself. It is an invitation to lay down the comfortable lies we have believed, the religious traditions we have inherited uncritically (often from people who were as broke as they were sincere), and the poverty mindsets we have been baptized with spiritual language. It is a challenge to return to Scripture with fresh eyes, willing to be corrected, willing to be enlarged, willing to discover that God might be far more generous than our theology has allowed Him to be.

What follows in these pages will offend religious sensibilities. Good. Jesus offended the religious establishment of His day by declaring truths that contradicted their traditions, by healing on the Sabbath, by dining with tax collectors, and by suggesting that their meticulous rule-keeping had somehow missed the heart of God entirely. Truth is not concerned with comfort; it's concerned with liberation. And if your religious sensibilities have been shaped more by tradition than by Scripture, then yes, they need to be offended. They need to be challenged. They need to be demolished and rebuilt on the foundation of God's Word alone.

As you turn these pages, you will be confronted repeatedly with the inevitability of choice:

- Will you believe what God has said, or will you retreat into what you have always been told and always believed to be true?
- Will you allow the Bible to shape your understanding of prosperity, or will you force prosperity passages to conform to your predetermined conclusions?
- Will you follow Scripture wherever it leads, even if it leads you out of your denominational comfort zone, even if it means admitting that perhaps the people who warned you against "those prosperity preachers" were themselves operating from unexamined assumptions?

The journey ahead requires courage. It requires the humility to admit that perhaps, just perhaps, the caricatures you have heard about prosperity preaching bear little resemblance to what Scripture actually teaches. It requires the honesty to examine whether your objections are truly biblical or merely cultural, truly theological, or merely traditional, truly rooted in Scripture or merely parroting what you heard some seminary professor say who himself was parroting what his seminary professor said in an unbroken chain of inherited assumptions stretching back to the Dark Ages.

But most of all, it requires a settled conviction that Scripture alone must be the final arbiter of truth. Not your pastor's opinion, however respected he may be. Not your denomination's statement of faith, however historic it may be. Not your personal history of unanswered prayers, however painful it may be. Not your grandmother's folk theology, however sincere she may have been. Scripture. Alone. Supreme. Authoritative. Sufficient. Final.

This is where we must begin. Everything else flows from this decision. If you cannot trust Scripture on this, you have no foundation to trust it on anything. The authority of God's Word is indivisible, and it stands or falls as a whole. You cannot pick and choose which promises to believe based on which ones fit comfortably within your existing worldview. You cannot selectively apply literal interpretation to passages about hell while spiritualizing passages about blessing.

The same Holy Spirit who inspired Paul to write about justification by faith also inspired him to write that godliness with contentment is a great gain and that God supplies all our needs according to His riches in glory (see Philippians 4:19).

Choose this day whom you will believe: God, or the gatekeepers of religious tradition who have spent centuries explaining why God didn't really mean what He clearly said. It's time to lay our experiences and our opinions on the altar and say, "From this day forward, I make the Bible my final authority." This is where we must begin. Everything else flows from this decision.

Now that we've anchored ourselves in the supremacy of Scripture, I need to tell you why this book exists and why these truths have gripped my heart so profoundly that I couldn't stay silent.

I'm going to start where all authentic theology begins: with a personal encounter with God's Word. I want to take you into my own journey, not because my story validates the truth, but because it illustrates how the Spirit takes eternal truths and makes them burn within us. No matter how powerful our experiences may be, no matter how convinced we become through personal revelation, truth is never authenticated by testimony alone. It must be tested, proven, and established by the unchanging Word of God. *Our experiences can awaken us to truth, but only Scripture can anchor us in it.*

So, before we dive into the biblical examination that forms the foundation of everything I'm about to share, let me pull back the curtain on my own heart. Let me show you why this subject doesn't just interest me intellectually, but why it burns like fire in my bones, demanding to be proclaimed.

Alan DiDio
Charlotte, North Carolina

PART ONE

FISH COME FIRST

1

THE COST OF SILENCE

It was a cold winter night in January 2015, a Wednesday evening, and I was in my office preparing for our midweek Bible study. My office at that time was a concrete cellar in my home, the place where I spent all my time.

I'm not like some ministers who thrive on social interaction. I'm the biggest introvert you'll ever meet in your entire life. I would be happy being alone in a room for months on end and feel like I haven't missed out on anything. That's just how I'm wired. My wife and kids are the social ones in the DiDio family. But me? Give me a basement, a Bible, and some time, and I'm totally at home.

A REBUKE AND A RESET

That Wednesday, we were in the middle of a series on the miracles of Jesus. We had just covered the wedding at Cana where Jesus turned water into wine. What fascinated me about that miracle was that it wasn't a miracle of need, but of desire. The Bible says they wanted wine; they didn't actually need it.

They were having a party, and the wine had run out. Jesus set the tone for the tenor of His entire ministry by supplying a desire, not a dire necessity. Some have suggested that Jesus performed this miracle to protect the host's reputation. Others have suggested that Jesus did it to honor His mother. Whatever the reason was, it was undoubtedly a miracle of provision.

Now we were ready to talk about the second miracle, the one recorded in Luke 5, where Jesus called the disciples by the Sea of Galilee. Most people have a cursory knowledge of this story. They think Jesus just walked along the shore, saying, *"Follow me, and I will make you fishers of men"* in some hypnotic tone, and the disciples' eyes started to twirl, and they dropped everything and followed Him.

But that's not what happened. What I was about to discover is that the encounter in Luke 5:10 was actually His third call to Peter. This was the third time He had said, *"Follow me."*

Peter's first encounter was when his brother Andrew brought him to Jesus. One day, John the Baptist was talking to two men, one of whom was Andrew, Peter's brother.

They began following Jesus, who invited them to His home. On the way, Andrew stopped to get his brother, Peter. When they met up with Jesus, the first thing Jesus did was prophesy over Peter, calling him a stone (or rock). The Bible doesn't specifically say that Jesus asked Peter to follow Him during this encounter, but the context certainly implies it.

The second time was an instance recorded in both Matthew 4 and Mark 1. When Jesus was walking one day by the sea of Galilee, he saw Andrew and Peter working on their fishing equipment. Jesus said, *"Follow me, and I will make you fishers of men"* (Matthew 4:19; see also Mark 1:17). That brings us to the third encounter, which I will discuss more in the next chapter. Before that, I need to lay some background for you so just stay with me, and keep that third call in mind as we move forward.

I was studying and studying, and it was getting closer and closer to service time. I didn't have it. You know what that's like? When it is just not clicking? I mean, I can preach on anything. But if it's not hot off the griddle in my spirit, I just can't bring it to life. If it's not hot, I can't serve it.

I had preached from Luke 5 many, many times. Every commentary I'd ever read on this passage inevitably went to evangelism, missions work, winning the lost. And that's fine, but for some reason that night, it just wasn't clicking. I was trying to put the pieces together and something was off.

And then, in one of those "suddenly" moments, the glory of God came into my office in one of the most profound ways I think I've ever experienced in my entire life.

The glory of God came into that basement and literally picked me up out of my chair and threw me to the floor. The weight of it was so heavy, it was almost pushing my face into the carpet. I immediately began weeping in the presence of God—and He was rebuking me.

It was a moment that turned my destiny away from destruction and toward life. That's what a rebuke is. It's a loving nudge from darkness into light. And I'm trying to do the same thing for you right now through this chapter.

My face was on the floor. I was weeping, and it was an ugly cry. I'm not an emotional person unless the presence of God is involved, or I'm watching *Little House on the Prairie,* but this was heavy. This was real. This was terrifying and glorious all at once. I didn't even understand what was going on. I was just studying about evangelism, getting ready for a regular Bible study. There was nothing dramatically wrong in my life, at least nothing of which I was aware.

But here's what I haven't told you yet: I had just come off the mission field. I had spent from about 2007 all the way through to that moment working with the persecuted Church around the world. In doing that work, I had learned something about ministry that many people don't realize: pastors are constantly under assault, and it's wise to pick your battles. It's one of the most burned-out professions that exists on the planet.

People put enormous demands on pastors. Some think the service is too loud. Others think it's too quiet. Some think the message went too long. Others think it didn't go long enough. And there's constant scrutiny about what we're wearing, what kind of shoes we have on, and how much we paid for them.

I just wanted to focus on evangelism, missions, and revival. After spending so much time on the mission field, I had identified certain words that were radioactive. When these words are mentioned, they make the religious hair on the back of the devil's neck stand up. If you mention these radioactive terms people get suspicious and judgmental. When that happens they are less likely to hear your message. All I wanted was to see the Spirit of God poured out and to launch churches in other nations. If I could help that along by dodging certain land mines, then so be it.

We had launched more than 400 churches internationally, and I knew that missions work was something anybody could get behind. Even unbelievers appreciate missions, and I didn't want to do anything to jeopardize those relationships. There were certain subjects I had started to avoid as a result. And certainly one of the most controversial subjects in the American Church revolves around one word.

The moment I say it, you're going to feel that religious spirit rise up. Are you ready? *Prosperity!*

I knew what the Bible said about it. I believed what the Bible said about it. However, I understood there were certain battles you just got tired of fighting. As someone who focused on the mission field and evangelism, I just wanted to keep the main thing the main thing without any distractions. So I spent an entire year without mentioning it, without receiving an offering in my own church. I had other leaders do it, but I never touched it. I wasn't going to talk about it.

And so there I was, minding my own business in my office when the glory of God came in. The overwhelming force of it picked me up, threw me to the floor, and proceeded to rebuke me for not receiving offerings or talking about prosperity.

DRAMA AND DISCLAIMER

As much as the encounter with God I'm about to describe impacted me, I know that we are not to be led by dramatic encounters, prophetic words, dreams, and visions alone. As I stated earlier, the Word of God is our principal source of instruction, the infallible guide for our lives.

The Bible warns us about false prophets and deceptive dreams, reminding us to test every spirit and hold fast to what is true (see 1 John 4:1; 1 Thessalonians 5:21). Prophetic words like this, while potentially powerful, must always be measured against the truth of Scripture, and their value is in their ability to arrest our attention and bring our focus back to the Word of God.

Prophetic words that point us to the Bible—words that confirm God's teachings and align with Scripture—can be significant and should not be ignored.

Prophetic words can serve as reminders, warnings, or encouragements, prompting us to dig deeper into Scripture and drawing us closer to Him. But they can never be allowed to replace the Bible as our primary source of truth. Dreams, visions, and prophecies must always direct us to the Bible.

The Word of God must be our final authority. I'm simply telling you what caused me to look back at the Bible and to study these things in Scripture. What follows is not based on my encounter, but on what that encounter drove me to discover in God's Word.

If you've ever had an encounter with God, you know it's like the voice of many waters. There are many things happening at one time, many deposits being made simultaneously. It's amazing that these downloads can take place instantaneously.

I remember the Holy Spirit asking me very strongly:

"If everyone in your church were unsaved, how much would you preach on salvation?

"I would preach salvation hard. I would preach it until I got a good number of them saved."

"If everyone in your church were sick, what would you do?"

"I would preach on healing. Not only would I preach on healing, but I would also bring nutritionists in. I would bring doctors in. I would hit it from every angle. If everyone in my church were sick, it would be a dereliction of duty not to address it."

And then He asked me this rhetorical, yet riveting, question:

"How many people in your church are in debt or struggling financially?"

Of course, I knew the answer. You know the answer, too.

"How are they supposed to get victory if you don't preach it? Faith comes by hearing, and hearing by the Word of God."

I had no answer. I was like Job. I had been a foolish man. And then these words came to me like waves of glory hitting me. I had no clue what they meant. I quickly grabbed a legal pad and began to write through the tears. The pen was actually going through the wet paper that my tears were staining as I wrote these three words: ***Fish Come First***.

I didn't even know what it meant. He had confronted me with my failure to receive offerings (I thought I was somehow being diplomatic or humble when, in actuality, I was giving in to the fear of man). He gave me these three words, and then that overwhelming presence was gone.

I didn't know what to do with those words. I didn't even know where to begin. So I grabbed my Bible and started in Genesis 1. If you don't know where to start, start at the beginning! What I discovered that night changed everything. It changed my ministry. It changed my church. It changed lives. And it's about to change yours.

TERRIFIED PREACHERS

Here's a truth that most pastors won't admit: we know what the Bible says about money, but we're terrified to preach it. We'll preach on sin. We'll preach on hell. We'll preach on repentance and holiness and dying to self. But mention prosperity, mention financial blessing, mention God's desire to increase His people, and watch the room go cold. Watch the arms cross. Watch people mentally check out or, worse, walk out.

Why? Because somewhere along the way, the word *prosperity* became synonymous with *greed*. The excesses of some teachers poisoned the well for all of us, and now any mention of biblical prosperity gets lumped in with the charlatans.

So we avoid it. We dance around it. We talk about *blessing* in vague, spiritual terms that never touch the practical realities of rent payments, medical bills, and putting food on the table. We've become experts at preaching a gospel that saves souls but leaves people broke.

And here's the tragic irony: while we're busy avoiding the subject to maintain our credibility, the people in our congregations are drowning. Consider this:

- Forty-three percent of Americans spend more than they take in every single month.[1]
- The majority of Americans say that finances cause the most stress in their lives.[2]

Marriages are being destroyed. People are losing sleep. They're battling depression and anxiety. They're making decisions out of desperation rather than wisdom. And the number one cause? Money, or in actuality, the lack of it.

But we're afraid to talk about it because we don't want to be associated with "those" preachers.

Let me tell you what I learned that Wednesday night in 2015: silence isn't neutrality; silence is surrender. When we refuse to address what the Bible clearly teaches about God's provision, we're not protecting people from error; we're abandoning them to bondage.

THE FEAR OF MAN IS A SNARE

After years on the mission field, I had developed a strategy. I wanted to see revival. I wanted to see churches planted. I wanted to see the Kingdom advance. And I knew that certain subjects created controversy that could jeopardize relationships and opportunities. So I made a calculated decision: I would focus on the non-controversial stuff.

Salvation, yes. Healing, absolutely. The Great Commission, of course. But money? Prosperity? Financial breakthrough? Those were lightning rods. Those would alienate people. Those would make donors uncomfortable and cause other ministers to distance themselves from me.

For an entire year—by not receiving an offering myself in the church—I had avoided the subject entirely. I had thought I was being wise, strategic, and humble. I was actually operating in the fear of man. Proverbs 29:25 says: *"The fear of man bringeth a snare: but whoso putteth his trust in the Lord shall be safe."*

I had fallen into that snare. I was more concerned with what people thought about me than what God had commanded me to do. I was more worried about protecting my reputation than equipping God's people for victory. And God had to knock me to the floor to wake me up.

THE COST OF SILENCE

Here's what I didn't realize until that night: my silence wasn't just hurting me. It was hurting the people I was called to serve. When I didn't preach on financial prosperity, the people couldn't discover that it was

God's will for them. When I failed to teach biblical principles of stewardship, sowing, and reaping, they had no tools to break free from the cycles of debt and poverty that were crushing them.

> *So then faith comes by hearing, and hearing by the word of God* (Romans 10:17 NKJV).

If people don't hear the Word on a subject, they can't have faith for breakthrough in that area. If I'm not preaching it, God's people are not hearing it. If they're not hearing it, they can't believe it. And if they can't believe it, they can't receive it. My fear of controversy was costing my people their freedom. It was a dereliction of duty. It was pastoral malpractice. And I was guilty of it.

You don't realize how much the stress of your financial situation is hindering the miraculous in your life. When you're divided, when you're worn out trying to make ends meet, when you're using all your mental and emotional energy just to survive, you're sapped of your strength. You're sapped of your energy. You're sapped of your faith.

Then, when you come into the house of God, and it's time to believe for healing, you only have about 5 percent of your strength left because you used it all up just to pay the electric bill. You want to believe for revival in your city, but you're tapped out just trying to cover your mortgage.

The spirit of mammon (see Matthew 6:24) knows that if it can oppress you financially, it can limit you spiritually. It can restrict your generosity. It can shrink your vision. It can keep you in survival mode instead of advancement mode. It can make you so stressed and anxious that you can barely lift your head up in worship, much less believe God for breakthrough. And the Church has played right into this strategy by treating *prosperity* like a dirty word.

Try saying the word *prosperity* in the privacy of your own home. The religious conditioning is so deep and the cultural programming so strong that for many, it feels awkward just speaking it aloud.

Prosperity is Bible language. It's God's language. Moses used it. David sang about it. Solomon wrote about it. The prophets promised it. Jesus demonstrated it. Paul prayed for it. John wished it for his friends.

If the word is good enough for the Holy Spirit to inspire and preserve in Scripture, it's good enough for us to preach. And if we're too afraid to use it because of what people might think, then we need to repent of the fear of man and get back to fearing God alone.

Some will attempt to excuse their vicious maligning of this biblical concept by pointing to the errors out there. But two wrongs don't make a right, and the solution to bad teaching isn't more bad teaching—it's good teaching. The way to answer the prosperity gospel lies and abuses isn't to abandon the subject. It's to reclaim it, define it biblically, and preach it with integrity. Two counterfeits don't cancel out the genuine. And our discomfort with the subject doesn't change what Scripture clearly teaches.

That Wednesday night, face down on the carpet, I made a decision. I repented for my fear. I repented for my silence. And I committed to preach the whole counsel of God, even the parts that make people uncomfortable, even the subjects that might cost me relationships or opportunities. Because here's what I discovered: when you preach truth—even controversial truth—with love and biblical integrity, hungry people respond. Bound people get free. Struggling people find breakthrough.

Within a year of that encounter, our church saw millions of dollars in financial miracles. Not in the church budget but in people's lives! Debts were supernaturally canceled. Jobs were opened up. Businesses were blessed. Inheritances were released. People who had been stuck for years suddenly experienced breakthrough. And it all started with breaking the silence. It all started with having the courage to say what the Bible says about God's desire to prosper His people.

Provision comes before revival. Financial breakthrough precedes spiritual breakthrough.

Not because money is more important than the anointing, but because stressed, broke, anxious believers can't fully walk in the freedom and power God has for them. The people of God deserve to hear the truth. And the truth is, God wants to prosper you. Let me show you what I discovered in the Word that night.

2

FISH AND FINANCES

With tears still streaming down my face and those three mysterious words written on my legal pad, I didn't know where to begin. *Fish come first.* What did that even mean? So I went back to the beginning. I opened my Bible to Genesis 1 and started reading.

If God had given me a word, surely He would help me understand it. And if *fish* were significant, maybe I needed to see where fish first showed up in Scripture and what God had to say about them. I began reading through the creation account, and something jumped off the page that I had read a thousand times but never really seen.

THE FIRST-BLESSED IN ALL CREATION

Genesis 1:20-22 records the fifth day of creation:

> *And God said, Let the waters bring forth abundantly the moving creature that hath life, and fowl that may fly above the earth in the open firmament of heaven. And God created great whales, and every living creature that moveth, which the waters brought forth abundantly, after their kind, and every winged fowl after his kind: and God saw that it was good. And God blessed them, saying, Be fruitful, and multiply, and fill the waters in the seas, and let fowl multiply in the earth.*

Do you see it? The very first thing that God blessed in all of creation was fish. Not man. Not land animals. Not even the plants that would feed everything else. The first recipients of divine blessing, the first creatures to hear the words *"be fruitful and multiply"* were the creatures of the sea: *Fish come first.*

I sat there staring at that passage, and something began to dawn on me. In Scripture, fish consistently represent provision and abundance. They represent supply that exists in an unseen realm. Think about it: fish live in water—hidden beneath the surface—invisible until they're brought up into the seen world. They represent resources that exist in the spiritual dimension that can be pulled into the natural dimension.

God blessed the fish first because provision must be established before anything else can flourish. You can't multiply if you can't eat. You can't be fruitful if you have no resources. You can't fill the earth if you're starving. The blessing on the fish isn't random—it's foundational. It's God establishing from the very beginning that He is the God of supply, the God of abundance, the God who provides more than enough.

WHAT MAN IS GIVEN DOMINION OVER FIRST

I kept reading. Genesis 1:26-28 says:

> *And God said, Let us make man in our image, after our likeness: and let them have dominion over the fish of the sea, and over the fowl of the air, and over the cattle, and over all the earth, and over every creeping thing that creepeth upon the earth. So God created man in his own image, in the image of God created he him; male and female created he them. And God blessed them, and God said unto them, Be fruitful, and multiply, and replenish the earth, and subdue it: and have dominion over the fish of the*

sea, and over the fowl of the air, and over every living thing that moveth upon the earth.

Now catch this: when God gives man dominion, the very first creatures listed—the first area over which man was given authority—were the fish of the sea.

***Fish come first*:** not just in blessing, but in dominion. God is making a statement here; He is establishing a principle. Before man can properly exercise authority over anything else, he must first have dominion over provision. He must first understand how to tap into the supply that God has made available in the unseen realm. This is divine order. This is God's blueprint for how His Kingdom operates.

WHY FISH? WHY PROVISION FIRST?

Here's what I began to understand that night, and what I need you to grasp right now: money must often come before the miraculous. Provision must often precede revival. Financial breakthrough often has to happen before you can fully walk in the spiritual breakthrough God has for you. This isn't about making money an idol. This isn't about putting mammon ahead of God. This is about understanding that God, in His wisdom, has structured things so that when His people are *financially* free, they're *spiritually* free to pursue His purposes without hindrance.

In the same way that the soul must be healed for physical healing to fully manifest and remain, financial stress must be broken for the miraculous to flow freely in your life.

You may not realize how much the spirit of mammon, how much depending on some other source for your finances, how much the stress of your financial situation is blocking the supernatural in your life. The joy of the Lord is your strength (see Nehemiah 8:10). But when you're divided, when you're worn out trying to make ends meet, you're sapped of your strength and sapped of your energy and sapped of your faith.

This is why God blessed the fish first in creation. This is why He gave man dominion over fish first. He was establishing a pattern that would run through all of Scripture: I am the God who provides; and when My people understand My provision, they're free to pursue My purposes.

As I kept reading through Genesis that night, I started seeing this pattern everywhere. God always supplies before the need arises:

- He created water before He created fish...*that needed it to swim in.*
- He created grass before He created cattle...*that needed it to eat.*
- He created light before He created eyes...*that needed it to see.*
- He created air before He created lungs...*that needed it to breathe.*

God is always ahead of the need. He's always preparing the supply before the demand shows up. He's never scrambling. He's never caught off guard. He's never looking around saying, "Oh no! They need something, and I don't have it ready."

That's not how He operates. That's not who He is. He is El Shaddai, the God who is more than enough. Not El Cheapo, the God who barely gets by. El Shaddai, the God of abundance, the God of overflow, the God who supplies before you even know you have a need.

Because it's true that God always supplies before there's a need, here's the revelation that will change your life: if you have a need right now, that need is a prophecy that the supply already exists.

Let that sink in. Your need is not evidence that God has not provided. Your need is evidence that somewhere, in the unseen realm, God has already prepared the supply. Your job isn't to manufacture it. Your job is to tap into it by faith.

FISH, FISH, AND MORE FISH

Once you start looking for it, you see fish showing up at critical moments throughout Scripture, and they're always connected to supernatural provision.

When Jonah was running from God's call and got thrown into the sea, God had his means of rescue already prepared: *"Now the Lord had prepared a great fish to swallow up Jonah..."* (Jonah 1:17).

Even in judgment, even in correction, God provides. The fish that swallowed Jonah became the very vehicle of his salvation and restoration.

When Jesus wanted to pay the temple tax for Himself and Peter, what did He do? He told Peter:

> *...go thou to the sea, and cast an hook, and take up the fish that first cometh up; and when thou hast opened his mouth, thou shalt find a piece of money: take that, and give unto them for me and thee* (Matthew 17:27).

Provision comes from the unseen realm, pulled up by faith. When Jesus fed the 5,000, remember what He multiplied?

> *And they say unto him, We have here but five loaves, and two fishes* (Matthew 14:17).

He took an insufficient supply and multiplied it into an abundant provision.

After the resurrection, when Jesus appeared to the disciples on the shore, look at what He provided:

> *Jesus saith unto them, Come and dine. And none of the disciples durst ask him, Who art thou? knowing that it was the Lord. Jesus then cometh, and taketh bread, and giveth them, and fish likewise* (John 21:12-13).

Even in His resurrected glory, He still provided fish. The pattern is consistent. Fish represent the provision of God. They represent supply from the unseen realm. They represent the abundance that God releases to His people.

Sitting in my basement office that night, with my Bible open and tears drying on my face, I began to understand what God was showing me. When His people:

- ...are financially free
- ...are not stressed by the constant pressure of lack
- ...have more than enough
- ...then they are positioned to receive everything else He wants to give them. They can dream big because they're not limited by poverty thinking.

Fish come first: not because fish are more important than the many other things that God wants to do in a believer's life, but because financial breakthrough removes the barriers that keep people from fully walking in those things. This is why the enemy fights so hard to keep God's people broke. This is why there's so much controversy around this subject. This is why religious spirits rise up every time prosperity is mentioned.

The devil knows something that the Church has forgotten: when God's people prosper, they're dangerous. When they have resources, they can fund the gospel. They can build churches. They can support missionaries. They can meet needs. They can demonstrate the goodness of God in tangible, undeniable ways. But...

- ...if the devil can keep them broke
- ...if he can keep them stressed
- ...if he can keep them trapped in debt and anxiety
- ...if he can keep them in bondage to fear

- ...he can limit their impact. He can restrict their influence. He can keep them so busy trying to survive that they never get around to advancing the Kingdom.

Fish come first: It's not a statement about priority. It's a statement about order. Get your finances right, and everything else becomes possible (see Luke 16:11).

That Wednesday night, sitting alone in my basement, I finally understood what God was trying to tell me. And I knew what I had to do. I had to go back to my congregation and repent. I had to break the silence. I had to preach what the Bible actually says about God's heart to prosper His people.

But first, I needed to understand the full scope of what the Scriptures taught. I needed to see how this pattern of provision plays out in the lives of God's people.

And what I discovered in Luke 5 solidified everything.

THE THIRD CALL

With the Genesis revelation burning in my spirit, I turned back to Luke 5, the passage I had been preparing to preach that very night. But now I was reading it with completely different eyes.

Luke 5:4-10 records what most people think is Jesus' first encounter with the disciples.

> *Now when he had left speaking, he said unto Simon, Launch out into the deep, and let down your nets for a draught. And Simon answering said unto him, Master, we have toiled all the night, and have taken nothing: nevertheless at thy word I will let down the net.*
>
> *And when they had this done, they inclosed a great multitude of fishes: and their net brake. And they beckoned unto their partners, which were in the other ship, that they should come and*

> *help them. And they came, and filled both the ships, so that they began to sink.*
>
> *When Simon Peter saw it, he fell down at Jesus' knees, saying, Depart from me; for I am a sinful man, O Lord. For he was astonished, and all that were with him, at the draught of the fishes which they had taken: and so was also James, and John, the sons of Zebedee, which were partners with Simon. And Jesus said unto Simon, Fear not; from henceforth thou shalt catch men.*

Here's what I discovered that many people miss: this wasn't the first time Jesus had called them. This was the third time. Go back and trace the timeline. Jesus had already called these men to follow Him. They had attended His meetings. They had seen Him minister. They had even witnessed miracles in their own homes.

In fact, Jesus had come into Peter's house and healed his mother-in-law of a great fever (see Luke 4:38-39). Think about that. Jesus was in Peter's house. He had performed a miracle for Peter's family, and then He left. And Peter let Him go. Why? Because Peter had bills to pay. He had a fishing business. He had partners. He had obligations. He had overhead. So even though Jesus was right there, even though the power of God was manifesting in his own home, Peter stayed behind when Jesus moved on to the next town.

Can you imagine? Jesus moving in your house, and you let Him leave because you have bills to pay? Of course, you can imagine it. Because that's exactly what most of us do every single week. We encounter God on Sunday, but by Monday morning we're back to chasing the almighty dollar.

- We experience His presence…
- We feel the tug to go deeper…
- We sense Him calling us to something more…
- …but we let Him go because we have a mortgage, car payments, credit card debt, and student loans.

We want to follow Jesus. We want to pursue His purposes, but we're trapped by financial obligations. We're bound by the need to make money. We're limited by the very thing that should be under our dominion.

WHAT MADE THIS CALL DIFFERENT? FISH!

This time, Jesus doesn't just call them. He gets in their boat. He gets into their business with them. They've been fishing all night, and they have caught nothing. They're exhausted. They're frustrated. They're cleaning their nets, probably calculating how they're going to make ends meet with no catch to sell. And Jesus shows up and starts teaching from Peter's boat. He gives Peter an instruction that makes no sense from a fishing perspective:

> *...Launch out into the deep, and let down your nets for a draught* (Luke 5:4).

Peter's response reveals everything: *"Master, we have toiled all the night, and have taken nothing"* (Luke 5:5).

Translation: "We're professionals. We know what we're doing. We've already tried; it didn't work. The fish aren't biting."

But then Peter says something that changes everything: *"Nevertheless **at thy word** I will let down the net."* At His word. Not at my understanding. Not at my experience. Not at my professional judgment. At His word.

And when Peter obeys, the nets break. Both ships start sinking from the weight of the catch. Supernatural abundance shows up when Peter acts on the word of the Lord.

Now here's the part that confused me for years. When Simon Peter saw the miraculous catch, he didn't celebrate. He didn't throw a party. He didn't start counting his money. He fell down at Jesus' knees and said, "Depart from me; for I am a sinful man, O Lord."

- Why would a financial miracle produce repentance?
- Why would abundance lead to conviction?

It happened because in that moment, Peter received a revelation. He realized that he had been depending on his own ability to provide. He had been trusting in his fishing skills, his hard work, his professional network, his partners, his boats, and his nets. He had been trusting in the arm of the flesh. And Jesus had just proven that provision doesn't come from your job—it comes from Him.

All those times when Peter had stayed behind because he had bills to pay, all those opportunities he missed to follow Jesus because he was afraid of losing income, all that stress and anxiety and toil through the night with nothing to show for it. It was all because he was looking to the wrong source.

The apostle Paul would later articulate what Peter learned in that moment: *"But my God shall supply all your need according to his riches in glory by Christ Jesus"* (Philippians 4:19).

Not my job. Not my boss. Not my business. Not my education. Not my network. Not my hustle. My *God* shall supply.

This miracle reveals how God operates. Notice Jesus didn't just meet their need. He didn't give them just enough fish to break even for the night. He gave them so many fish that their nets broke and their ships started sinking. That's abundance. That's overflow. That's more than enough. That's prosperity.

And notice when it happened. Not when they were working all night in their own strength. Not when they were using their professional expertise and experience. It happened when they obeyed a word from Jesus that didn't make natural sense. *At Your word.*

God's provision often comes through instructions that contradict your experience, challenge your understanding, and require faith to obey.

Launch out into the deep in the middle of the day…when every fisherman knows fish don't bite.

Let down your nets…when you've tried all night and caught nothing. Do what I say even when it doesn't make sense.

And when you obey, nets will break from the blessing.

FOR PETER, FISH STARTED IT ALL!

This is the miracle that launched the disciples into full-time ministry with Jesus. After this, Luke 5:11 says: *"And when they had brought their ships to land, they forsook all, and followed him."*

Why? Because they finally understood that if they followed Jesus, their provision was secure. They didn't have to choose between following God and paying their bills. Following God was the way to have their bills paid.

This wasn't the first time Jesus called them, but it was the first time they freely responded. The financial breakthrough removed the barrier that had kept them tied to their boats, their nets, and their limited thinking.

Here's what you need to catch: this miracle of provision happened so they could follow Jesus into ministry. The fish weren't the goal; the fish were the means! God prospered them so they could pursue His purposes without hindrance.

That's what biblical prosperity is for. Not so you can hoard it. Not so you can live in luxury while others suffer. It's so you can be free to follow Jesus wherever He leads, to do whatever He calls you to do, to be as generous as He moves you to be, without the limitations of lack holding you back.

Fish come first: not as the end, but as the beginning. Not as the destination, but as the launching pad.

What was the first thing blessed in all creation?

Fish.

What was the first thing over which man was given dominion?

Fish!

What was the first miracle that launched Peter into ministry?

Fish!

Fish come first: and you haven't even heard the most amazing scriptural connection yet.

God blessed the fish first in Genesis so everything else could flourish. Jesus provided the fish in Luke 5 so the disciples could launch into their calling. And He's ready to do the same thing for you. But you have to be willing to let down your net at His word, even when it doesn't make sense, even when your experience says otherwise, even when you've already tried it, and it didn't work.

At Your word, Lord. That's the key.

3

PROSPERITY PREACHER REPENTS

Here's what hit me that night in my office: if the enemy is using financial pressure this effectively as a weapon against believers, then breaking that pressure must be a Kingdom priority. This isn't about materialism. This is about spiritual warfare. The enemy knows this—why doesn't the Church?

Fish come first: not because fish matter more than souls, but because until the financial burden is broken, most believers will never have the capacity to fully pursue what God has called them to. And if we won't…

- *…teach it*
- *…preach it*
- *…and equip people to walk in it,*
- *…**we are complicit in their bondage.***

PROSPERITY BEFORE REVIVAL?

That night in my office, as I was processing everything God was showing me about *fish come first*, I told the Lord, "I just want to preach Joel 2:28. That's what I want to preach. I want to preach about the outpouring of Your Spirit."

And the Holy Spirit said, "Okay, let's go there."

I flipped to Joel 2:28, thinking I knew this passage inside and out. This is Pentecostal shouting ground. This is where we go when we want to talk about revival and about God pouring out His Spirit on all flesh:

> *And it shall come to pass afterward, that I will pour out my spirit upon all flesh; and your sons and your daughters shall prophesy, your old men shall dream dreams, your young men shall see visions.*

Beautiful. Powerful. Every believer's heart cry. We want the outpouring. We want revival. We want to see God move in power. But then the Holy Spirit asked me a question that stopped me cold: "When does it come to pass?"

I read it again.

And it shall come to pass ***afterward****....*

Afterward. After what?

I backed up to verse 23, and what I saw there rocked my theology. Here's what must come before the outpouring:

> *Be glad then, ye children of Zion, and rejoice in the Lord your God: for he hath given you the former rain moderately, and he will cause to come down for you the rain, the former rain, and the latter rain in the first month.* ***And the floors shall be full of wheat, and the vats shall overflow with wine and oil. And I will restore to you the years that the locust hath eaten.... And ye shall eat in plenty, and be satisfied****, and praise the name of the Lord your God, that hath dealt wondrously with you: and my people shall never be ashamed. And ye shall know that I am in the midst of Israel, and that I am the Lord your God, and none else: and my people shall never be ashamed. And it shall come to pass afterward, that I will pour out my spirit upon all flesh...* (Joel 2:23-28).

Look at the sequence. Before the outpouring, there must be:

- Fullness (*the floors shall be full of wheat*)
- Overflow (*the vats shall overflow with wine and oil*)
- Restoration (*I will restore to you the years the locust hath eaten*)
- Plenty (*ye shall eat in plenty*)
- Satisfaction (*and be satisfied*)

And then, ***afterward***, *"I will pour out my spirit."*

The financial breakthrough precedes the spiritual outpouring. The material restoration comes before the revival. The abundance is established first, and then the anointing is poured out.

WHY THE ORDER MATTERS

This isn't arbitrary. This is divine wisdom. Because here's what happens when God pours out His Spirit in a place where there's no financial capacity: the revival dies where it started. It can't spread. It can't be sustained. It can't reach the nations.

But when He pours out His Spirit where there's fullness, where there's overflow, where there's plenty, then equipment can be purchased to broadcast that anointing around the world. Buildings can be constructed to contain larger gatherings. Missionaries can be sent. The poor can be fed. The gospel can be funded.

Revival without resources becomes a local phenomenon that fizzles out. Revival with resources becomes a global movement that transforms nations.

God knows this. That's why He establishes the order the way He does.

THE LOCUST YEARS

Notice that God promises to restore the years the locust has eaten. This is significant because many believers have lost years—even decades—to financial devastation. Bad decisions. Economic downturns. Unexpected crises. Generational poverty. The enemy has eaten their resources, their opportunities, their potential.

But God says, *"I will restore."* He promises to:

- Restore what was taken.
- Give back what was lost.
- Compensate for the wasted years.

It means *your past losses don't disqualify you from future abundance.* The fact that the locusts came doesn't mean that they won. God is in the restoration business, and He specializes in turning devastation into abundance.

The floors will be full. The vats will overflow. You will eat in plenty and be satisfied. And then, *afterward,* the Spirit will be poured out.

Right now, we are beginning to see the outpouring in the United States and around the world. Reports are coming in from every continent about how God is moving in unprecedented ways. Salvations. Healings. Miracles. People encountering Jesus in dreams and visions. Churches are exploding with growth.

And if Joel 2 is the pattern, do you know what that means? It means there's a great catch of fish awaiting every one of us. It means that the abundance precedes the anointing, which means that the abundance is already being released. The fact that we're seeing the outpouring is proof that God is releasing the overflow.

Your job isn't to make it happen. Your job is to position yourself to receive it:

- To break agreement with poverty thinking.
- To reject the religious lies that say lack is holy.
- To start declaring that it is God's pleasure to prosper His servants.

PENTECOST PROSPERITY

Think about the book of Acts. After the Day of Pentecost, thousands were saved. The Church exploded. What did they need immediately? Resources. Food. Housing. Organization. Leadership. Facilities. Acts 2:44-45 says:

> *And all that believed were together, and had all things common; and sold their possessions and goods, and parted them to all men, as every man had need.*

They had the capacity to meet the need because God had prospered them beforehand. Nobody lacked because the blessing was already in place. Acts 4:34-35 reinforces it:

> *Neither was there any among them that lacked: for as many as were possessors of lands or houses sold them, and brought the prices of the things that were sold, and laid them down at the apostles' feet....*

The revival didn't create the resources. The resources enabled the revival to spread and be sustained.

That's Joel 2 in action: fullness, overflow, restoration, plenty, satisfaction—and *then* the Spirit is poured out, and the movement has everything it needs to go global.

God is about to move in ways we've never seen before. The outpouring Joel prophesied is happening right now. Your sons and daughters are going to prophesy. Dreams and visions are going to increase. The supernatural is going to become normal. But you need to be financially positioned to participate. Not to hoard, not to consume—to deploy.

When God moves, and people get saved, somebody has to disciple them. When miracles happen and crowds gather, somebody has to organize, feed, and house them. When the harvest comes in, somebody has to fund the workers. That somebody is you. But not if you're broke. Not if you're stressed. Not if you're barely surviving.

Fish come first: the provision precedes the outpouring so that when the outpouring comes, you're equipped to steward it.

Joel 2 isn't just prophecy. It's instruction. Get your finances in order. Break free from debt. Position yourself to receive the overflow. The Spirit is about to be poured out, and God wants you ready to move with Him when it happens.

The floors are about to be full. The vats are about to overflow. And then, afterward, the greatest move of God you've ever seen is coming. Are you ready?

THE HIDDEN MYSTERY

After His resurrection, Jesus could have appeared to the disciples anywhere, in any way, and said anything. But look at what He chose to do, and when He chose to do it. John 21:1-3 sets the scene:

> *After these things Jesus shewed himself again to the disciples at the sea of Tiberias; and on this wise shewed he himself. There were together Simon Peter, and Thomas called Didymus, and Nathanael of Cana in Galilee, and the sons of Zebedee, and two other of his disciples. Simon Peter saith unto them, I go a fishing. They say unto him, We also go with thee. They went forth, and entered into a ship immediately; and that night they caught nothing.*

Here they are, post-resurrection, and Peter's going fishing. The others follow. They work all night and catch nothing. Sound familiar? It's Luke 5 all over again. Same scenario, same frustration, same failure. But this time, there's a critical difference in the timing.

This encounter in John 21 happens approximately ten days before Pentecost. Jesus has already told them to wait in Jerusalem until they are endued with power from on high (see Luke 24:49 and Acts 1:4-5).

The Day of Pentecost is coming, and they need to be in position to receive it. But here's the problem: waiting in Jerusalem for ten days with 120 people costs money. A lot of money.

You can't just gather that many people and expect them to live on air. They need food. They need lodging. They need provisions. If you've ever tried to take a ten-day vacation and feed everyone, you know it's expensive. Now multiply that by 120 people who are supposed to stay put and pray until the Holy Spirit shows up. Somebody has to fund that. Let's go on to verse 4 in John 21:

> *But when the morning was now come, Jesus stood on the shore: but the disciples knew not that it was Jesus.*

They've been working all night with no results. They're exhausted, frustrated, and probably calculating how they're going to make ends meet with nothing to show for their labor. Does that sound like your life sometimes?

And Jesus calls out to them: *"'Children, have ye any meat?' They answered him, 'No'"* (John 21:5).

Then, echoing His instructions to them that we looked at in Luke 5, He says: *"Cast the net on the right side of the ship, and ye shall find."*

I guarantee you Peter had a flashback in that moment. He'd heard this before. Three years earlier, a similar instruction produced a similar result. And something in his spirit probably whispered, "That's Him."

They cast the net, and verse 6 says: *"...they were not able to draw it for the multitude of fishes."*

Now watch Peter's reaction this time. John 21:7 says:

> *Therefore that disciple whom Jesus loved saith unto Peter, It is the Lord. Now when Simon Peter heard that it was the Lord, he girt his fisher's coat unto him, (for he was naked,) and did cast himself into the sea.*

Three years earlier, Peter needed a sign to believe. Matthew 14:28 (NKJV) tells us that he needed proof, he needed confirmation: "*...Lord, if it is You, command me come to You on the water.*"

But now? The moment Peter suspects it might be Jesus, he doesn't wait for confirmation. He doesn't need to walk on water. He doesn't even care if he has to swim. He's getting to Jesus, period.

That's maturity. That's what happens when you've walked with the Lord long enough that you don't need constant signs and wonders. You don't need every step proven. You just jump in and go.

THE 153 GREAT FISH

John 21:11 records the interesting, albeit enigmatic (to some) result:

> *Simon Peter went up, and drew the net to land full of great fishes, an hundred and fifty and three: and for all there were so many, yet was not the net broken.*

There were 153 large fish. Scholars have debated the significance of that number for centuries. Some say it represents all the known species of fish at the time. Others see numerical symbolism. But here's what matters for our purpose: it was a massive, supernatural catch.

Here's the key: the haul wasn't for eating. Look at John 21:9:

> *As soon then as they were come to land, they saw a fire of coals there, and fish laid thereon, and bread.*

Jesus already had fish prepared for them on the shore. He had breakfast ready. They didn't need the 153 fish to eat. So what were they for?

That catch of fish was for selling. It was provision. It was the financial supply needed to sustain 120 people in Jerusalem for ten days while they waited for the outpouring.

Do you see it now? Before Pentecost, there had to be supernatural provision. Before the greatest outpouring of the Holy Spirit the world had ever seen, Jesus made sure His disciples had the resources to sustain it. This truly fulfilled Joel's chapter 2 pattern.

Fish come first. The catch preceded Pentecost. The provision enabled the outpouring.

This wasn't random. Jesus could have provided in a hundred different ways, but He chose to do it through a miracle of abundance that directly addressed their immediate need while also funding the future move of God.

Did you know that this was the *first* miracle Jesus performed after His resurrection? That's right, even with Jesus, *fish come first*!

Fast-forward ten days. Acts 2. The Day of Pentecost. The Holy Spirit falls. Peter preaches. Three thousand souls are saved in one day (see Acts 2:41). And what happens immediately after that? Acts 2:44-47 tells us:

> *And all that believed were together, and had all things common; and sold their possessions and goods, and parted them to all men, as every man had need. And they, continuing daily with one accord in the temple, and breaking bread from house to house, did eat their meat with gladness and singleness of heart, praising God, and having favour with all the people. And the Lord added to the church daily such as should be saved.*

Nobody lacked. Why? Because the provision was already in place. The catch of fish funded the initial gathering. The overflow continued as God prospered believers, and they shared generously. The financial foundation supported the explosive growth of the Church.

That's what happens when provision comes first. The revival doesn't get choked out by lack. It spreads because there's capacity to sustain it.

God is preparing His Church for an outpouring like we've never seen. Reports from around the world confirm it. The Spirit is moving. Revival is breaking out.

And just like in Acts, just like in Joel 2, God is releasing supernatural provision ahead of the move. He's preparing His people financially so that when the anointing falls, they're equipped to steward it.

The 153 fish weren't just for the original disciples. They're a prophetic picture for us. God is about to release great catches, supernatural abundance, and financial miracles that seem impossible by natural means.

Your job is to let down your net at His word. To obey even when it doesn't make sense. To believe that He's already prepared the supply before the need shows up.

Because *fish come first.* The catch comes before the outpouring. And the outpouring is on its way! Are you ready to pull in your net?

4

EVERY NEED IS A PROPHECY

I want to reiterate something here that will change how you see every challenge you face: if you have a need right now, that need is a prophecy of a supply that already exists. Your need isn't evidence that God has forgotten about you. Your need is evidence that, somewhere, God has already prepared the answer. He's already set aside the provision. He's already made the way.

Your job isn't to create the supply. Your job is to tap into what He's already prepared. This is where faith comes in. Not faith that God will provide someday, somehow, some way. But faith that believes He has *already* provided, and you're simply positioning yourself to receive what He has *already* released. It's the difference between begging and believing. Between anxiety and expectation. Between desperation and confident trust. Here is what I mean:

- When Peter let down his net at Jesus' word, the fish were already there. They didn't appear because Peter obeyed. They were swimming in those waters all along. Peter's obedience simply positioned him to catch what was already prepared.
- When Jesus told Peter to go fishing and find a coin in the fish's mouth to pay the temple tax (see Matthew 17:27), that coin was already there. The supply existed before Peter cast his line.

- When Elijah told the widow to make him a cake first and promised that her jar of meal and cruse of oil wouldn't run empty (see 1 Kings 17:13-14), the ongoing supply was already secured before she took the step of obedience.

The pattern is consistent: God prepares the supply, then gives you instructions that will position you to receive it.

You can't manufacture provision, but you can position yourself for it. You can obey His instructions. You can sow when He tells you to sow. You can give when He tells you to give. You can launch out into the deep when He tells you to go. And when you do, you'll discover what was already there waiting for you.

He created the provision. He secured the resources. He made the way. Now He's inviting you to step into what He's already prepared. Let's look back a moment:

What was the first thing blessed in all creation?

Fish.

What was the first thing over which man was given dominion?

Fish.

What was the first miracle that launched Peter into ministry?

Fish!

What was the first miracle Jesus performed after His Resurrection?

FISH!

Fish come first: not because you earned them. Not because you deserve them. Not because you figured out the perfect formula. But because God, in His wisdom and love, prepares a supply before you even know you need it. Because He's El Shaddai. Because He's your Father and good fathers provide for their children.

The supply is there. The fish are in the water. The breakthrough is prepared. The provision exists. Now let me show you what to say until you see it.

SAY THIS CONTINUALLY!

With all these revelations flooding my mind and heart that Wednesday night, the Holy Spirit led me to one more passage that would become the battle cry for everything I was learning. It is found in Psalm 35:27:

> *Let them shout for joy, and be glad, that favour my righteous cause: yea, let them say continually, Let the Lord be magnified, which hath pleasure in the prosperity of* ***his servant.***

Read that last part again. The *Lord* has pleasure in the prosperity of His servant.

Not tolerance, not reluctant permission: pleasure. He delights in it. He takes joy in it. He's pleased when His servants prosper.

And notice what we're commanded to do: say it continually. Why continually?

Here's what I've discovered after pastoring for more than two decades and praying for more than 100,000 people—one of the most common questions believers ask is, "What do I say when I pray? I don't know what to say."

Well, here's your answer. Here are explicit instructions from Scripture about what you should be saying, and how often you should be saying it.

Say continually: "The Lord takes pleasure in my prosperity."

Not once. Not occasionally when you feel spiritual. Not just when you're in church. Continually. Why? Because you've been so propagandized by poverty theology, so conditioned by religious tradition, so beaten down by the spirit of mammon that it's going to take a washing and a renewal of your mind to break free. Romans 12:2 says:

> *Be not conformed to this world: but be ye transformed by the renewing of your mind.*

Your mind has been conformed to a worldview that says poverty is holy and prosperity is suspect. That needs to be renewed. And renewal happens through the Word spoken continually.

Notice that Psalm 35:27 says: *"his servant."* It is singular, personal, which refers to how God wanted people to pray and say for King David. God wants these prayers prayed over you. Make it a declaration. Say it aloud right now:

- "The *Lord* takes pleasure in my prosperity."
- Again: "The Lord takes *pleasure* in my prosperity."
- And again: "The Lord takes pleasure in *my* prosperity."

Feel that resistance rising up? That religious discomfort? That's exactly why you need to say it continually. Because every time you declare it, you're breaking agreement with the lies you've believed and aligning yourself with what God actually says.

A PROSPERITY PREACHER REPENTS

After that Wednesday night encounter, I went before my congregation and repented. I threw my notes in the air and told them I had been wrong to avoid this subject. I had been operating in the fear of man instead of the fear of God. And I made them a promise: We were going to dig into biblical prosperity, and we weren't going to stop until everyone in the congregation understood what God says about it.

Within weeks, "The Lord takes pleasure in my prosperity" became a mantra in our church. Anytime I told the congregation to turn to a passage in their Bibles, you'd hear people like popcorn popping, shouting out, "The Lord takes pleasure in my prosperity!" Someone on one side of the room would start it; someone on the other side would finish it.

It created an atmosphere. It shifted the culture. It broke the religious stranglehold that had kept people in poverty thinking. And within a year, we saw millions of dollars in financial miracles in people's lives.

The same thing can happen for you, but you have to break the silence in your own life. You have to start declaring what God says instead of agreeing with what religion, tradition, and poverty theology have programmed into you.

Make this your habit:

- When you wake up in the morning: "*The Lord takes pleasure in my prosperity.*"
- When you're driving to work: "*The Lord takes pleasure in my prosperity.*"
- When you're facing a bill you don't know how to pay: "*The Lord takes pleasure in my prosperity.*"
- When the enemy whispers that you're going to lose everything: "*The Lord takes pleasure in my prosperity.*"

Say it when you feel it. Say it when you don't. Say it when your bank account agrees. Say it when your bank account is empty. Say it until it gets down into your spirit. Say it until you believe it. Say it until the evidence shows up in your life.

This isn't positive confession trying to manipulate reality. This is agreeing with what God has already said about you. This is renewing your mind with His truth. This is speaking God's Word over your situation until your situation lines up with God's Word.

Continually means continually. Not sometimes. Not when it's convenient. Not just during the offering. Continually, because the propaganda is deep. The lies are strong. The religious conditioning is real. And it's going to take continual declaration of truth to break free. That's why I wrote a book titled *101 Prosperity Confessions: Daily Decrees That Release God's Abundance*. In that book, I walk you through 101 Bible verses for 101 days to renew your mind. I encourage you to get it!

BREAKING THE ORPHAN SPIRIT

That Wednesday night in January 2015 changed everything for me. The glory encounter. The rebuke. The three words that I didn't understand but that unlocked a biblical revelation I'd been missing my entire ministry: *Fish come first.*

I've watched the same breakthroughs happen everywhere I've shared this message. I've shared it in congregations across America. I've shared it with pastors, leaders, and churches around the world, including the underground and persecuted churches around the world that we work with. When people get this revelation, when they understand that *fish come first*, and that God takes pleasure in their prosperity, breakthrough follows.

An orphan doesn't expect provision. An orphan doesn't assume the father cares. An orphan lives in survival mode, scraping by, making do with whatever they can get on their own. But you're not an orphan. You're a son. You're a daughter. And your Father cares about every area of your life, including your finances. Romans 8:15 says:

> *For ye have not received the spirit of bondage again to fear; but ye have received the Spirit of adoption, whereby we cry, Abba, Father.*

Abba is the most intimate term for father. It's like saying *Papa* or *Daddy*. It's a child's cry as the child runs to greet a father who loves and provides for his child.

That's your relationship with God. Not a distant deity who might throw you a bone if you beg hard enough. Your Abba. Your Papa. Your Father who takes pleasure in blessing His children. The orphan mentality says:

- You're on your own.
- You have to make it happen.

- Provision is something you earn rather than receive.
- It's wrong to desire to prosper.

Until you break agreement with the orphan mentality, you'll struggle to walk in the abundance God has for you.

So right now, I break that orphan spirit off your life in Jesus' name. I declare that you are a son, you are a daughter, and your Father cares about your finances. He cares about your needs. He cares about your bills and your debts and your dreams. And He has provision prepared for you that you haven't even tapped into yet, in Jesus' name!

The same gospel that forgives your sins is the same gospel that will get you out of debt. The same power that heals your body is the same power that can break financial bondage. The same Jesus who set you free from the penalty of sin wants to set you free from the tyranny of poverty.

This isn't two different gospels. This is one gospel with comprehensive implications. Jesus came to give you an abundant life (see John 10:10), not barely-getting-by life. Abundant life. Life that overflows. Life that has more than enough. Life that is free to pursue God's purposes without the limitations of lack.

If we are going to preach the whole gospel, we have to include this part. Not as the main thing, but as part of the whole package of what Jesus came to give us.

So here's my challenge to you: stop apologizing for prosperity. Stop retreating from promises God made.

Start declaring what God says. Start believing that He takes pleasure in your prosperity. Start positioning yourself to receive the overflow He's already prepared.

Fish come first. Not as the goal, but as the foundation. Not as the end, but as the means. Not to make you comfortable, but to make you dangerous for the Kingdom.

When you're financially free, you're spiritually free to pursue everything God has called you to. You can give without limitation. You can go without hesitation. You can build without restriction. You can bless without constraint.

That's what biblical prosperity is for. And that's what God wants to release in your life.

The supply has already been prepared. The fish are already in the water. Will you break agreement with poverty thinking? Will you start declaring continually that the Lord takes pleasure in your prosperity?

The encounter I had that Wednesday night wasn't just for me. It was for every believer who's been held back by financial stress, limited by lack, and robbed of their full potential because they didn't know what God says about prosperity.

Now you know. Now you've seen it in Scripture. Now you understand the pattern: *Fish come first.* And the God who blessed them in Genesis, who multiplied them for Peter in Luke 5, who provided them before Pentecost in John 21, is the same God who wants to release supernatural abundance in your life right now.

PART TWO

DEFINING OUR TERMS

5

WHAT IS PROSPERITY?

Say the word *prosperity* in a room full of Christians and watch what happens. Eyes narrow. Arms cross. Someone mutters "health and wealth gospel" under their breath like it's an incantation that will protect them against evil spirits. The word has become radioactive, so toxic that many believers treat it like profanity, something to be avoided in polite theological company.

But here's the scandal: prosperity isn't a marketing slogan invented by televangelists in the 1980s. It's Bible language. It's God's language. And when we treat a word that the Holy Spirit chose to use hundreds of times across Scripture as if it were inherently corrupt, we're not protecting orthodoxy, we're surrendering vocabulary that belongs to the Kingdom of God. Think about that for a moment. The same Spirit who inspired Moses to write this:

> *...that the Lord thy God may bless thee in all that thou settest thine hand to...."* (Deuteronomy 23:20).

And moved the apostle John to pray this:

> *"I wish above all things that thou mayest prosper and be in health..."* (3 John 1:2),

somehow gets overruled by our cultural squeamishness.

THE PENDULUM SWINGS

We've allowed the excesses of some teachers and the cynicism of others to rob us of a valid biblical category. That's not discernment; that's capitulation.

The backlash is understandable. We've all seen the abuses, the manipulative schemes that prey on desperate people. The word *prosperity* became shorthand for spiritual shallowness, for a version of Christianity that looks more like greed in a Sunday suit than the gospel of the crucified and risen Lord.

So the pendulum swung. Hard. In reaction to all the prosperity excesses, many Christians embraced the idea that lack is somehow holier than provision because all that prosperity jargon just makes us feel "icky."

But here's the problem with pendulums: they don't find truth, they just swing from one error to another. Rejecting prosperity and the biblical means to attain it doesn't get us closer to Scripture; it just trades one ditch for another.

There is only one question we should ask if we're serious about building our lives on the Word rather than on our own reactions. We should not ask what our experience, our tradition, or even our understandable revulsion toward greedy preachers says.

The real question is: What does God say in the text He gave us? If church history teaches us anything, it is this: every time we let culture, tradition, or reaction interpret Scripture, we end up in trouble.

The Pharisees added to the Law until they crushed people under unbearable burdens. The medieval Church created an entire theology of suffering, turning poverty and pain into sacraments. The Reformers had to break through centuries of accumulated tradition just to let people hear the gospel again. And we are not immune.

GOING BACK TO BASICS

Every generation has to do the hard work of going back to the text, not to find what we want to find, not to proof-text our preferences, but to let Scripture interrogate us. To let God's Word sit in judgment over our assumptions, our experiences, and yes, our reasonable concerns about how other people have misused biblical language.

So before we write off *prosperity* as a compromised term, before we cede the vocabulary of increase, blessing, and abundance to false teachers, before we decide that the language of Deuteronomy 28 and Psalm 35:27 and 2 Corinthians 9:8 is off-limits to the people of God, maybe we should actually read what those passages say.

Maybe we should do the hard, unglamorous work of examining the original Hebrew and Greek. Maybe we should trace the theme from Genesis to Revelation and see if God's heart on this matter is as clear as His heart on holiness or justice or grace. Maybe we should ask whether the Bible's own vocabulary supports a theology of divine provision and covenant increase, or whether we've been reading the text through the lens of our Western guilt and our reactions to American excess.

That's what this chapter is about. Not defending charlatans. Not justifying greed. This chapter is about reclaiming biblical language from both those who abuse it and those who abandon it. We'll be looking at it all in this book.

If *prosperity* is God's word, and we're about to see that it is, then treating it as greed is, in itself, a kind of blasphemy. It's calling unclean what God has called clean. It's rejecting vocabulary that the Holy Spirit has chosen, inspired, and preserved for us across centuries, languages, and cultures.

The word itself isn't the problem. Our misuse of it is. Our failure to define it biblically is. Our tendency to import cultural greed or medieval asceticism into the text instead of letting the text speak for itself is. So let's go back to the Book. Let's open the Hebrew lexicons and the

Greek concordances. Let's read Moses and David and Solomon and Isaiah and Jesus and Paul and John with fresh eyes and honest hearts. Let's see what they meant when they used the language of blessing and increase and provision and, yes, prosperity.

And let's be prepared to repent if we've been wrong—not because some preacher convinced us, but because the Word of God demands it. That's the standard. Not experience. Not tradition. Not reaction. Scripture alone.

Let's see what it says. How does the Bible define prosperity? Not the caricatures pushed by critics who build their case on a few bad actors. Not the poverty-soaked version handed down by religious tradition. But the real one, the one written in Hebrew and Greek, woven into the covenants, and taught by Jesus and His apostles.

We need to get these definitions settled. Every truth about blessing, stewardship, and abundance stands on this foundation.

IF PEOPLE MATTER, PROSPERITY MATTERS

Why spend an entire chapter defending a word that makes people uncomfortable? Why fight this battle when it would be easier to just avoid the term and talk about *blessing,* or provision instead?

Because words matter. Vocabulary matters. And when we surrender biblical language to critics and abusers, we lose more than a word. We lose a whole category. We lose a piece of the gospel.

Here's the bottom line: if people matter, money matters. If you care about human beings—their health, their families, and their futures, then you have to care about the resources required to meet their needs. Love isn't abstract. Love is concrete. Love pays bills. Love funds food. Love prints Bibles. Love sends missionaries. Love builds hospitals. Love digs wells. Love educates children. Love rescues the trafficked. Love shelters the homeless. And all of that costs money.

You can have the purest heart in the world, the deepest passion for souls, and the most Spirit-filled prayers, but if you don't have resources, your impact is limited. Ministry requires money. Mercy requires money. Missions require money. Making disciples requires money.

You can't run a church, support a missionary, or feed the hungry on good intentions alone. That is why prosperity matters.

Not because money is the point, but because people are the point. And people have needs that require resources to meet. God prospers His people so they can be the answer to someone else's desperation. He increases their capacity so they can extend His Kingdom. He blesses them so they can be a blessing.

Prosperity is about love. It's about having the means to do what love demands. It's about being equipped to meet needs, to seize opportunities, to respond when the Spirit says "go" or "give" or "build."

It's about being a conduit of God's provision instead of a bottleneck. The world is full of need. Millions are hungry. Millions are enslaved. Millions have never heard the gospel. Millions are sick, oppressed, and dying without hope. And God's plan to reach them isn't to rain down manna from Heaven again. His plan is to prosper His people and send them out as His hands and feet into the darkness.

That's the vision. That's the "why." That's the reason for biblical prosperity.

RECLAIMING THE LANGUAGE

This brings us to a point that needs to be made: it's time to stop using the term *"prosperity gospel"* as a pejorative.

Since *prosperity* is a biblical term that reflects God's will for His children, using it to label what some perceive as error is both misleading and unfortunate. It unfairly taints something that aligns with God's desire. It hinders His children from receiving what He wants to give them. Every time we treat *prosperity* like a dirty word, we're conditioning believers to recoil from a promise that God Himself made.

If the issue is greed, call it what it is—the *"greedy gospel"* or the *"materialism gospel"* or the *"self-centered gospel."* Those terms address an actual problem. But don't slander a biblical word by attaching it to the perversion.

It would be like calling false teaching about grace the *"grace gospel"* and then training Christians to be suspicious every time someone mentions the word *grace*. That's insane. Grace is good. The abuse of grace is bad. We don't stop preaching about grace because some people twist it into license. We correct the distortion and keep preaching the truth.

The same applies here. Prosperity is good. The abuse of prosperity teaching is bad. But the solution isn't to abandon the word or treat it like blasphemy. The solution is to define it biblically, guard it carefully, and reclaim it from those who've misused it.

Using *"prosperity gospel"* as a blanket negative promotes division rather than unity. It creates misrepresentations. It trains believers to reject what God wants them to embrace. And it does damage to the very people it's supposedly trying to protect, because it cuts them off from understanding a key dimension of God's covenant faithfulness.

If the real issue is *greed,* then call it greed. If the issue is *manipulation,* call it manipulation. If the issue is a shallow, cross-less Christianity, call it what it is. But don't misuse a divine and biblically endorsed word as if it's synonymous with error. That's intellectually dishonest, and it's spiritually harmful.

GOD'S PROSPERITY, GOD'S WAY

Here's the truth we need to lock in: God wants you to prosper. But He wants you to prosper His way, not yours. His way includes the Cross. His way includes obedience. His way includes generosity. His way includes wisdom, work, and stewardship. His way includes seasons of testing, sacrifice, and learning to trust Him when you can't see the provision yet. His way includes aligning your ambitions with His purposes, your resources with His Kingdom, your heart with His heart.

As long as you put His Kingdom and His righteousness first (see Matthew 6:33), you have no reason to fear the word *prosperity*. You have no reason to shrink back from God's promises of increase, blessing, and abundance. You have no reason to settle for poverty when God has called you to be a conduit of His provision.

The issue has never been whether God wants to prosper you. The issue is whether you'll define prosperity the way He does—as a covenant capacity to fulfill His will and to love His people well.

So let's stop apologizing for biblical language. Let's stop retreating from promises God made. Let's stop letting the abusers and the critics define the terms.

Prosperity is Bible language. It's covenant language. It's Kingdom language. And it's time the people of God reclaimed it.

WHAT THE BIBLE ACTUALLY SAYS

If we're going to reclaim the language of prosperity, we need to know what we're reclaiming. That means doing the work of lexicography: cracking open the Hebrew and Greek dictionaries, examining how words are actually used in Scripture, and letting the biblical authors define their own terms instead of importing our assumptions.

When Paul prays that believers would *"prosper"* or when Moses promises that God will make His people *"prosperous,"* what exactly are they saying? What concepts are buried in those words? What mental pictures would ancient Hebrew or first-century Greek speakers have had when they heard these terms? The answers might surprise you.

Because what we're about to discover is that the Bible's vocabulary of blessing, increase, and provision is neither as crass as its critics claim nor as shallow as its abusers have made it. It's covenant language, earthy and spiritual, material and relational, individual and communal. It's the vocabulary of the God who blesses His people so they can be a blessing, who provides so they can be generous, and who increases them so they can advance His purposes on earth.

6

THE LANGUAGE OF INCREASE

Every line of business has its own vocabulary. There are words, phrases, and references that are clear to those within that business, but which may not be understood by the general public. The same is true with the biblical concept of prosperity. My purpose in this section is to bring insight and clarity to the vocabulary—both Hebrew and Greek—that makes up the biblical study of prosperity.

IMPORTANT HEBREW WORDS CONCERNING PROSPERITY

Tsalach: The primary Hebrew verb for *prosper* is צָלַח (*tsalach*, pronounced tsah-LAKH). It appears more than 60 times in the Old Testament, and its core meaning is vivid: to push forward, to advance, to break through, to succeed.

The word *prosper* is not passive. It's about forward momentum, progress, and breakthrough. Most importantly, it is always something God grants or enables.

The standard Hebrew lexicons define *tsalach* as, "to advance, prosper, succeed; causatively, to make prosperous."[3] The causative form is critical because it keeps God in the center of the action. You don't *tsalach* by your own power. God makes you *tsalach*. He's the One pushing you forward. He's the One granting success.

Look at how Scripture uses it. When Joseph is in Potiphar's house, the text says:

> *The Lord was with Joseph, and he was a prosperous man...* (Genesis 39:2).

The Hebrew is literally "he was a *tsalach* man" or "a man who was advancing, succeeding, breaking through obstacles." Because "the Lord was with him, and that which he did, the Lord made it to *tsalach*" (see Genesis 39:3). God was the cause. Joseph was the beneficiary.

Sakal: It was the same with David. When he went out to fight:

> *David behaved himself wisely in all his ways; and the Lord was with him* (1 Samuel 18:14).

The word that is translated "behaved wisely" is *sakal* in Hebrew, which means, "to act or behave wisely, prudently, and with circumspection, which often leads to success or prosperity as a result of divine favor."[4]

Although slightly different from *tsalach*, the ideas overlap. David was succeeding, prospering, and advancing—and the text is explicit that the Lord was the reason.

Later, when David's mighty men are listed, we read about those who *"helped David"* and how *"the Lord of hosts was with him"* (1 Chronicles 11:9). The pattern is consistent: God's presence produces *tsalach*. His blessing generates forward movement.

Consider Hezekiah. After he cleansed the temple and restored proper worship, the text says:

> *And in every work that he began in the service of the house of God, and in the law, and in the commandments, to seek his God, he did it with all his heart, and prospered* (2 Chronicles 31:21).

That's *tsalach* again. Hezekiah advanced. He succeeded. His projects bore fruit—it happened because he aligned himself with God's purposes.

This is what biblical prosperity looks like in Hebrew: God-given forward movement in your calling. It's tied to covenant faithfulness and divine purpose. You prosper in what God called you to do, and you prosper because He's with you. This includes material wealth and abundance.

Shalvah: Another key term is שַׁלְוָה (*shalvah*, pronounced shal-VAH), which means, "ease, prosperity, security, tranquility."[5] It shows up in passages including Psalm 122:7:

> *Peace be within thy walls, and prosperity within thy palaces.*

The word evokes rest, safety, and well-being. It's the prosperity of a city at peace, a nation under God's protection, and a life marked by stability rather than chaos.

Shalvah is closely related to the more well-known word *shalom*, which means peace; however, it carries connotations of completeness, wholeness, and yes, material well-being. When the prophets promise *shalom,* they're not just talking about the absence of war. They're talking about flourishing crops in the field, safety in the streets, children playing, elders honored, justice flowing. It's comprehensive prosperity, the kind that touches every area of life.

So here's the working definition we can draw from the Hebrew:

- Biblical prosperity is God-given forward movement, success, security, and fruitfulness in one's calling under His blessing.
- It's active *(tsalach)* and restful *(shalvah).*
- It's about advancing God's purposes while enjoying His peace.
- It's increase that comes from covenant, not hustle. Blessing that flows from obedience, not manipulation.

SUFFICIENCY WITH OVERFLOW

When we move into the New Testament and into the Greek, the vocabulary shifts but the concepts stay consistent.

Euodoō: The primary Greek verb for *prosper* is εὐοδόω (*euodoō*, pronounced yoo-oh-DAH-oh). It's a compound word: *eu* (good) + *hodos* (way or journey). Literally, it means "to have a good journey," and by extension, "to prosper, to succeed."[6]

The word appears most famously in 3 John 1:2, where the apostle writes: *"Beloved, I wish above all things that thou mayest prosper and be in health, even as thy soul prospereth."*

That's *euodoō*, the prayer that your physical and material life would advance and succeed in the same way your spiritual life is advancing. John doesn't pit the two against each other. He wants them in sync. He wants the believer to prosper.

Greek lexicons emphasize that *euodoō* carries the idea of success granted by God.

It's not self-made success; it's divinely enabled prospering. God grants the good journey. He gives the breakthrough. And significantly, John prays this for a fellow believer as a matter of course, not as something scandalous or exceptional, but as a normal Christian desire.

Perisseuō: Another critical term is περισσεύω (*perisseuō*, pronounced peh-ris-SYOO-oh), which means "to abound, to overflow, to have more than enough."[7]

Paul uses it repeatedly in 2 Corinthians 9 when he's receiving an offering and talking about generosity in giving:

> *And God is able to make all grace abound toward you; that ye, always having all sufficiency in all things, may abound to every good work* (2 Corinthians 9:8).
>
> *Being enriched in every thing to all bountifulness...* (2 Corinthians 9:11).

The language here is extravagant. All grace abounding. All sufficiency in all things. Enriched in everything. This isn't bare-minimum provision. This is overflow. Abundance. More than enough. Notice the purpose: *"that ye... may abound to every good work."* God supplies abundantly so you can give abundantly.

Autarkeia: This brings us to αὐτάρκεια (*autarkeia*, pronounced ow-TAR-kay-ah), meaning "sufficiency, contentment, competence."[8]

Paul uses it in the same passage: *"having all sufficiency"* (2 Corinthians 9:8). He also uses it in 1 Timothy 6:6: *"But godliness with contentment is great gain."*

The word doesn't mean, "barely scraping by." It means having enough, and in the context of 2 Corinthians 9, it means having enough to overflow into generosity.

Autarkeia is about being adequately resourced for the mission God's given you. *Fish come first!* Not lacking. Not in want. Not dependent on others in a way that cripples your ability to serve. You're sufficient. You're competent. You have what you need.

Ploutos: Finally, there's πλοῦτος (*ploutos*, pronounced PLOO-tos), the straightforward word for "riches" or "wealth."[9] Paul uses it both literally and metaphorically. He talks about *"the riches of his glory"* (Philippians 4:19) and *"the unsearchable riches of Christ"* (Ephesians 3:8). But he also promises that:

> *My God shall supply all your need according to his riches in glory by Christ Jesus* (Philippians 4:19).

The riches are real. They're God's resources, yes, but they supply your real needs in the real world.

So here's the working definition from the Greek:

Biblical prosperity is God-supplied sufficiency with overflow for every good work.

It's enough *(autarkeia)* that becomes more than enough *(perisseuō)* because God causes you to succeed *(euodoō)* so that His riches *(ploutos)* can flow through you to meet needs and advance His Kingdom.

GLORY AND SUBSTANCE

Kabod: There's one more Hebrew term we need to examine, and it might be the most surprising of all: דוֹבָּכ (*kabod*, pronounced kah-VODE), the word most often translated "glory."[10]

We're used to thinking of glory in purely spiritual terms: God's radiant presence, His majesty, His honor. *Kabod* certainly carries those meanings. But here's what many Christians don't know: the root meaning of *kabod* is "weight" or "heaviness," and in common usage it often referred to wealth, riches, and substantial possessions.[11]

The verb form, *kabad*, means "to be heavy, weighty, burdensome."[12] In ancient Near Eastern culture, one of the primary ways a person's weight or substance was measured was by their material resources.

Look at how Scripture uses it. In Genesis 31:1, Laban's sons complain about Jacob:

> *...Jacob hath taken away all that was our father's; and of that which was our father's hath he gotten all this glory.*

The word there is *kabod*. They're not talking about some abstract spiritual honor. They're talking about wealth, flocks, and herds—the visible, material substance that makes a man weighty in his community.

Similar language is used in Genesis 45:13 when Jacob sends for his father:

> *And ye shall tell my father of all my glory in Egypt....*

What is Joseph's glory? It is his position, yes, but it is also his resources, his authority, and his ability to provide. His *kabod* in Egypt was demonstrated by the grain stored in the storehouses, the power at his disposal, and the provision he can extend to his family.

Even when God Himself is described with *kabod*, the physical and material dimensions aren't absent. When Moses asks to see God's glory in Exodus 33:18, he's asking to see the fullness of who God is.

The manifestations of God's glory consistently include tangible, visible, weighty realities. The cloud fills the tabernacle with such heavy presence that the priests can't stand (see 1 Kings 8:11). The glory of the Lord appears as *"a consuming fire"* (Exodus 24:17). Glory has substance. It has weight. It's real in every sense of the word.

Wealth was a visible manifestation of a person's standing, their honor, their glory in the community. To have *kabod* was to have both honor and the substance to back it up.

This isn't to say that glory equals wealth in some crude one-to-one equation. However, in Hebrew thought, you cannot completely separate the two in every instance. A man of *kabod* was a man of substance, spiritual and material, honor and resource, character and capacity. Glory wasn't abstract. It was earthy. It had weight.

Psalm 24:10 declares: *"...The Lord of hosts, he is the King of glory."*

He's not just talking about ethereal majesty. He's talking about the God of infinite substance, infinite resource, and infinite weight.

Here's why this matters for our discussion: if kabod can include the idea of substantial wealth and tangible resource, then the dichotomy we've created between "spiritual" blessing and "material" blessing collapses.

In the Hebrew worldview, they're not opposites. They're dimensions of the same reality. The God of glory is the God of substance. A people who reflect His glory will, by extension, carry the weight of spiritual authority, as well as the resources and capacity to accomplish His purposes on earth.

When Paul writes about *"the riches of his glory"* (see Ephesians 3:16), he's tapping into this Hebrew concept. Glory isn't just bright light; glory is the weight of God's inexhaustible presence and resource.

The glory of God and the prosperity of God aren't competing concepts. They're connected. Because glory, at its root, means weight. A people who carry God's glory will not only carry His substance in character, but also in capacity. In wisdom and in resource. In spiritual authority as well as in practical provision. God's glory is weighty and He intends for His people to carry that weight into the world.

The question has never been whether the Bible talks about prosperity. The question is whether we'll let the Bible define what prosperity means in our lives or whether we'll let the culture (either the greedy version or the guilty version) do the defining for us.

Now we have the vocabulary. We know what the words mean. In the next section, we'll trace the story from Eden to the early Church, and see how God's commitment to prospering His people unfolds across the entire biblical narrative.

7

THE PROSPERITY PATTERN

Prosperity isn't a random theme that shows up in a few scattered verses. It's woven into the fabric of redemptive history from the very first chapter of Genesis to the final pages of Revelation. It's part of God's original design, His covenant promises, His restoration plans, and His ultimate vision for redeemed humanity. To see this, we need to trace the story following the narrative arc that Scripture itself lays out.

What we're about to discover is that God's heart for prospering His people is a consistent thread that runs through every major epoch of biblical history. The vocabulary changes. The covenant administration develops.

But the core commitment remains: God blesses His people so they can be a blessing. He provides for them so they can provide for others. He increases them so His name can be magnified and His purposes advanced on earth.

Let's walk through the story.

THE EDEN BLUEPRINT

Before sin, before the Fall, before poverty or scarcity or lack existed in the human experience, God gave humanity its marching orders, saying:

> *Be fruitful, and multiply, and replenish the earth, and subdue it: and have dominion over the fish of the sea, and over the fowl of*

> *the air, and over every living thing that moveth upon the earth* (Genesis 1:28).

Read that again. The first divine command to humanity is a prosperity mandate. Be fruitful. Multiply. Fill the earth. Subdue it. Exercise dominion. This is increase language. This is expansion language. This is the vocabulary of growth, development, cultivation, and abundance.

God didn't create Adam and Eve to merely survive. He created them to flourish. He placed them in a garden that was already *"pleasant to the sight, and good for food"* (Genesis 2:9). He surrounded them with resources—gold, bdellium, onyx (see Genesis 2:11-12) and commissioned them to extend Eden's order and beauty over the whole earth.

The original human vocation was creative, productive, and expansive.

This is the blueprint. Prosperity is baked into creation itself. It's God's design for image-bearers operating in a world He called *"very good"* (Genesis 1:31).

And then came the Fall.

WHERE POVERTY ENTERS

Genesis 3 changed everything. When Adam and Eve rebelled, the curse that followed was devastatingly material. God tells Adam:

> *...cursed is the ground for thy sake; in sorrow shalt thou eat of it all the days of thy life; thorns also and thistles shall it bring forth to thee...* (Genesis 3:17-18).

Work became toil. Provision became struggle. The ground resisted. Scarcity entered. For the first time, humanity faced lack, frustration, and death. The prosperity of Eden gave way to the poverty of a fallen world.

This is critical: poverty was not part of God's original design. It's a consequence of sin. It's part of the curse. And everything God does from Genesis 3 forward is aimed at reversing the curse, restoring what was lost, and bringing humanity back into the abundance He always intended.

After Adam, we see God's provision and blessing throughout the generations. The same command to increase and prosper that was given to him was given again to Noah and his descendants.

COVENANT RESTORES BLESSING

God's answer to the Fall is covenant. When He established His covenant with Abraham, prosperity language was front and center:

> *And I will make of thee a great nation, and I will bless thee, and make thy name great; and thou shalt be a blessing: and I will bless them that bless thee, and curse him that curseth thee: and in thee shall all families of the earth be blessed* (Genesis 12:2-3).

Notice the repetition: *bless, blessing, bless, bless, blessed.* This is covenant vocabulary. God is committing Himself to prosper Abraham tangibly. He promises land, descendants, protection, and a great name. And significantly, the blessing isn't just for Abraham's benefit—it's so Abraham can be a blessing to others. The prosperity is purposeful. It's meant to flow through Abraham to the nations.

Later, the text notes that *"Abram was very rich in cattle, in silver, and in gold"* (Genesis 13:2). This isn't incidental. It's evidence that God keeps His promises. The covenant blessing shows up in Abraham's flocks, his wealth, his capacity to host guests, and his ability to negotiate with kings. His prosperity is visible, material, and directly tied to God's faithfulness.

The same pattern repeats with Isaac:

> *Then Isaac sowed in that land, and received in the same year an hundredfold: and the Lord blessed him. And the man waxed great, and went forward, and grew until he became very great* (Genesis 26:12-13).

And with Jacob, despite Laban's attempts to cheat him:

> *And the man increased exceedingly, and had much cattle, and maidservants, and menservants, and camels, and asses* (Genesis 30:43).

The patriarchal narratives establish a principle: covenant faithfulness produces tangible blessing.

God prospers His people. He makes them fruitful. He increases what they steward. It's evidence that God is with them and that He keeps His Word.

TORAH BLESSING

When God gives Israel the Law at Sinai, He makes the connection between obedience and prosperity explicit. Deuteronomy 28 lays it out in stark detail: blessings for obedience, curses for disobedience.

The blessings include abundant crops, multiplied livestock, full barns, victory over enemies, and lending to nations rather than borrowing (see Deuteronomy 28:1-14). The curses include famine, disease, defeat, and debt (see Deuteronomy 28:15-68).

This isn't a mechanical formula where good behavior automatically produces wealth; rather, it is a covenant framework. God ties material flourishing to covenant faithfulness because He's establishing a people who will display His character and His blessing to the watching world. When Israel obeys, they prosper and the nations take notice. When they rebel, they suffer and God's name is dishonored.

Deuteronomy 8:18 makes the purpose clear:

> *But thou shalt remember the Lord thy God: for it is he that giveth thee power to get wealth, that he may establish his covenant which he sware unto thy fathers....*

God gives the ability to generate wealth. Why? To establish His covenant. Prosperity serves covenant purposes.

The wisdom literature reinforces this. Proverbs repeatedly links diligence, integrity, and the fear of the Lord to material blessing:

> *The blessing of the Lord, it maketh rich, and he addeth no sorrow with it* (Proverbs 10:22).

> *Honour the Lord with thy substance, and with the firstfruits of all thine increase: so shall thy barns be filled with plenty...* (Proverbs 3:9-10).

Wise people prosper because they align themselves with God's order.

This is what many miss. Prosperity is as much a principle as it is a promise. More on this later.

At the same time, the Law and the prophets are relentless in their concern for the poor, the widow, the orphan, and the stranger. Justice and generosity are nonnegotiable.

The point is not to hoard wealth but to steward it righteously. Prosperity in the biblical framework always includes the responsibility of blessing others.

When Israel falls into idolatry and injustice, the prophets announce judgment. But they also announce restoration. The language of restoration is saturated with prosperity themes.

Isaiah envisions a day when:

> *They shall build houses, and inhabit them; and they shall plant vineyards, and eat the fruit of them. They shall not build, and another inhabit; they shall not plant, and another eat...* (Isaiah 65:21-22).

This is security, provision, and fruitfulness restored.

Jeremiah promises:

> *For I know the thoughts that I think toward you, saith the Lord, thoughts of peace, and not of evil, to give you an expected end* (Jeremiah 29:11).

The word *peace* in this verse is *shalom*, which comprehensively involves well-being, prosperity, and flourishing.

Ezekiel prophesies about the river flowing from the temple, bringing life wherever it goes:

> *And by the river upon the bank thereof, on this side and on that side, shall grow all trees for meat, whose leaf shall not fade, neither shall the fruit thereof be consumed...* (Ezekiel 47:12).

Prosperity imagery saturates the vision of restoration.

The prophets don't promise a return to Eden exactly, but they do promise that God will reverse the curse, restore His people, and bring them into a place of abundance and security. The hope is spiritual, material, social, and economic. It's the full restoration of *shalom*.

THE KINGDOM BREAKS IN

When Jesus arrives, He announces that the Kingdom of God is at hand (see Mark 1:15). And what does the Kingdom look like? Blind eyes opened. Deaf ears unstopped. Lame people walking. Lepers cleansed. Hungry crowds fed. Water turned to wine. Nets so full they nearly break (see Luke 5:6). A coin in a fish's mouth to pay taxes (see Matthew 17:27).

Jesus didn't spiritualize material blessings in an effort to explain them away. He multiplied loaves and fish because people were hungry and He had compassion on them (see Matthew 14:14-21). And then, He gave the one who sowed the loaves and fish an overflowing blessing. He turned water into wine because a wedding host was in need (John 2:1-11).

The Kingdom brings provision. It meets real needs in the real world.

At the same time, Jesus warned against greed, hoarding, and anxiety: *"Take no thought for your life, what ye shall eat, or what ye shall drink"* (Matthew 6:25).

The issue isn't whether God provides. The issue is whether we trust Him and will use what He gives for His glory.

Jesus taught a Kingdom economy: *"Give, and it shall be given unto you; good measure, pressed down, and shaken together, and running over shall men give unto your bosom..."* (Luke 6:38).

Jesus tells parables about wise stewardship and increase (see Matthew 25:14-30). He rebukes the servant who buried his talent instead of investing it. The Kingdom expects fruitfulness. It expects multiplication. It expects a return on what's been entrusted.

And then Jesus says something stunning: *"...I am come that they might have life, and that they might have it more abundantly"* (John 10:10).

The word *abundantly* is *perisseuō,* meaning overflow, superabundance, more than enough.

Jesus came to bring abundant life. Not barely-getting-by life. Not survival life. Abundant life!

Later in Luke 22:35, Jesus asked His disciples a simple but revealing question: "*...When I sent you without purse, and scrip, and shoes, lacked ye any thing? And they said,* ***Nothing***."

Their answer was as brief as it was powerful.

That single word should shake anyone who has swallowed the propaganda of the poverty gospel.

These men had left everything to follow Christ, yet they lacked nothing.

The early Church lived out this Kingdom reality. Acts 2 and 4 describe a community where: *"Neither was there any among them that lacked..."* (Acts 4:34).

They shared resources. They met needs. They took care of widows (see Acts 6:1-7). The Church wasn't marked by poverty, it was marked by radical generosity flowing from sufficiency.

Paul's letters reinforced the theme. He told the Philippians: *"But my God shall supply all your need according to his riches in glory by Christ Jesus"* (Philippians 4:19).

> *He promised the Corinthians: "And God is able to make all grace abound toward you; that ye, always having all sufficiency in all things, may abound to every good work"* (2 Corinthians 9:8).

He prayed that they were: *"Being enriched in every thing to all bountifulness…"* (2 Corinthians 9:11).

This is New Covenant prosperity. God supplies. Believers have sufficiency. They abound in good works. They're enriched so they can be generous.

The pattern is consistent: provision produces generosity, which produces more provision, which produces more generosity. It's a cycle of blessing.

John wrote to Gaius: *"Beloved, I wish above all things that thou mayest prosper and be in health, even as thy soul prospereth"* (3 John 1:2).

The apostle wanted his friend to prosper materially and physically in proportion to his spiritual growth. It's not either/or. It's both/and.

THE THROUGH-LINE

From Eden to the early Church, the story is consistent: God created humanity to flourish. Sin brought poverty and a curse. God responded with covenant promises of blessing and increase.

He prospered Abraham, Isaac, and Jacob. He gave Israel a land flowing with milk and honey. He promised restoration through the prophets. Jesus announced abundant life. The apostles taught provision, sufficiency, and generosity.

Prosperity is part of how God reverses the curse, restores His image-bearers, and advances His Kingdom purposes on earth. The question has never been whether God wants to prosper His people. The question is whether we'll define prosperity the same way He does.

The Bible's prosperity pattern is clear. However, lurking on the other side of the spectrum is poverty. Far from being a virtue, is actually part of the curse we're meant to resist.

POVERTY IS FROM HELL

We need to say something clearly and without apology: poverty is from hell. It's not romantic. It's not noble. It's not a pathway to holiness. It's a degrading, destructive force that crushes human dignity, shortens lives, fills prisons, fuels addiction, and drives people to desperation.

The Bible never calls poverty a *virtue*. Never. What it does call poverty is a *curse*.

Let's start where Scripture starts: Genesis 3. When sin enters the world, God pronounces judgment, and part of that judgment falls on the ground itself:

> *...cursed is the ground for thy sake; in sorrow shalt thou eat of it all the days of thy life; thorns also and thistles shall it bring forth to thee; in the sweat of thy face shalt thou eat bread...* (Genesis 3:17-19).

This is the origin of lack, of scarcity, of grinding toil that doesn't produce enough. Poverty's DNA is in the curse.

Move to Deuteronomy 28, where God lays out the blessings of obedience and the curses of disobedience. The curses include famine, nakedness, debt, and dependence:

> *Thou shalt carry much seed out into the field, and shalt gather but little in…* (Deuteronomy 28:38).
>
> *The stranger that is within thee shall get up above thee very high; and thou shalt come down very low. He shall lend to thee, and thou shalt not lend to him…* (Deuteronomy 28:43-44).

Poverty isn't presented here as a spiritual discipline. It's presented as a covenant curse.

Proverbs reinforces this: "*…the destruction of the poor is their poverty*" (Proverbs 10:15).

Not their sin. Not their pride. Their poverty itself is destructive: "*The poor is hated even of his own neighbour…*" (Proverbs 14:20).

Poverty isolates. It marginalizes. It robs people of dignity and community.

This is what poverty does in the real world. It degrades the image of God in people. It shortens lifespans. It increases infant mortality. It limits access to education, healthcare, and opportunity. It creates environments where crime becomes rational, where addiction offers escape, where prostitution seems like the only option.

Poverty fills prisons with thieves and murderers because when people can't provide for themselves or their families through legitimate means, desperation drives them to illegitimate ones.

I've talked with physicians who told me they'd have a fraction of their patient load if it weren't for the stress and anxiety that comes from financial pressure.

Poverty creates a kind of psychological disease that borders on insanity. The constant worry, the sleepless nights, the humiliation of not being able to feed your kids or keep a roof over their heads. This isn't character building, it's soul-crushing.

And poverty doesn't just destroy individuals. It destabilizes societies.

Socialism, one of the most destructive ideologies of the 20th century, gains its foothold through poverty. When people are desperate and see no way out, they become vulnerable to promises of forced redistribution and state control. Poverty creates the conditions for tyranny because desperate people will trade freedom for the promise of bread.

THE HUMAN COST

The global statistics on poverty are staggering. As of recent estimates, more than 700 million people still live in extreme poverty, surviving on less than $2.15 per day—roughly 10 percent of humanity.[13]

Another 240 million workers globally are considered "working poor," meaning they have jobs but still can't escape poverty's grip.[14]

When you measure poverty multidimensionally, including lack of access to education, healthcare, and basic living standards, the number climbs to over 1.1 billion people.[15]

These are human beings made in the image of God. They are mothers watching their children go hungry. They are fathers unable to provide. They are kids who will never learn to read, never get the medicine they need, never have a chance to develop the gifts God put in them.

Poverty kills. It kills through malnutrition, preventable disease, unsafe water, and lack of medical care. It kills through violence in communities where desperation breeds crime. It kills through the slow grind of hopelessness that saps the will to live.

And yet, in some Christian circles, we've romanticized poverty and enabled it by not preaching what the Bible says about prosperity. Shame on us! We've treated it as if it were spiritually superior to prosperity.

We quote *"blessed are the poor"* (see Matthew 5:3) out of context and ignore the fact that Jesus immediately went about healing the sick, feeding the hungry, and setting people free from every form of bondage, including economic bondage. Jesus blessed the poor because they were poor, because they needed the Kingdom's intervention, not because poverty itself is holy.

This brings up questions:

1. If it's okay to be poor, why would Jesus instruct us to help people out of poverty?
2. How can we help someone out of poverty if we are poor ourselves?

Poverty is not a virtue; it's a vice. It's a condition to be resisted, overcome, and eliminated wherever possible. The Bible commands us to care for the poor (see Deuteronomy 15:11, Proverbs 19:17, James 1:27), but caring for the poor doesn't mean celebrating poverty. It means working against it.

The only antidote to poverty is prosperity. Not socialism. Not government redistribution. Not charity alone. Prosperity. The Bible's answer to lack is increase. The answer to scarcity is abundance. The answer to curse is blessing.

And here's where most Christians miss it: *just enough* doesn't fix poverty. *Just enough* enables it. If all you have is just enough for yourself, you can't help anyone else. You can't hire. You can't give. You can't invest in someone else's breakthrough. You become part of the problem because you're stuck in survival mode.

Christians must learn that it's their responsibility to get more than enough because there's always somebody who doesn't have enough. You can't lift someone out of poverty if you're barely treading water yourself. You can't fund missions if you're in debt. You can't be generous if you're broke.

This is why 2 Corinthians 9:8 says God makes grace abound so that you *"may abound to every good work."* The prosperity isn't the end. It's the means.

God gives you more than enough so that you can be the answer to someone else's prayer. God prospers you so that you can be a conduit of His provision.

None of this means that we despise the poor. Scripture is relentless in its commands to show mercy, practice justice, and care for the vulnerable:

> *He that hath pity upon the poor lendeth unto the Lord; and that which he hath given will he pay him again* (Proverbs 19:17).

> *Pure religion and undefiled before God and the Father is this, To visit the fatherless and widows in their affliction...* (James 1:27).

Having compassion for the poor is not the same as glorifying poverty. We show compassion precisely because poverty is evil, because it's destructive, and because it's part of the curse that Christ came to break. We don't leave people in poverty and call it spiritual. We work to get them out. God's heart has always been to lift people out of lack and into abundance.

That's what the Jubilee year was about in Leviticus 25: restoring land, canceling debts, giving people a fresh start. That's what the gleaning laws were about: providing a way for the poor to work and eat with dignity (see Leviticus 19:9-10).

That's what Jesus was doing when He fed the 5,000, healed the sick, and cast out demons that tormented people. He was pushing back the curse. He was restoring what the Fall had stolen. That is what the Church is called to do—not to manage poverty, but to destroy it.

Not to make peace with lack, but to wage war against it in Jesus' name. Not to settle for just *enough*, but to pursue the kind of biblical prosperity that creates the capacity to bless, to give, to build, to liberate. Poverty is a curse. Prosperity is the antidote. And the only question is whether we have the courage to say so.

8

WHAT PROSPERITY IS NOT

We have established what prosperity means in Scripture. Now we need to be equally clear about what it *doesn't* mean, because the fastest way to discredit a biblical truth is to let it get twisted into something Scripture never intended.

Years ago, the Lord impressed upon my heart a principle that has guided my discernment ever since: Pay careful attention to the doctrines that are mocked, maligned, and misused, for those are often the very areas where I am moving.

If there is one doctrine that fits all three—abused by some, attacked by many, and ridiculed by the world, it is the doctrine of prosperity.

The prosperity gospel has earned its bad reputation honestly, and it's not because the Bible doesn't teach prosperity. It's because some teachers have divorced prosperity from covenant responsibility, character, sacrifice, and the Cross. They've turned blessing into vending machine theology: insert faith, receive Mercedes. That is *not* the gospel. So let's draw some hard lines.

IT'S NOT A GUARANTEE

The Bible never promises that you can be lazy, foolish, and undisciplined and still prosper. In fact, it promises the opposite:

> *The soul of the sluggard desireth, and hath nothing: but the soul of the diligent shall be made fat* (Proverbs 13:4).

> *He becometh poor that dealeth with a slack hand: but the hand of the diligent maketh rich* (Proverbs 10:4).

Prosperity requires stewardship. It requires wisdom; it requires work. You don't plant corn and expect to harvest wheat. You don't sow laziness and expect to reap abundance. God gives seed to the sower (see 2 Corinthians 9:10), but you still have to sow. You still have to cultivate. You still have to manage what He gives you with intelligence and integrity.

Never forget this: prosperity is as much a principle as it is a promise. Many misread the book of Proverbs as if it were a collection of divine guarantees, when in fact it is a compendium of divine principles.

A promise is immediate and it depends solely on the faithfulness of the One who gave it. A principle, however, requires partnership. It demands application, discipline, and endurance. A principle means that when consistently practiced over time, it produces predictable results.

That is the essence of biblical prosperity. It is not a spiritual lottery or a shortcut to wealth. It is the cumulative result of aligning one's life with God's covenant laws of stewardship, generosity, diligence, and faith. Those who apply these truths faithfully will, in due season, walk in the prosperity of God.

PROSPERITY IS NOT PERMISSION TO BE GREEDY

Jesus could not have been clearer: "*...Take heed, and beware of covetousness: for a man's life consisteth not in the abundance of the things which he possesseth*" (Luke 12:15).

Paul warns that: *"For the love of money is the root of all evil..."* (1 Timothy 6:10).

James condemns the rich who hoard and oppress: *"Go to now, ye rich men, weep and howl for your miseries that shall come upon you"* (James 5:1).

Biblical prosperity is never about accumulation for its own sake. It's never about luxury while your brother goes hungry. It's never about building bigger barns so you can say: "*...Soul, thou hast much goods laid up for many years; take thine ease...*" (Luke 12:19).

That's the fool's prosperity, and God calls him a fool to his face.

The biblical model is generosity. You're blessed to be a blessing. You're increased so you can increase others. You receive so you can give.

The moment prosperity stops flowing and starts pooling, it becomes toxic. Stagnant water breeds disease; flowing water brings life.

PROSPERITY IS NOT A DENIAL OF SEASONS, SUFFERING, OR SACRIFICE

Nowhere does Scripture promise that every believer will be wealthy at all times.

- Paul said he knew how to abound and how to be abased (see Philippians 4:12).
- Job lost everything and still blessed the name of the Lord (see Job 1:21).
- Jesus had nowhere to lay His head (see Matthew 8:20).
- The apostles were often in need, sometimes hungry, sometimes beaten, sometimes imprisoned (2 Corinthians 11:23-28).

Biblical prosperity doesn't erase hardship. It doesn't mean you'll never go through a lean season, never face loss, never be called to sacrifice. Abraham was prosperous, but he still lived in tents. Joseph was prosperous, but he spent years in prison first. David was anointed king, but he ran for his life before he ever sat on a throne.

The prosperity promise isn't, "You will never struggle." It's, "God will sustain you, supply your needs, and ultimately fulfill His purpose in your life."

PROSPERITY IS NOT INCOMPATIBLE WITH SIMPLICITY OR CONTENTMENT

Paul says, "*Godliness with contentment is great gain. …having food and raiment let us be therewith content*" (1 Timothy 6:6,8).

Some read these verses and conclude that wanting more than food and clothing is sinful. But that's not what Paul is saying.

Contentment isn't the same as complacency. Contentment means you're not anxious, not driven by greed, not measuring your worth by your net worth.

It means you trust God whether you have little or much. But contentment doesn't mean you can't desire increase for Kingdom purposes. It doesn't mean you shouldn't work toward greater capacity. It doesn't mean ambition is sin.

Paul was content in every circumstance, yet he still worked with his hands to provide for himself and others (see Acts 20:34). He was content, yet he still took offerings for the poor in Jerusalem. He was content, yet he still told the Corinthians that God wanted to make them rich in generosity (see 2 Corinthians 9:11).

Simplicity and contentment are about posture, not poverty. They're about freedom from materialism, not a vow of destitution.

PROSPERITY IS NOT ABOUT MANIPULATING GOD

We're not talking about treating the Creator of the universe like a cosmic ATM.

God is not a means to an end. He is the end. You don't use God to get stuff. You seek God and trust Him to provide for you. There's a massive difference between *faith* that trusts God's character and *presumption* that tries to control God's actions.

- The Bible does teach sowing and reaping (see Galatians 6:7).
- The Bible does teach that generosity produces return (see Luke 6:38).
- The Bible does teach that God rewards those who diligently seek Him (see Hebrews 11:6).

But these are covenant principles, not mechanical levers. You can't manipulate God. You can only trust and obey Him.

PROSPERITY IS NOT AT ODDS WITH THE CROSS

Prosperity teaching doesn't suggest that persecution is always avoidable. That's not the gospel Paul preached:

- "*I am crucified with Christ....*" (Galatians 2:20)
- "*...I die daily.*" (1 Corinthians 15:31)

Paul counted his privileges as *"dung"* compared to knowing Christ (see Philippians 3:8). The Cross is central. Death to self is non-negotiable. You can't bypass Calvary on your way to Pentecost.

But here's what's equally important—the resurrection follows the crucifixion. Death leads to life. The grain of wheat that falls into the ground and dies bears much fruit (see John 12:24). Jesus endured the Cross *"...for the joy that was set before him..."* (Hebrews 12:2).

Biblical prosperity includes the willingness to lose everything for Christ. But it also includes the promise that what you lose for His sake, you gain a hundredfold (see Mark 10:29-30). You hold everything with open hands, willing to surrender it if He asks. And ironically, it's those open hands that God fills most freely.

THE BALANCE SCRIPTURE DEMANDS

Biblical prosperity walks a tightrope. On one side is the ditch of greed, materialism, and self-indulgence. On the other side is the ditch of false humility, poverty piety, and economic fatalism. Scripture calls us to walk the narrow road between them.

That road includes work and rest, giving and receiving, faith and wisdom, ambition and contentment, abundance and sacrifice. It's held in tension by the Spirit, governed by the Word, expressed in love.

When we keep these guardrails in place, prosperity stops being a stumbling block.

THE ILLUSION OF PROSPERITY

Picture this, a banker in a three-piece suit strutting down Wall Street, Italian leather shoes clicking against the pavement, gold Rolex catching the sunlight, briefcase full of contracts worth millions. Now picture a tribesman walking across the sun-scorched African plains, barefoot, wearing nothing but a loincloth and a wide-brimmed straw hat, carrying a walking stick and a gourd of water.

To our modern eyes, it's obvious who's prosperous, right? The banker has everything. The tribesman? He's barely surviving. Let's flip the script. Drop that same banker in the middle of the Sahara at high noon: no Starbucks, no air-conditioned office, no Uber coming to save him.

Suddenly that tailored suit becomes a death trap, soaking him in sweat. Those polished shoes? Useless torture devices on burning sand. That gold watch? Can't buy him a single drop of water. Within hours, he's desperate, dehydrated, dying, and everything he thought made him rich is worthless.

Meanwhile, the tribesman, the one we pitied moments ago, looks like a billionaire. That straw hat is a portable oasis. His tough feet in those sandals know how to walk on fire. His simple gourd is worth more than the banker's entire stock portfolio. In this environment, he's the wealthy one. His knowledge, his tools, his wisdom—all perfectly suited for his world.

Prosperity isn't about appearance or possessions. It's about having what you actually need when you actually need it and having more than enough. It's about adaptability. It's about wisdom.

PROSPERITY ISN'T AUTOMATIC

At this point, someone might ask, "Okay, if God wants to prosper His people, how does it actually happen? Is it automatic? Do I just wake up one day and find abundance in my bank account?"

The answer is no. Biblical prosperity isn't automatic, and it's not predetermined in a way that bypasses human responsibility. It's not fatalistic—"if it's God's will, it'll happen no matter what I do."

That's not how covenant works. That's not how any of God's promises work.

Think about marriage. God's will is for marriages to thrive, for husbands and wives to experience love, unity, and fruitfulness. But a good marriage doesn't just happen because you said, "I do."

There are principles. There are patterns. There are ways to tap into what God designed for your marriage: communication, sacrifice, forgiveness, intimacy, commitment. You have to learn them. You have to practice them. You have to steward the relationship.

Prosperity works the same way. There are biblical mechanisms. There are Kingdom principles. There are ways to position yourself under God's blessing and ways to block it. Wisdom matters. Diligence matters. Generosity matters. Obedience matters. Stewardship matters.

Scripture gives us examples throughout:

- Joseph's administrative genius in Egypt.
- Bezalel's creative skill in building the tabernacle.
- The Proverbs 31 woman's business acumen.
- Lydia's trade network in Philippi.

These weren't people sitting around waiting for manna to fall. These were people who combined faith with action, who stewarded gifts and opportunities, who sowed and reaped according to God's design.

We're going to unpack all of this in detail later in the book including the practical mechanisms of biblical prosperity, the principles of sowing and reaping, the role of wisdom and work, the power of generosity, the importance of aligning yourself with God's purposes. This chapter is about establishing the foundation: prosperity is biblical. The chapters that follow will show you how to walk in it and to address other unanswered questions.

Now, just understand that prosperity is a covenant capacity that you steward, not a lottery ticket that you wait on.

God gives you the power to get wealth (see Deuteronomy 8:18), but you still have to get it. He supplies seed to the sower (see 2 Corinthians 9:10), but you still have to sow. He opens doors, but you still have to walk through them.

The *how* matters. And we'll get there. But first, let's make sure we have clear definitions locked in.

QUICK REFERENCE DEFINITIONS

The following are the key terms we've established, with biblical definitions distilled for clarity:

Prosperity: God-given sufficiency with overflow to fulfill His purpose and bless others. It is covenant capacity, spiritual, material, relational, secured in Christ, stewarded by faith, expressed in generosity.

Blessing: God's empowering presence that produces fruitfulness, increase, security, and peace across every domain of life. Blessing is both spiritual and material, both internal and external. It flows from covenant relationship with God and is meant to extend through His people to the world.

Poverty: A curse-state of deprivation and lack rooted in the Fall and reinforced by disobedience, oppression, injustice, or broken systems. Poverty degrades human dignity, limits potential, and hinders the flourishing God designed for image-bearers. It is to be resisted, relieved, and overcome—not romanticized.

Stewardship: Managing God's resources according to God's wisdom for God's purposes. Stewardship recognizes that everything we have belongs to Him and is entrusted to us for Kingdom advancement. Good stewards multiply what they're given. Poor stewards bury it.

Glory: *(Kabod):* The weight, substance, and honor of God's presence. In Hebrew thought, glory includes both spiritual radiance and tangible resources. A person or people carrying God's glory will reflect His character and His capacity, wisdom and wealth, authority and provision, holiness and influence.

Generosity: The outflow of biblical prosperity. God blesses us so we can bless others. Generosity is the proof that prosperity is functioning as God intended—not as a dead-end reservoir, but as a flowing river that brings life wherever it goes.

Covenant Increase: The biblical pattern in which God multiplies what His people steward faithfully. From Abraham's flocks to the early Church's resources, God increases what is aligned with His purposes. Covenant increase is not random; it follows obedience, wisdom, and faithful stewardship.

Sufficiency *(Autarkeia):* Having enough for the task God has assigned. Sufficiency isn't barely scraping by; it's being adequately resourced to accomplish what God has called you to do without dependency that cripples mission.

Abundance *(Perisseuō):* More than enough. Overflow. The surplus that allows believers to *"abound to every good work"* (2 Corinthians 9:8). Abundance is the margin that makes generosity possible.

These definitions form the foundation. When we use these terms, this is what we mean.

PART THREE

WHAT IS SO IMPORTANT ABOUT PROSPERITY?

9

DOES GOD WANT YOU TO BE A MILLIONAIRE?

If you study this subject in the Bible, you will notice that satan keeps using the same playbook: corrupt the offering, control the cash flow, cripple the influence.

Look at Cain. What corrupted him? His offering was rejected. Instead of repenting, he murdered his brother. The first murder in human history was tied to worship and the prosperity/favor of God on Abel's life.

Fast-forward to Judas. What turned the trusted treasurer of Jesus' ministry into a traitor? Thirty pieces of silver. He had access to the money bag, yet he was stealing from it (see John 12:6). His corruption was financial.

And look ahead to the antichrist. Revelation 13 makes it crystal clear: the ultimate tool of global control won't be military might alone, it will be economic dominance.

No one will be able to buy or sell without the mark of the beast (see Revelation 13:17). Think about that. The final enemy doesn't just want to deceive your doctrine; he wants to control your bank account. Why?

The devil knows what too many Christians have forgotten: money is influence, and influence is power.

He doesn't need to shut down revival if he can just bankrupt the revivalists. He doesn't need to silence the gospel if he can defund the messengers. Control the Church's cash flow, and you control the Church's impact.

THE LEAVEN OF WRONG THINKING

Jesus warned us in Matthew 16:6 to *"beware of the leaven of the Pharisees and Sadducees."* Leaven works invisibly. You don't see it doing its work, you just wake up one day and the whole loaf has risen.

This is how satan operates in the minds of believers: he plants tiny thoughts that grow into toxic theologies.

Satan whispers: Money is the root of all evil.

It's not. The *love* of money is, according to 1 Timothy 6:10.

Satan suggests: Jesus was poor, so you should be, too.

He wasn't. Jesus had a treasurer, wore expensive clothing, and was supported by wealthy women (see Luke 8:3).

Satan insinuates: If you're blessed, you're probably greedy.

Tell that to Abraham, Isaac, Jacob, Job, Solomon, and Joseph of Arimathea.

Over time, these little lies become accepted doctrine. Revelation gets replaced with resentment. Believers start viewing prosperity as *suspicious* instead of *scriptural.* And before long, the Church is working against the very tool God designed to fund the advancement of His Kingdom.

THE SPIRIT OF SOCIALISM AND COMMUNISM

Here's where it gets uncomfortable, but we need to say it: the same spirit that birthed socialism and communism has infiltrated the Western Church's theology about wealth. Both ideologies operate on the same premise: demonize the prosperous and shame the successful. Their slogan? "Everyone should have enough, but no one should have abundance."

Sound familiar? It should. Because that's the exact spirit Judas operated in when Mary broke the alabaster box of expensive perfume and poured it on Jesus' feet. Judas was indignant: "Why this waste? This perfume could have been sold for more than a year's wages and given to the poor!" (see Matthew 26:8-9). We'll dive deep into this in another chapter.

This spirit has false compassion. Fake outrage. But Jesus rebuked Judas publicly:

> *... Why are you bothering this woman? She has done a beautiful thing to me. The poor you will always have with you, but you will not always have me* (Matthew 26:10-11 NIV).

Now listen to how this plays out in modern church culture:

"That preacher talks about money too much."

"They should sell that and give it to the poor."

"Do they really need a jet?"

"I don't think Jesus would drive that kind of car."

Judas is alive and well, sitting in the third pew, disguising envy as righteousness.

According to a 2019 Pew Research study, 59 percent of Americans believe the economic system in the US unfairly favors the wealthy, and nearly half of younger evangelicals express sympathy toward socialist economic policies.[16]

That's a spiritual crisis. The Church has adopted the slogans of a godless ideology and baptized it in religious language. Proverbs 10:15 (NIV) says: *"The wealth of the rich is their fortified city, but poverty is the ruin of the poor."*

Poverty doesn't just limit options—it destroys lives. It breaks families. It silences voices. It keeps the gospel landlocked when it should be going global.

Satan knows this. If he can get you to reject prosperity, he doesn't have to fight your influence because you won't have any.

CRITICIZING PROSPERITY PREACHERS

I was talking with a pastor who was complaining about some preacher on TV and the nice watch he had on his wrist. I asked, "Is it wrong to have a nice watch?"

"Well, no," he answered.

"Okay. Is a cheap watch more moral than a quality one?"

"I guess not."

"So, if quality isn't the issue, who gets to decide the price limit on righteousness? Is there a dollar amount where a watch stops being acceptable and starts being sinful? $100? $500? $5,000?"

Silence.

"And what if someone gave you that watch as a gift? What if you bought it honestly with money you earned ethically? What if you got a $25,000 watch for $500 because of a relationship or favor, does it become sinful when you tell people what it's worth?"

By now, the pastor was squirming. I'd just exposed the flaw in their entire argument: there is no consistent standard for wealth-shaming. It's all arbitrary opinion dressed up as moral superiority and virtue signaling.

Jesus wore a seamless robe so valuable that Roman soldiers gambled for it at the foot of the Cross (see John 19:23-24). According to ancient historians, seamless garments were expensive, often worn by priests and people of means. Jesus didn't dress like a pauper; He dressed appropriately for His mission.

WHO DRAWS THE LINE?

Here's the problem with the prosperity police: they can never tell you where the line is.

They'll criticize the preacher with the private plane but say nothing about the pastor with the $80,000 SUV. They'll mock the evangelist with the Rolex but wear a $300 Apple Watch themselves.

They'll condemn the prophet who flies first class but think nothing of their own annual beach vacation that costs a pretty penny.

Who gets to set the dollar limit on righteousness? Who appointed these moral referees? And why do their standards always seem to apply to everyone except themselves? I've heard people say, "I just don't think Jesus would wear something that nice. Oh, really? Based on what? Your feelings? Your upbringing? Your income level?

Your opinion cannot be the standard for my obedience.

Let me say that again for the people in the back: your personal conviction about money does not get to become my moral obligation. Romans 14:4 (NIV) puts it this way:

> *Who are you to judge someone else's servant? To their own master, servants stand or fall. And they will stand, for the Lord is able to make them stand.*

In other words, back off. God didn't appoint you as the financial watchdog over someone else's calling.

WHAT ABOUT PRIVATE JETS?

I was at a pastors' meeting where everyone started gossiping about a well-known minister who was raising money for a ministry airplane. They were all appalled. "Can you believe they're asking people to help buy a plane? That's outrageous!"

I spoke up and addressed the lead grumbler in the group by saying, "You know, when you look at that plane in proportion to that ministry's annual budget, it's the equivalent of you owning a $30,000 car. Do you own a $30,000 car?"

The pastor went silent. I continued.

"So if we're going to condemn them for having a plane, we'd have to condemn you for having that car. If you think they should sell that plane and give the money to missions, then by the very same logic, you could sell your car and do the same."

Game over.

See, wealth-shaming always backfires when you apply it consistently. *Wealth-shaming exposes envy more than it exposes ethics.*

There are practicing Christians who believe it is morally wrong for pastors to live in affluence, yet those same Christians often own luxury items themselves.

The contradiction is glaring: we judge leaders by a standard we refuse to live by ourselves.

And here's the real kicker: we don't actually care about the poor when we criticize prosperity. If we did, we'd sell our own stuff first. What we care about is feeling morally superior without having to sacrifice anything ourselves.

Judas didn't care about the poor either. John 12:6 tells us plainly that he was a thief. His indignation over the expensive perfume wasn't compassion; it was envy wrapped in false piety.

And that same spirit is alive in the Church today. People will often quote Judas by saying, "That money should have been given to the poor!" They think they're quoting Jesus, not realizing they're operating in the wrong spirit.

CLARIFYING THE QUESTION

Let's cut through the noise and ask the question that makes everyone uncomfortable: Does God want every Christian to be a millionaire?

Now before you answer, let me clarify what we're actually asking here. We're not debating whether God wants His people to prosper in general. That question is already settled in Scripture:

- Deuteronomy 8:18 tells us: *God gives us the power to get wealth.*
- Psalm 35:27 says: *The Lord takes pleasure in the prosperity of His servant.*

- Proverbs 10:22 declares: *The blessing of the Lord makes rich and adds no sorrow with it.*
- Psalm 112:1-3 promises: *Wealth and riches shall be in the house of the righteous.*

That's not up for debate.

What we're asking is more specific: Does God want every believer to have seven figures in the bank? Does He desire monetary abundance—not just spiritual or relational blessing, but actual financial wealth—for all His children?

This question reveals how we understand the character of God Himself. Is He stingy or generous? Does He ration blessing or pour it out abundantly? Does He keep His promises?

According to a 2025 report by Ramsey Solutions, 49 percent of Americans say they live paycheck to paycheck, and many Christians report feeling financial stress that directly impacts their ability to give, serve, or respond to God's leading.[17] That's not prosperity. That's a consequence of either poor stewardship, wrong teaching, or spiritual attack.

THE LAW OF NATURE AND OF NATURE'S GOD

The phrase "the Laws of Nature and of Nature's God" comes from the opening lines of the Declaration of Independence (1776):

> *When in the Course of human events, it becomes necessary for one people to dissolve the political bands which have connected them with another, and to assume among the powers of the earth, the separate and equal station to which the Laws of Nature and of Nature's God entitle them....*

This phrase points to the knowable will of a moral Creator. The founders believed that divine truth isn't buried in mystery, accessible only to prophets or priests, but written into the fabric of creation itself.

The same God who authored Scripture also authored the natural order, and both testify to His will.

This means that by observing creation, reason, and human conscience, we can discern something of God's intentions for mankind. He is not arbitrary or hidden. His character is consistent in both revelation and reality.

That's why the founders could appeal to "self-evident truths." They recognized that certain moral laws such as justice and liberty are visible to any honest mind. Scripture confirms this. God's invisible attributes are clearly seen in the things He has made (see Romans 1:20).

The order of creation reflects the order of its Creator. When we study nature, human relationships, and the moral instincts He implanted within us, we discover the God who wills for His children to flourish. He designed ecosystems to multiply, seeds to bear fruit, and human societies to thrive through unity and virtue. In both revelation and reason, increase—not deprivation—is the mark of His design.

Because God's will can be seen in the structure of creation, then prosperity—understood as wholeness, fruitfulness, and well-being—is not a human *invention* but a divine *intention.* Even our natural parental instincts echo this truth. Every parent longs to see their children grow, succeed, and live abundantly. That desire didn't originate with us. It reflects the nature of the One whose image we bear. Jesus addressed this directly in Matthew 7:11:

> *If ye then, being evil, know how to give good gifts unto your children, how much more shall your Father which is in heaven give good things to them that ask him.*

The Creator placed within human hearts a reflection of His own goodness, so that by simply understanding how we love our children, we may glimpse how He loves us.

To deny that God wants His people to increase is to deny what both Scripture and creation declare. It's imagining that the Father of lights—from whom every good and perfect gift proceeds—delights in scarcity rather than abundance.

Ask any parent anywhere in the world, doesn't matter if they're in Tokyo or Nairobi, Beijing or Buenos Aires. Ask them this simple question: "Do you want your child to be wealthy?"

The answer is universal: "Yes!"

Not because they're greedy; not because they worship money. Their answer is "Yes!" because love naturally desires abundance for those it cares about. No father hopes that his daughter will struggle. No mother prays that her son will barely survive. Parents want their children to excel, to thrive, to have more opportunities than they had. It's hardwired into us.

Think about the logic here. If fallen, broken, selfish human beings still want the best for their children, what does that say about a perfect, loving, infinitely generous God? It means His desire to bless His children far exceeds anything we can imagine.

The generic answer is that God's ultimate will for His children is an emphatic "Yes!" He desires prosperity for you.

Isaiah 48:17 (NKJV) declares: *"Thus says the Lord, your Redeemer... 'I am the Lord your God, who teaches you to profit, who leads you by the way you should go.'"*

Notice the word *profit.* God Himself teaches us how to increase, how to gain, how to multiply. Psalm 23:5 (NKJV) paints the picture: *"You prepare a table before me in the presence of my enemies; You anoint my head with oil; my cup runs over."*

Not just full. Not just enough. Overflowing. Psalm 112:1-3 (NKJV) promises:

> *...Blessed is the man who fears the Lord, who delights greatly in His commandments. His descendants will be mighty on earth;*

> *the generation of the upright will be blessed. Wealth and riches will be in his house, and his righteousness endures forever.*

The apostle Paul wrote in Philippians 4:19 (NKJV): *"And my God shall supply all your need according to His riches in glory by Christ Jesus."*

All your need. Not some. Not most. All.

And here's one people love to skip over. Deuteronomy 28:11-12 (NIV) promises that if you obey God's voice:

> *The Lord will grant you abundant prosperity.... The Lord will open the heavens, the storehouse of his bounty, to send rain on your land in season and to bless all the work of your hands. You will lend to many nations but will borrow from none.*

Lenders, not borrowers. Abundant, not adequate. Overflow, not just enough. The biblical pattern is undeniable. From Genesis to Revelation, God blesses those who walked with Him:

- Abraham became extremely wealthy.
- Isaac reaped a hundredfold.
- Jacob left Laban with massive flocks.
- Joseph became second in command of Egypt.
- Solomon's wealth was legendary.
- Job was restored double.
- The early Church had no lack.

God's default setting is blessing. His heart is generosity. His nature is abundance. So yes, the generic answer is clear: God desires that His children prosper.

10

THE PROPHETIC ANSWER

Now here's where we need to get honest. God's desire and God's timing are not the same thing. Every parent wants their child to be wealthy. But no sane parent would hand a two-year-old a million dollars. At age 2, or even 10, giving them full control would destroy them. They would choke on coins, set the house on fire, or get exploited by the first stranger who smiled at them.

The problem isn't the money. The problem is the maturity to manage it.

Same principle applies in the Kingdom. Some believers aren't ready to steward great wealth. And God, in His wisdom and love, withholds what would harm them until they're prepared to handle it.

ABUNDANCE DELAYED

There are legitimate reasons God may delay abundance in someone's life, and none of them have to do with Him being stingy. Let's look at several of those reasons:

Lack of financial integrity. If you can't tithe on $50,000, why would God trust you with $500,000? If you're dishonest with your taxes, late on your bills, or careless with your credit line, you're proving you're not ready for more.

Unbroken addictions. Money amplifies whatever is already in you. If you have a gambling problem, a shopping addiction, or substance abuse issues, wealth won't fix that. It will fund it. God loves you too much to finance your destruction.

Selfish consumption. James 4:3 (NKJV) says, "*You ask and do not receive, because you ask amiss, that you may spend it on your pleasures.*"

Some people want wealth for indulgence, not influence. They want the boat, the vacation home, the status. God's not interested in funding your ego; He's interested in building His Kingdom.

Spiritual immaturity. Proverbs 20:21 (NKJV) warns: "*An inheritance gained hastily at the beginning will not be blessed at the end.*"

Quick money in immature hands leads to ruin. Just look at the statistics on lottery winners.

According to a study by the National Endowment for Financial Education, approximately 70 percent of people who win a lottery or receive a large windfall end up broke within a few years.[18] Why? Because they were never taught stewardship.

God won't give you what you're not ready to carry. That's not punishment. That's protection. He has your provision in a trust fund, waiting on you to grow up.

THE EXAMPLE OF ISRAEL

Did God want Israel to enter the Promised Land? Absolutely. He promised it to Abraham in Genesis 12. But when the time came in Numbers 13, they weren't ready. They sent 12 spies into Canaan, and ten came back with a bad report. They saw giants and said, "We can't take the land."

God didn't change His mind about the promise. He delayed their entry because they weren't mature enough to possess it. An entire generation died in the wilderness, not because God was cruel, but because they refused to grow up. Forty years later, their children walked into the same land with the same promise. Same God. Same inheritance. Different mindset.

The promise was delayed by immaturity. Sound familiar?

Here's the bottom line: God's ultimate will is wealth. His immediate will depends on your stewardship.

Every act of obedience moves you closer to that readiness. Every tithe you give in faith. Every debt you pay off with discipline. Every generous seed you sow when it doesn't make sense. Every budget you stick to. Every impulsive purchase you resist. In Luke 16:10 (NKJV), Jesus lays it out clearly: *"He who is faithful in what is least is faithful also in much; and he who is unjust in what is least is unjust also in much."*

You don't get promoted to wealth by complaining about lack. You get there by proving you can handle little with the same integrity you'd handle much.

Stop asking God for a million dollars when you haven't been faithful with a thousand. Stop praying for overflow when you're wasting what's already in your hand.

The prophetic answer is this: Yes, God wants you wealthy. But not until you're ready to steward it for His glory.

MOCKING PROSPERITY = MOCKING GOD

Asking if it's God's will for every Christian to prosper is like asking if it's God's will for every Christian marriage to be successful. Of course it's His will for Christians to stay married. However, there are failed marriages everywhere.

Divorce rates hover around 42 percent, according to a 2025 study by the Institute for Family Studies.[19] Does that mean God approves of divorce? Does the existence of failure prove that God doesn't desire success? Of course not.

The existence of broken marriages doesn't reveal God's will. It reveals humankind's disobedience to His principles. The same logic applies to poverty. Just because believers are broke doesn't mean God wants them that way. It means they're violating financial principles, operating under wrong teaching, or are in process and on their way to prosperity.

God's desire is clear: He wants wholeness in your marriage, health in your body, peace in your mind, and provision in your finances. The fact that people experience the opposite doesn't change His will.

It exposes their choices, the enemy's attacks, and the curse of this world. Stop using other people's failure as proof of God's intention.

If someone's marriage is in shambles, what advice would you give them? You would tell them to go back to church, go to counseling, study what the Bible says about marriage, apply those principles, etc. This is a no-brainer. If your marriage is struggling, you need to zero in on it like a laser and have a hyperfocus.

The same is true when it comes to prosperity. The difference is that if you do attempt to focus on it, you're labeled a heretic.

What you secretly believe is unholy, you will unconsciously avoid. If deep down you think wealth is worldly, you'll sabotage every opportunity to gain it. If you believe rich people are greedy, you'll repel the very increase God is trying to send your way. If you're convinced that struggling financially is more spiritual than thriving, you'll never step into the abundance God has for you.

Your subconscious won't let you become what you've been taught to despise.

That's why so many believers live beneath their potential. They've been programmed to associate prosperity with carnality. They quote: *"It is easier for a camel to go through the eye of a needle than for a rich man to enter the kingdom of God"* (Matthew 19:24 NKJV).

They ignore verse 26 where Jesus continues: *"With man this is impossible, but with God all things are possible."*

They focus on the warning about wealth and miss the promise that God can make you both wealthy and righteous. You can't steward what you secretly resent. When the Church rejects prosperity, it surrenders influence.

Ecclesiastes 9:16 says: "*...the poor man's wisdom is despised, and his words are not heard.*"

The poor man's wisdom is despised. Not because his wisdom is wrong, but because poverty strips credibility. Fair or not, that's reality. A broke person giving financial advice isn't taken seriously. A struggling ministry calling for societal change gets ignored.

When believers forfeit prosperity, they forfeit their microphone. The world listens to those who have something they want. If Christians are perpetually broke, constantly begging, and barely surviving, why would the world listen to us about anything?

Proverbs 22:7 puts it bluntly: "*...the borrower is servant to the lender.*"

If the Church is in debt, who's really in control? If ministries are dependent on government grants or corporate sponsorships, whose agenda are they serving?

A 2023 report by Lifeway Research found that 31 percent of churches in America are not sure of how many weeks of cash reserves they have—and 44 percent of those who do know have less than 16 weeks of reserves.[20] That means a significant number of congregations are one crisis away from closing their doors. That's financially irresponsible.

How can we tell the world about the God who supplies all our needs when we can't even pay our own bills?

STATISTICAL CONTEXT

Let's talk numbers because most Christians operate with a poverty mindset built on false scarcity. They think there's just not a lot of money out there, but I can assure you that there's plenty to go around.

According to the "2024 Global Wealth Report" by *UBS,* there are approximately 52 million millionaires worldwide.[21] In the United States alone, there are more than 24 million millionaires, which means roughly 1 in every 11 American adults has a net worth exceeding one million dollars.[22]

There are more than 3,028 billionaires globally, with a combined wealth exceeding $16.1 trillion, according to *Forbes* 2025 Billionaires List.[23]

But here's the part that should blow your mind: according to Giving USA's 2023 annual report, American individuals, estates, foundations, and corporations gave an estimated $557 billion to charity in 2023. Of that, $374 billion came from individuals. Religious organizations received the largest share at 26 percent of total giving: approximately $146 billion.[24]

If that money were distributed evenly among the roughly 300,000 churches in America, each church would receive nearly $500,000 annually. But we all know that's not happening. The issue isn't lack of money. The issue is lack of faithful stewards positioned to receive it and distribute it according to Kingdom purposes.

The world operates on scarcity. Wall Street runs on supply and demand. Economists preach limited resources. Governments hoard wealth and ration blessing. Socialism says, "There's only so much to go around, so let's make sure no one has too much."

But the Kingdom doesn't operate by scarcity. It operates by multiplication. Jesus didn't look at five loaves and two fish and say, "Well, that's all we've got, so let's divide it equally and everyone gets a crumb."

No, He blessed it, broke it, and multiplied it until 5,000 men (plus women and children, likely over 15,000 people total) were fed with 12 baskets left over (see Matthew 14:13-21).

That's Kingdom economics: supernatural multiplication, not natural division.

In 2 Kings 4, a widow came to Elisha with nothing but a jar of oil and a mountain of debt. Elisha didn't tell her to adjust her budget or apply for government assistance. He told her to gather empty vessels and start pouring. And as long as she had containers, the oil kept flowing. When she ran out of jars, the oil stopped (see 2 Kings 4:1-7).

The limitation wasn't due to God's supply. It was due to her capacity to receive. *There is no moral ceiling to prosperity in the Kingdom.*

God is not rationing blessing. He's not worried about running out. He's already given us a blank check—we just have to learn how to make the withdrawal according to His Word. The issue is whether you have the vessels, the vision, and the obedience to receive what He's pouring out.

According to a 2023 study by the International Monetary Fund, global GDP exceeded $105 trillion. The total wealth in the world is estimated at over $450 trillion.[25] And we serve the God who owns the cattle on a thousand hills (see Psalm 50:10), who laid the foundations of the earth, and filled it with resources we haven't even discovered yet.

The wealth is there. The question is, are you positioned, prepared, and obedient enough to steward it?

GOD WANTS YOU WEALTHY

Like any loving parent, God wants all His children to be financially prosperous. Not every believer is ready for it, but that doesn't change His desire. Here's the truth some people don't want to hear: just because God desires it, doesn't mean you are prepared to receive it.

A two-year-old can't handle a million dollars. A teenager can't manage a corporation. A person in bondage to addiction can't steward overflow without destroying themselves. God loves you enough to withhold what would harm you until you're mature enough to multiply it.

Your current financial state isn't a reflection of God's willingness. It's a reflection of your readiness.

Stop blaming God for what you haven't prepared for. Stop resenting others who walked in obedience while you complained. And stop using your struggle as proof that prosperity isn't God's will. Wealth follows stewardship. Increase follows integrity. Overflow follows obedience. Abundance often identifies Jesus.

Stop policing others' prosperity. Their obedience is between them and God, not you and your opinion. Would it be that maybe if you spent half the energy stewarding your own finances instead of critiquing someone else's, you'd already be walking in the blessings God has for you?

Start pursuing the wisdom that qualifies you for increase. Read Proverbs. Study principles of multiplication. Tithe faithfully. Give generously. Budget wisely. Work diligently. And stop making excuses for why you're stuck. God's plan is not selective abundance—it's collective overflow. He doesn't have favorites. He has faithful stewards.

Heaven's resources are not running low. The vaults are full. The storehouses are stocked. The supply is unlimited. God is ready—are you?

> *Blessed be the Lord, who daily loadeth us with benefits, even the God of our salvation. Selah* (Psalm 68:19).

11

WHY PREACHERS MUST PREACH PROSPERITY

THE MYTH OF AUTOMATIC PROSPERITY

Some believers treat prosperity as if it were automatic, as though blessing will somehow drift into their lives without any effort on their part. They say things like, "If God wants me to have it, He'll give it to me." That's not faith; that's fatalism in religious language. If you followed that logic through the rest of life, you'd be in serious trouble.

If God wanted you to brush your teeth, would He come down and do it for you? Imagine showing up at church saying, "I'm waiting on the Lord to brush my teeth." Everyone would keep a polite distance.

The same applies to your marriage, your career, and your finances. If you want a strong marriage, you apply the principles that make one. If you want a good job, you show up and work. And if you want to prosper, you must practice the principles of prosperity that God has established.

God's promises are perfect, but His principles require partnership.

When you ignore that, you forfeit results and blame Him for what you never pursued. Heaven does not reward passivity. Faith without works is still dead, and dead faith never produced a living harvest.

Prosperity is not a matter of waiting for God to act; it is the result of acting on what God has already said.

PROMISE VERSUS PRINCIPLE

One of the greatest misunderstandings in the Church is the failure to distinguish between a promise and a principle. We have already discussed this previously, but I want to revisit the third concept to make sure it is clear.

A promise depends entirely on God's faithfulness. A principle depends on our faithfulness to obey what He has already established. Salvation is a promise. Prosperity is rooted in a promise, but it operates by principle.

When God promises something, He alone fulfills it. When He gives a principle, He invites us into partnership. Deuteronomy 8:18 says, "*...it is he that giveth thee power to get wealth....*"

Notice, He didn't say He gives *wealth*. He gives power—the ability, wisdom, and opportunity—to obtain it. That power must be exercised, or it produces nothing.

The book of Proverbs is filled with principles:

> *...the hand of the diligent maketh rich* (Proverbs 10:4).
>
> *He that tilleth his land shall have plenty of bread...* (Proverbs 28:19).

These verses don't describe automatic outcomes; they reveal consistent patterns. When diligence is practiced, prosperity follows. When laziness is tolerated, poverty grows. God's blessing rests upon the principle.

A promise guarantees divine intention. A principle guarantees divine results only when applied. The person who lives by principle aligns with the order of creation itself. Prosperity then becomes predictable, not mysterious. To walk in God's blessing is not to wait for something to happen but to work with the truths He has already revealed.

THE LAWS OF SOWING AND REAPING

Everything God created operates on a rhythm of seedtime and harvest. Genesis 8:22 declares that as long as the earth remains, this law will never cease. God built increase into creation itself. Every living thing multiplies according to its kind. A farmer plants a seed expecting a harvest, not because he hopes for a miracle, but because he understands a principle.

The same law governs spiritual life. You cannot sow disobedience and reap blessing. You cannot sow neglect and reap abundance. You cannot sow *nothing* and expect *everything*. God designed increase to respond to action. That means the outcome of your life is not random, it is cultivated.

Even Jesus explained His ministry through this same law. He said, *"Except a corn of wheat fall into the ground and die, it abideth alone: but if it die, it bringeth forth much fruit"* (John 12:24).

He was showing that life itself flows through the pattern of sowing, dying, and multiplying. Everything in God's Kingdom follows that design—your giving, your service, your prayers, and even your words.

When believers sow their faith through obedience and consistency, they activate Heaven's economy. It isn't luck, and it isn't chance. It is the result of cooperation with the structure God built into His world. Seedtime and harvest are proof that prosperity is not accidental, it is agricultural. What you sow determines what you grow.

IS IT POSSIBLE TO LOSE YOUR HARVEST?

Prosperity is predictable when the principles of God are honored, but it can also be delayed or completely lost, when they are ignored. The Bible shows several ways believers forfeit their harvest.

Laziness

Proverbs 10:4 says, *"He becometh poor that dealeth with a slack hand, but the hand of the diligent maketh rich."*

God is not against the poor; He is against idleness. Diligence is the currency of increase. A farmer may have the best seed and the best field, but if he never goes out to work it, he starves. You can give, tithe, and even confess the Word, but if you don't act on it, you are asleep during harvest.

Distraction

Ecclesiastes 11:4 warns: *"He that observeth the wind shall not sow; and he that regardeth the clouds shall not reap."*

Distraction is one of the enemy's most effective tools. He points to the economy, the news, or someone else's opinion until your faith hesitates. You stop sowing because the conditions don't look perfect. Faith doesn't study the forecast, it obeys the Word.

Discouragement

Galatians 6:9 promises: *"...we shall reap, if we faint not."*

The little word *if* carries enormous weight. Many faint right before the season turns. Every harvest has a time of waiting, and every believer is tested by it. The farmer who gives up before the rain never gathers what he planted. Endurance is the price of manifestation.

Apathy

Proverbs 10:5 calls for action: *"He that gathereth in summer is a wise son: but he that sleepeth in harvest is a son that causeth shame."*

Some Christians have sown faithfully but have never gone out to collect what is theirs. They left their field full because they mistook God's promise for automatic provision. A harvest left unattended will rot.

God's laws of prosperity work perfectly, but they require your participation. You can sow your seed, but you must also gather your increase. Faith expects; diligence collects.

HARVEST VERSUS HARVESTING

One of the greatest confusions among believers is the assumption that the harvest and reaping are the same. They are not. *The harvest is **what comes in**—it is what grows from the seed you sow. Harvesting, or reaping, is **what you bring in**.*

The harvest represents what God has produced through your obedience, but reaping is the act of claiming it and carrying it home.

Mark 4:26-29 compares the Kingdom of God to a man who casts seed into the ground. The seed grows *"he knoweth not how,"* but when the fruit appears, the farmer still must *"put in the sickle."* The plant didn't harvest itself. God caused the growth, but the man was responsible for gathering what grew.

The Hebrew word for *harvest* is *qatsar*, meaning "to cut off" or "to claim as mine." It pictures the moment when a man looks at what has matured in his field and says, "That belongs to me."

Reaping is not waiting; it is taking possession. It's not pride to say, "That's mine." It's agreement with the covenant we have with the Lord of the Harvest.

The same is true of the blessings that God has promised you. If you don't claim them, the enemy will gladly keep them uncollected. Many believers have harvests rotting in their fields, opportunities unclaimed, favor unspoken for, provision unreceived. God's part is to grow it; your part is to gather it. Harvest happens when God provides, but reaping begins when you act.

Faith alone believes that God will do what He said. Action proves that you believe it. These two must always work together. Faith without action is like having a seed and never planting it. It may contain life, but it will never produce fruit.

Mark 11:24 says, "*...What things soever ye desire, when ye pray, believe that ye receive them, and ye shall have them.*"

The word *receive* here means "to take hold of." Believing without taking hold is like standing in a field and admiring ripe grain while refusing to pick it.

Throughout Scripture, God required faith and action. Israel was promised the land of Canaan, but they still had to march, fight, and claim it. The blind man had to walk to the pool and wash. The widow had to pour oil into empty vessels. God performs the miracle, but He demands movement.

Faith doesn't work on a timer, it works through persistence. True faith steps out, speaks out, and stays at it until what is believed becomes visible.

Every time you act on God's Word, you are giving your faith hands. You are saying, "Lord, I trust You enough to move." Heaven always responds to movement. Prosperity comes to those who don't just believe the promise but behave as though it's already done.

EVERYTHING GOD CREATED REQUIRES STEWARDSHIP

From the beginning, God tied prosperity to stewardship. When He placed Adam in the Garden, He didn't hand him a finished paradise to admire, He gave him a project to manage. Genesis 2:15 says, "*The Lord God took the man, and put him into the garden of Eden to dress it and to keep it.*"

Even in perfection, Adam had work to do. God supplied the soil, the seed, and the sun, but Adam supplied the stewardship.

God's pattern has not changed. He blesses what you manage, not what you neglect. The same God who provided manna in the wilderness later commanded His people to cultivate the land. He will rain provision into your life, but He expects you to build the storehouses to contain it.

Increase without management turns into waste.

Many believers ask God to bless their finances while refusing to budget, invest, or plan. They pray for promotion but fail to prepare. That's not faith, that's carelessness cloaked in spirituality.

God prospers good stewards because stewardship proves readiness. Jesus said, *"He that is faithful in that which is least is faithful also in much…"* (Luke 16:10).

Faithfulness is the bridge from promise to possession.

Stewardship means order, accountability, and diligence. It's not only about money, but it is also about managing every resource God entrusts to you: your time, your relationships, your energy, and your influence. When you handle what you have as if it belongs to God, you position yourself for Him to release more.

Prosperity doesn't come to the person who prays for more but to the one who proves faithful with what they already have.

DON'T GET WEARY

Every harvest demands endurance. You can plant the right seed in the right soil and still lose the crop if you give up before it matures. Galatians 6:9 says, *"…in due season we shall reap, if we faint not."*

The phrase *due season* means there is an appointed time for manifestation. Your harvest will come, but not necessarily on your schedule. Patience is the proof that faith is still alive.

The enemy works to wear down believers before their breakthrough arrives. He points to the calendar, the bank balance, or the slow pace of progress, hoping you'll faint in the field. Yet the farmer doesn't dig up his seed to check its progress.

He waters it, protects it, and waits. He knows the process is working even when he can't see it. Prosperity is no different. You sow the Word, you act on the Word, and you hold steady while it grows.

Discouragement is often the final test before manifestation. It whispers: What you believed isn't working. Giving and tithing were pointless. Your faith failed.

But faith never fails; the impatient heart fails. Your consistency must outlast your emotions.

Focus keeps you from being swayed by appearances. Perseverance carries you through the season between sowing and reaping. If you refuse to quit, the law of seedtime and harvest will not fail you. God's principles are as sure as gravity. Those who stay the course will always see results.

Prosperity is not limited to finances. The same divine principles that govern increase in your bank account also govern peace in your home, health in your body, and progress in your purpose. God designed all of life to respond to the law of sowing and reaping.

In marriage, you reap what you sow. Sow kindness, patience, and forgiveness, and you will harvest intimacy and stability. Sow criticism, neglect, and resentment, and you will harvest distance and conflict. God's principles are universal and impartial. They work for whoever works them.

The prayer of faith cannot substitute for the principle of stewardship. In your health, the same rule applies. You can't mistreat your body and pray for divine energy. Rest, proper diet, and discipline are also spiritual acts of obedience. Your body is the temple of the Holy Spirit, and it responds to how you manage it.

In your work or business, the principle is identical.

When you sow:

- Diligence
- Integrity
- Excellence

You will reap:

- Opportunity
- Favor
- Increase

Employers and clients may think they are rewarding you, but in truth, it is God's law of increase honoring your faithfulness.

When you live by God's principles, every area of life becomes fertile ground. Prosperity ceases to be a financial pursuit and becomes a way of life. The same God who multiplies money multiplies peace, wisdom, and joy. Once you understand this, prosperity becomes predictable because it's not about what you have, but how you handle what you have.

PROSPERITY IS PREDICTABLE

Prosperity is not mysterious, random, or reserved for a select few. It is the natural result of honoring the laws God established from the beginning.

When you obey the principle, you can expect the promise. The same way gravity pulls objects to the ground, obedience pulls blessing into your life.

Many pray for what God has already provided. The harvest is waiting, but Heaven will not do your part. God gives the seed, the soil, and the season, but He will not swing the sickle for you. You must act. You must plan, plant, and persevere. Prosperity does not come to the wishful but to the willing.

When people say, "If God wants me to have it, He'll give it to me," they misunderstand both God's nature and His system. He already wants you to prosper. He already made provision. The question is whether you will apply His principles. Waiting for *God* to do what He told *you* to do is not humility, it's disobedience with a religious excuse.

Everything God made operates by design, not chance. Prosperity is no exception. When you:

- Sow diligently
- Guard against distraction
- Refuse to faint, and
- Act on the Word ...then increase become inevitable.

You won't have to chase prosperity, it will begin to chase you. God's will for you is not survival but success, not lack but abundance, not dependence but dominion. The moment you stop waiting for Him to brush your teeth and start working His Word, your life will begin to change.

This is precisely why biblical prosperity principles must be proclaimed from every pulpit across America and around the world. When we fail to teach God's financial wisdom, believers remain ignorant of Kingdom economics and continue living in bondage to debt, lack, and poverty mindsets.

But the consequences extend far beyond personal finances. When the body of Christ doesn't prosper, we lack the resources to fulfill the Great Commission. Souls hang in the balance. Missions go unfunded. The gospel's advance is hindered *not by the power of darkness, but by the poverty of God's people.*

The math is sobering: far more people will suffer eternally because we didn't have the funds to reach them than will ever be harmed by the excesses or abuses of prosperity teaching.

The greater sin is silence. When we refuse to equip believers with God's principles for increase, we leave them defenseless against the spirit of poverty. We rob the Kingdom of the resources needed to advance. Consider the true casualties of our silence on prosperity: the souls lost because a church couldn't afford to send missionaries; the communities left in darkness because believers lacked the means to establish a presence there.

Let's preach the whole counsel of God's Word, including His desire for His children to prosper and be in good health, even as their souls prosper.

12

THE PROSPERITY-PERSECUTION PARADOX

One of the most common objections to biblical prosperity is: "But didn't Jesus promise that we would suffer persecution?"

He did, but He never said we would suffer from self-imposed unpaid bills or financial chaos. There's a vast difference between *persecution* and the *pain* caused by poor stewardship. To confuse the two is to dishonor those who have truly suffered for the gospel.

Persecution is external; it comes from the world's hostility toward righteousness. Financial disorder, on the other hand, is internal; it comes from neglecting the principles of diligence, giving, and management that God has clearly established. Jesus promised persecution for standing for truth, not for failing to budget.

Some believers take pride in their financial struggle, calling it their "cross to bear." But the Bible never equates disorganization or debt with discipleship.

When Christians in free nations confuse persecution with the consequences of ignoring divine principles, it trivializes the blood of martyrs who died for the faith. It's one thing to be hated for Christ's sake—it's another to suffer because we refused to live by His wisdom.

The fires that burned the saints in history were ignited by man's hatred, not by overdue payments. Jesus never called us to glorify lack; He called us to glorify Him in every season, whether in plenty or in persecution.

Jesus was clear about persecution. He said that all who *"live godly in Christ Jesus shall suffer persecution"* (2 Timothy 3:12). He didn't say "might," He said *"shall."*

It's not optional for those who stand for truth in a world that hates it. Persecution is the inevitable collision between righteousness and rebellion, between light and darkness. It is the world's reaction to a believer's obedience.

Mark 10:29-30 records that after Peter reminded Jesus of all they had sacrificed to follow Him, the Lord responded:

> *...There is no man that hath left house, or brethren, or sisters, or father, or mother, or wife, or children, or lands, for my sake, and the gospel's, but he shall receive a hundredfold now in this time... with persecutions, and in the world to come eternal life.*

The blessing and the backlash arrive together. Prosperity and persecution are not opposites, they are traveling companions.

When the favor of God rests visibly on your life, it provokes those who despise His ways. The moment you walk in obedience, darkness looks for a way to strike back. That's why the enemy often attacks believers through ridicule, accusation, or financial pressure. The accuser of the brethren often finds people to partner with him in the Church!

We are not to fear persecution, but to expect it and stand in it. It is the price of being a shining light in a dark world. Yet make no mistake, suffering for righteousness is holy, but suffering from negligence is not. The fires of persecution refine faith; the fires of irresponsibility burn opportunity.

SUFFERING FOR CHRIST OR CHAOS?

To understand persecution, we must look at those who actually endured it. John Foxe's *Book of Martyrs* records men and women who faced death, not debt collectors; flames, not financial frustration. They didn't suffer because they mishandled their resources but because they refused to renounce Christ.

Consider Hugh Latimer and Nicholas Ridley, burned at the stake in Oxford in 1555. As the flames were lit, Latimer turned to Ridley and declared: "Be of good comfort, Master Ridley, and play the man; we shall this day light such a candle by God's grace in England, as I trust shall never be put out."[26]

Their suffering wasn't self-inflicted; it was the price of unwavering faith.

Or think of Thomas Cranmer, Archbishop of Canterbury, who recanted under pressure, then publicly withdrew that recantation, confessing Christ boldly before being led to the stake in 1556. When the fire was lit, he thrust his right hand into the flames, calling it: "That unworthy hand." His dying words were, "Lord Jesus, receive my spirit. I see the heavens open and Jesus standing at the right hand of God."[27] His agony was not the result of poor planning, it was the result of courageous conviction.

These believers faced persecution because they valued truth above comfort. They could have chosen compromise and lived, but they chose loyalty to Christ and died.

To compare their martyrdom to the financial disfunction of the average American Christian borders on blasphemy. Whenever you talk about prosperity and some brainwashed, backslidden Christian living in the top 1 percent of the wealthiest people on the planet sneers at you and says, "What about persecution? Do you think you're better than those who are hurting?"

Just look them right in the eye and say, "No, but unlike you, I actually want to be able to help them."

THE FALSE EQUIVALENCE

There is a dangerous tendency among believers to baptize every hardship as "my cross to bear." That mindset confuses persecution with personal mismanagement. These are often self-inflicted wounds. You don't get extra credit for suffering the results of ignoring divine order.

When someone in a free nation experiences financial chaos, yet claims, "I'm just being persecuted for my faith," they're mocking the faith of those who truly bled for Christ. The martyrs faced kings, inquisitors, and mobs. We face spreadsheets and impulse purchases. Confusing the two trivializes their witness and dulls our discernment.

The truth is simple: persecution purifies; negligence penalizes. One is spiritual warfare, the other is spiritual immaturity. God will comfort you through both, but He only rewards one. If you are being persecuted for righteousness' sake, Heaven applauds. If you are suffering from disobedience, Heaven calls you to repent and apply His wisdom.

God's Word produces predictable outcomes. Obedience brings blessing, and disorder brings loss. The only thing worse than confusing the two is calling the consequences of your choices "God's will."

THE ELDER BROTHER SYNDROME

In the parable of the prodigal son, the focus is often on the rebellious younger brother who squandered his inheritance. But hidden in that story is another lesson, one that reveals a kind of spiritual resentment that still surfaces today. It's actually the purpose of the parable.

When the younger son returned home, forgiven and restored, the elder brother refused to celebrate. Luke records that *"he was angry, and would not go in"* (Luke 15:28). He complained:

> *And he answering said to his father, Lo, these many years do I serve thee, neither transgressed I at any time thy commandment: and yet thou never gavest me a kid, that I might make merry with my friends: But as soon as this thy son was come, which hath devoured thy living with harlots, thou hast killed for him the fatted calf. And he said unto him, Son, thou art ever with me, and all that I have is thine* (Luke 15:29-31).

The older brother was suffering—but it was from jealousy.

That same spirit lives in the Church today. It's the voice that says, "Why should they be blessed? I've been faithful longer." It's the tone of bitterness that sneers at testimonies of increase, revival, or answered prayer. The elder brother resented the celebration because it exposed his unbelief. He had access to everything his father owned, yet he lived like a servant, not a son.

In many ways, this is what fuels criticism of biblical prosperity. It isn't always theological disagreement, it's resentment. Some believers feel guilty for succeeding when others have not.

Others refuse to rejoice when someone else is blessed, mistaking jealousy for humility. This is a form of spiritual survivor's guilt—the unease of being favored while others struggle.

But God never intended for His blessing to make us ashamed; He intended it to make us a channel. The elder brother could have joined the feast, but he chose to stand outside, sulking. The difference between resentment and rejoicing is revelation. When you understand that everything the Father has is yours, you celebrate another's blessing as evidence that yours is near.

THE HUNDREDFOLD WITH PERSECUTION

When Peter reminded Jesus that he and the other disciples had left all to follow Him, Jesus responded with one of the most remarkable promises in Scripture:

> *Verily I say unto you, there is no man that hath left house, or brethren, or sisters, or father, or mother, or wife, or children, or lands, for My sake, and the gospel's, but he shall receive a hundredfold now in this time...with persecutions; and in the world to come eternal life* (Mark 10:29-30).

Notice the balance in Jesus' words. He didn't just promise blessing; He promised blessing with backlash. The hundredfold increase was said to come with guaranteed resistance. Prosperity attracts persecution because favor magnifies faith. The same abundance that glorifies God also exposes rebellion in others.

The world and those in the Church influenced by it will often interpret your blessing as arrogance or greed. The same people who cheered when you gave will sometimes criticize when you prosper. The blessing provokes envy.

Persecution, then, is not proof that you've missed God—it's often proof that you've found His favor. The devil does not waste bullets on a barren field. A harvest worth gathering is a harvest worth guarding.

Jesus promised that increase and opposition arrive in the same package because visible blessing exposes hidden resentment.

To be blessed is to be envied. To be envied is to be targeted.

CAIN, JUDAS, AND THE ANTICHRIST

The first conflict in human history was also the first conflict over the blessing. In Genesis 4, Cain and Abel each brought an offering to the Lord. Abel's gift was accepted because it was offered in faith and obedience; Cain's gift was rejected because it lacked both. Instead of repenting, Cain turned his anger toward his brother.

Jealousy over divine favor led to murder. The spirit that despised Abel's blessed life has never left the earth—it is the same spirit that hates believers who walk in the visible blessing of God today.

That same pattern resurfaced in the life of Judas Iscariot, who kept the disciples' money bag. John's Gospel says Judas objected when Mary anointed Jesus with expensive perfume, pretending to care for the poor. Scripture then adds a revealing note:

> *He did not say this because he cared about the poor but because he was a thief; as keeper of the money bag, he used to help himself to what was put into it* (John 12:6 NIV).

Judas cloaked greed in religious language. The spirit that hates generosity always disguises itself as moral concern. It criticizes prosperity not because it loves holiness, but because it covets control.

This spirit will reach its climax in the coming antichrist. Revelation 13 foretells a global system *"so that they could not buy or sell"* (see Revelation 13:17 NIV) without allegiance to his rule. Once again, the enemy will weaponize money to persecute the righteous. From Cain's field to Judas' purse to the antichrist's economy, satan's strategy has remained consistent—use financial control to silence worship and restrict obedience.

The Bible calls this influence the spirit of mammon. It is not merely greed; it is the idolatrous power that seeks to replace trust in God with dependence on possessions. Jesus said plainly, *"You cannot serve God and mammon"* (Luke 16:13 NKJV). Mammon promises what only God can give: security, identity, and significance.

When you see the connection, it becomes clear why the enemy fights prosperity teaching so fiercely. Every believer who learns to handle money biblically becomes immune to manipulation. No wonder mammon resists it. The spirit of mammon hates prosperity preaching.

THE SPIRIT OF MAMMON

Mammon is not the possession of money but the worship of it. It is the belief that material resources can provide what only God can.

The spirit of mammon whispers two opposite lies. To the poor, it says, "If you only had more, you'd be secure." To the rich, it says, "You don't need God, you already have enough."

Either way, it builds dependence on wealth instead of on the Word. It corrupts both poverty and prosperity, twisting them into prisons of fear. The rich don't have a monopoly on greed. Often you'll find it more in the poor.

Mammon's goal has always been the same: to make people fear lack more than they fear disobedience. But God calls His people to master money, not to be mastered by it. When you tithe, give, sow, and steward resources in faith, you dethrone mammon and prove your trust in God's sufficiency. Prosperity God's way isn't about loving money, it's about demonstrating that money no longer owns you.

Giving is the only way to prove that money has no hold on you. The more believers learn to walk in true prosperity, the more this demonic system loses power. Every debt canceled, every business redeemed, and every gift given in obedience is a declaration that mammon has been defeated.

FAVOR ATTRACTS FIRE

The word *blessed* has been softened by modern religion; but in Scripture, it carries a weight that provokes both admiration and opposition. The Greek word *makarios* (used throughout the Beatitudes, see Matthew 5) means "happy, fortunate, or to be envied." To be blessed is to live so evidently favored that others notice. And when they do, some will be inspired, while others will be incensed.

From the beginning, blessing has stirred resentment. Abel's offering pleased God, and Cain's jealousy boiled over. Isaac reaped a hundredfold in famine, and the Philistines envied him. Joseph's dreams revealed divine favor, and his brothers hated him for it. Nothing attracts persecution like visible prosperity. Favor exposes the insecurity of those who refuse to obey the same God who gave it.

Jesus understood this perfectly, which is why He said, *"Blessed are you when they revile and persecute you…"* (Matthew 5:11 NKJV).

In other words, the proof of blessing is often found in the reaction it provokes. People don't persecute what they don't notice.

This helps explain why persecution often shadows prosperity. The world envies what the Church enjoys, but instead of humbling itself to learn the principles that produced it, it lashes out in bitterness. That same envy can even creep into the Church. Like the elder brother standing outside his father's house, some believers grow suspicious of joy and success. They convince themselves that visible blessing must mean hidden compromise.

Genuine prosperity is meant to be public, not hidden. It glorifies the Giver, not the receiver. And the envy of others does not cancel the favor of God—it only confirms it.

THE PROSPERITY PARADOX

A paradox is a statement that appears to contradict itself but, when examined, reveals a deeper truth. The Kingdom of God is full of them. You die to live. You give to receive. You humble yourself to be exalted. And here, we find another: prosperity and persecution can coexist. The world cannot comprehend how blessing and suffering can dwell in the same house, but Scripture insists that they do.

This is what Jesus revealed in Mark 10:30, *"...a hundredfold now in this time...with persecutions...."* The more visibly God blesses you, the more visible a target you become. Yet that very tension keeps prosperity pure. The blessing draws attention, but the persecution keeps pride from growing. It is both a gift and a guardrail.

There is another paradox worth considering, the hedonistic paradox. Philosophers use this term to describe how the *pursuit* of pleasure never produces *true* pleasure. When happiness becomes the goal, it vanishes. Only when a person pursues something higher than self does happiness follow.

The same principle applies to prosperity. Those who chase wealth for its own sake rarely find it or, if they do, it consumes them. But those who chase God, honor His Word, and apply His principles, find that prosperity follows them naturally.

This is the prosperity paradox: you do not get prosperity by pursuing prosperity. You get prosperity by pursuing the One who gives the power to get wealth.

It is not found in greed, but in godliness. Then, in our pursuit of Him, He will tell us to confess certain Scriptures, sow certain seeds, and anticipate certain results. It all must originate from a Divine command, rather than from the pursuit of personal comfort.

So when persecution comes because of the blessing, rejoice. It means the paradox is working. You are walking in abundance without being ruled by it, standing in favor while keeping your focus on the One who gave it.

ANSWERING THE AD HOMINEM

As the Church has continued to grow in revelation about God's will to bless His people, criticism has grown louder. The most predictable reaction to visible favor has always been accusation. The same spirit that moved Cain to envy Abel, that turned Judas against Jesus, and that will one day empower the antichrist, still operates today on social media with religious vocabulary.

Whenever believers begin to prosper God's way, the conversation shifts from Scripture to slander. Critics rarely argue the Word—they attack the person. That's the definition of an ad hominem, when you can't disprove the message, you discredit the messenger. The modern label "prosperity preacher" is often used this way—not as a theological category but as an insult meant to silence truth. Yet, if the Word of God is clear on the subject, then no amount of ridicule can rewrite it.

We will address these accusations in greater detail later because they deserve a thorough response, biblically, historically, and practically. But for now, remember this: persecution is proof that the blessing is visible.

So when you hear the jeers, the headlines, or the hashtags, don't be shaken. The same Jesus who promised the hundredfold also promised the persecution. Those two promises still stand side by side. The Church was never called to hide its blessing to avoid criticism, but to steward it well, and give God glory for it.

The paradox remains: the more blessed you are, the more opposition you will face, but both are signs that you're walking in the truth. In the chapters ahead, we go deeper into why this persecution rises, how the spirit of mammon fuels it, and how believers can answer it with wisdom, integrity, and undeniable fruit.

PART FOUR

EXPOSING ANTI-PROSPERITY LIES

13

COUNTERING LOGICAL FALLACIES

You can tell how radioactive a subject is by watching how fast preachers tiptoe past it. Money, giving, and prosperity are among the most avoided topics in the modern pulpit. You can hear entire sermon series on angels, marriage, or mental health, but suggest a message on God's will to bless His people and suddenly the room gets quiet. It is not because the Bible is unclear, it is because the mob is so loud.

Most pastors are terrified to preach about money—not because they don't know what *Scripture* says, but because they're afraid of what *people* will say. I've sat in ministerial gatherings where seasoned pastors, men who boldly preach the gospel week after week, confess in hushed tones that they avoid teaching on finances. If they preach a series on prosperity, the truth of it dies the death of a thousand qualifications as they constantly backpeddle, make excuses, and attempt to justify why they're not like those other "health and wealth" preachers.

They've watched what happens to colleagues who dare to address biblical prosperity. They've seen the social media pile-ons, the denominational whispers, the sudden loss of speaking invitations. Often pastors feel they cannot lead their congregations in financial matters because of their own financial struggles. Even those who are prospering often stay silent, not from guilt, but from fear. Fear of being labeled. Fear of being misunderstood. Fear of the "Christian cancel culture mob."

As many as one in seven verses in the Gospels touch on money or possessions. The Son of God, in His earthly ministry, devoted significant teaching time to financial matters; yet, the modern Church tiptoes around these topics "as if taking a walk through a minefield,"[28] as one writer put it.

The result? Financial illiteracy is epidemic among believers. Research from the Christian Stewardship Network reveals that 78 percent of American Christians live paycheck to paycheck.[29] Sixty percent couldn't cover a $1,000 emergency without going into debt.[30]

We have a generation of believers who have never heard clear, biblical teaching on God's desire to prosper His people, on the principles of sowing and reaping, or on the power God gives us to get wealth so that His covenant might be established on earth.

The silence in our pulpits has created a vacuum, and that vacuum has been filled with either secular financial advice devoid of Kingdom principles or religious tradition that sounds spiritual but contradicts Scripture.

CHRISTIAN CANCEL CULTURE

If you dare to teach biblical prosperity in today's climate, you'd better be prepared for the backlash. The moment you mention Deuteronomy 8:18 or 2 Corinthians 9, the accusations start flying:

- *"Prosperity gospel!"*
- *"Greedy charlatan!"*
- *"Name it and claim it!"*
- *"False teacher!"*
- *"Heretic!"*
- *"You're fleecing the sheep!"*

The reputation costs are real. Pastors who teach prosperity principles face accusations of manipulation and greed. It's not long before other ministers start distancing themselves. Denominational networks may revoke credentials. Social media becomes a courtroom where you're tried, convicted, and sentenced, all without a fair hearing of what Scripture actually says.

The institutional costs are equally severe. Speaking invitations dry up. Network relationships fracture. You find yourself labeled and blacklisted, not for denying the deity of Christ or rejecting the authority of Scripture, but for teaching what Moses, David, Solomon, Jesus, and Paul explicitly taught about God's provision for His people.

The internal cost may be the heaviest. Faithful pastors wrestle with being misunderstood, misquoted, and condemned by the court of public opinion all the time. They know they're standing on Scripture, but they watch as brothers and sisters in ministry treat them as the worst kind of heretics. When we allow fear and intimidation to silence biblical teaching on prosperity, entire congregations suffer.

This is why prosperity apologetics is so urgently needed right now.

WHY WE NEED PROSPERITY APOLOGETICS

The word *apologetics* comes from the Greek word *apologia,* which means, "a defense or a reasoned argument."[31] It's what Peter commanded us to do:

> *...Always be prepared to give an answer to everyone who asks you to give the reason for the hope that you have. But do this with gentleness and respect* (1 Peter 3:15 NIV).

We need prosperity apologetics for three critical reasons:

First: Scripture commands it. The Bible speaks clearly and repeatedly about God's desire to prosper His people. We cannot be faithful to the whole counsel of God while ignoring or downplaying these texts. When critics attack prosperity teaching, they're not just attacking preachers, they're attacking Scripture. We must defend what God has said.

Second: The opposition uses faulty reasoning. As we'll see in this chapter, the arguments against biblical prosperity are riddled with logical fallacies. These fallacies may sound convincing to the untrained ear, but they crumble under biblical and logical scrutiny. Believers need to be equipped to identify these errors so they're not deceived by arguments that sound good but prove nothing.

Third: There's a glaring double standard. Critics who condemn prosperity teachers as heretics somehow manage to honor Reformation figures who had far more serious—and documented—moral and theological failures.

Martin Luther wrote a 65,000-word treatise calling for the genocide of Jews, and questioned whether James, Jude, and Revelation belonged in Scripture.

John Calvin orchestrated the execution of theological opponents and oversaw a regime that falsely burned alive women purported to be witches. Yet these men are celebrated as heroes of the faith, while pastors who simply teach Deuteronomy 8:18 are branded as the worst kind of false teachers.

This inconsistency must be exposed—not to dishonor the Reformers, they made genuine contributions to Christian theology, but to reveal the intellectual dishonesty of critics who apply one standard to historical figures and a completely different standard to contemporary ministers.

In this chapter, you will learn to identify the most common logical fallacies used against prosperity teaching. Each fallacy is defined and shows you exactly how it's deployed in attacks on prosperity doctrine, explains why it's wrong, and gives you biblical responses. When someone accuses you of heresy, you can pinpoint the flaw in their reasoning and respond with clarity and confidence.

Finally, we provide ethical guardrails for teaching prosperity responsibly. Because yes, there have been abuses. By the time you finish this chapter, you will be equipped to defend biblical prosperity with confidence, to identify fallacious reasoning when you encounter it, and to teach God's people how to walk in the provision He desires for them.

Let's begin.

IDENTIFYING LOGICAL FALLACIES

Before we can effectively defend biblical prosperity, we need to understand how arguments work and how they break down. Most attacks on prosperity teaching aren't based on careful exegesis of Scripture. They're based on faulty reasoning that sounds convincing but proves nothing. These faulty patterns of reasoning are called *logical fallacies.*

A logical fallacy is an error in reasoning that undermines the validity of an argument.[32] Fallacies can be either structural (formal fallacies) or content-based (informal fallacies). They often involve arguments that seem persuasive on the surface but, upon closer examination, reveal underlying flaws.[33, 34]

Sometimes these fallacies are deployed deliberately to mislead, manipulate, or win arguments through emotional appeal rather than truth. As the *Internet Encyclopedia of Philosophy* notes:

"Fallacies often seem superficially sound, and they far too often retain immense persuasive power even after being clearly exposed as false."[35]

Let's look at exactly how critics deploy these errors, why they're wrong, and how to respond biblically.

FALLACY 1: AD HOMINEM

Attacking the Person, Not the Argument

Ad hominem is Latin for *to the person.* This fallacy occurs when someone attempts to invalidate an opponent's position by attacking a personal trait or fact about the opponent rather than addressing the actual argument they're making.[36] Instead of engaging with the substance of what's being taught, the critic attacks the teacher's character, lifestyle, appearance, or circumstances.[37]

You've probably heard these attacks:

- "Look at that pastor's car, watch, tennis shoes, (pick one!)—he's obviously just in it for the money."
- "That preacher has three private jets. That tells you everything you need to know about his theology."
- "She preaches about sacrifice while wearing a $5,000 dress. I don't need to hear another word she says."

Notice what's happening in each case. Critics never engage with what Scripture says about prosperity. They never address Deuteronomy 8:18 or 2 Corinthians 9. They simply point to the teacher's lifestyle and declare, "See? This proves the teaching is false."

But does it? Does the teacher's personal financial situation, whether abundant or lacking, have anything to do with whether Scripture teaches that God desires to prosper His people?

The ad hominem fallacy is wrong for several critical reasons:

First: Truth is independent of the messenger's circumstances. The validity of a doctrine doesn't depend on the personal life of the one teaching it. If I teach that two plus two equals four, that mathematical truth remains whether I'm rich or poor, educated or ignorant, virtuous or corrupt. The truth stands on its own merits.

Second: Scripture must be evaluated by Scripture, not by impression or opinon. When we're examining whether something is biblical, the question that should be asked is: "What does the Word of God say?" not, "What does this teacher's lifestyle look like?" You cannot determine biblical truth by examining a preacher's car, house, wardrobe, or even past mistakes. You can only determine it by carefully studying God's Word.

The personal attack distracts from the real question. By shifting the focus from "Is this doctrine biblical?" to "Do I like this person's lifestyle?" the ad hominem fallacy prevents honest examination of Scripture. It's a diversionary tactic that keeps people from engaging with what God's Word actually says.

In contrast, we should strive to be more like the Bereans. When Paul preached in Berea, the believers there *"...received the word with all eagerness, examining the Scriptures daily to see if these things were so"* (Acts 17:11 ESV).

They didn't evaluate Paul's teaching based on his travel arrangements or wardrobe. They searched the Scriptures. That's the model for us.

Additionally, Paul exhorts us to test everything: *"Test everything; hold fast what is good"* (1 Thessalonians 5:21 ESV).

How do we test? By Scripture. By fruit. By the Spirit's witness. Not by making assumptions based on someone's financial circumstances.

How Should I Respond?

When someone uses the ad hominem fallacy against prosperity teaching, here are ways you can respond:

- I understand you have concerns about [teacher's] lifestyle, but that's not the question we should be asking. The question is: What does Scripture actually teach?
- Does God give His people power to get wealth according to Deuteronomy 8:18?
- Does Jesus promise a hundredfold return in Mark 10:30?

These are the questions we need to answer from Scripture, so let's open the Bible together and see what God says.

FALLACY 2: STRAW MAN

Misrepresenting the Position

The straw man fallacy occurs when someone argues against a distorted, exaggerated, or oversimplified version of their opponent's position rather than engaging with what that person actually believes and teaches.[38] The term comes from the idea that a straw man is a flimsy, easy-to-knock-down replica of a real person. Instead of wrestling with the real argument, critics create a caricature and then attack that.

As one source explains: "A straw man argument is one that argues against a hyperbolic, inaccurate version of the opposition rather than their actual argument."[39]

Listen to how critics often characterize prosperity teaching:

- "Prosperity preachers say that if you have enough faith, you'll always be rich and never have problems."
- "Prosperity preachers claim that poverty is always a sign of sin or a lack of faith."
- "Prosperity gospel teaches that God is like a cosmic vending machine, you put in one dollar and get out a million."
- "Prosperity preachers promise you'll never suffer, never struggle, never face persecution if you just believe right and give enough."
- "Prosperity teachers tell you that if you're not wealthy, you're in sin or God is displeased with you."

Now, I want you to notice something crucial: these are not accurate representations of what responsible prosperity teachers actually teach. This is a straw man, a caricature designed to be easily demolished because the attacker is not well-versed enough in the Scripture to address it biblically.

The straw man fallacy is intellectually dishonest for several reasons:

First: It prevents genuine dialogue. When critics attack a position no one actually holds, they're not engaging in honest debate—they're shadow-boxing. Real discussion requires accurately representing what your opponent believes, then addressing that position with biblical and logical arguments.

Second: It's a form of bearing false witness. The ninth commandment says, *"You shall not bear false witness against your neighbor"* (Exodus 20:16 ESV). When we misrepresent what someone teaches—whether deliberately or through carelessness—we're violating this commandment. We're putting words in their mouth they never said and attributing positions to them that they don't hold.

Third: It keeps people from examining what Scripture actually says. If I can convince you that prosperity teaching is based on the theory, "God is a vending machine," you'll never take the time to study Deuteronomy 8:18 or 2 Corinthians 9 for yourself. The straw man keeps people away from the biblical text by making them *think* they already know what it says—but they don't.

Last: It judges a doctrine by its abuses rather than by its biblical foundation. Have there been teachers who took prosperity principles to unbiblical extremes? Unfortunately, yes. However, every doctrine in church history has been abused by someone. We don't judge a teaching by its worst representatives—we judge it by Scripture.

The Right Way

Scripture gives us clear principles for honest engagement. We should strive to accurately represent what others teach. Proverbs 18:13 (ESV) says: *"If one gives an answer before he hears, it is his folly and shame."*

We must hear, truly hear, what someone is teaching before we critique it. That means representing their actual position, not a distorted version of it.

Additionally, we should always endeavor to acknowledge nuance and balance. When Jesus was accused of casting out demons by the power of satan, He didn't respond to the straw man. He addressed the actual logical flaw: *"How can Satan cast out Satan? If a kingdom is divided against itself, that kingdom cannot stand"* (Mark 3:23-24 ESV).

He dealt with reality, not caricature. Conversely, Jesus also was the recipient of false accusations. They called Him "a glutton and a drunkard" (see Matthew 11:19) simply because He ate with tax collectors and sinners. Were the accusations true? No. The fact that Jesus was falsely accused doesn't mean His teaching was wrong; it means His critics were using straw man attacks. The same thing happens to prosperity teachers today.

Our task, then, must be to judge by Scripture, not by extremes. Paul warned about those who *"pervert the gospel"* (Galatians 1:7), but that didn't mean he rejected the true gospel. He made distinctions. We must do the same. Distinguish between abuses and accurate biblical teaching.

How Should I Respond?

When someone deploys a straw man argument against prosperity teaching, you may want to respond:

- I appreciate your concerns, but what you've described isn't what I teach nor is it what Scripture teaches.
- Let me clarify the actual position: (briefly state the biblical view).
- Now, if you want to critique this scriptural teaching, I'm happy to discuss it with you.
- Let's just make sure we're addressing what's really being taught, not a distorted version of it.

FALLACY 3: HASTY GENERALIZATION

Drawing Broad Conclusions from Small Samples

A hasty generalization occurs when someone draws a sweeping conclusion based on insufficient or biased evidence. It's making a universal claim based on a few examples, especially unrepresentative examples. It's rushing to a conclusion without having all the facts.[40, 41] This fallacy is sometimes called "leaping to conclusions" or "proof by anecdote."

You may have heard these arguments countless times:

- "I know a prosperity preacher who turned out to be corrupt. Therefore, all prosperity teaching is evil."
- "I saw a scandal involving a televangelist in the 1980s. That proves prosperity theology is false."
- "There was abuse in that one megachurch. This shows the entire prosperity movement is bankrupt."
- "Look at these three examples of excess. Obviously, anyone who teaches biblical prosperity is a fraud."

Notice the logical leap? The critic takes one example (or a handful of examples) and uses it to make a universal claim about everyone who teaches prosperity principles. That is like saying, "I once got food poisoning at a restaurant; therefore, all restaurants are dangerous and we should never eat out." The math doesn't work. The sample size is too small. The conclusion is too broad.

The hasty generalization fallacy fails on multiple levels:

First: You cannot judge an entire doctrine by individual failures. Every theological position in church history has had representatives who failed morally or taught erroneously. There have been corrupt Catholic priests, fallen Protestant pastors, abusive Pentecostal leaders, and greedy non-charismatic ministers. Does the failure of individuals invalidate the core doctrines? Of course not.

Second: The existence of counterfeits doesn't negate the authentic. If I show you three counterfeit twenty-dollar bills, does that prove that real twenty-dollar bills don't exist? No, it proves the opposite. Counterfeiters only attempt to replicate what is valuable and real. The fact that some have twisted prosperity teaching for personal gain actually suggests that there is something authentic worth counterfeiting.

Third: This fallacy assumes that if something has been misused or associated with bad actors, the doctrine itself must be bad. Scripture has been quoted by slave owners, tyrants, and false teachers throughout history. Does that make Scripture bad? Absolutely not.

Finally: It applies a standard to prosperity teaching that critics would never apply elsewhere. Consider this: there have been sexual scandals in every denomination, every theological tradition, every segment of Christianity. Yet no one says, "Because of these scandals, we should reject Reformed theology" or "These failures prove Baptist doctrine is false." We recognize that personal moral failure doesn't invalidate sound doctrine. Why isn't that same grace extended to prosperity teaching?

Protestant churches have prosperity-critical pastors who are greedy. Not every pastor who criticizes prosperity teaching is himself financially above reproach. There are non-charismatic pastors who've embezzled funds, lived lavishly while their churches struggled, or secretly accumulated wealth while preaching poverty theology. Does this invalidate Reformed doctrine or Baptist theology? Of course not.

Every denomination has scandals. Methodists, Presbyterians, Lutherans, Assemblies of God, Church of God in Christ—every tradition has had leaders who have fallen into sin. If we used the hasty generalization fallacy consistently, we'd have to reject all of Christianity because of individual failures. But we don't do that—nor should we.

The Bible teaches us to judge with wisdom and discernment: Jesus said, *"Do not judge by appearances, but judge with right judgment"* (John 7:24 ESV).

Right judgment requires looking at the whole picture, not just isolated examples. It requires evaluating doctrine by Scripture, not by individual failures.

Scripture also teaches us that tares grow among wheat. In Matthew 13:24-30, Jesus taught about the parable of the wheat and tares, acknowledging that false believers and true believers would grow together until the final harvest. The presence of tares doesn't mean there's no wheat. The presence of false teachers doesn't invalidate true teachers who preach the same general message.

As you work to judge with wisdom and discernment, remember not to let the minority define the majority. Most prosperity teachers are faithful pastors who genuinely love God's Word and God's people.

They're not getting rich off ministry, they're serving sacrificially, teaching stewardship, and helping believers break free from poverty mindsets. Unfortunately, we rarely hear about them because faithfulness doesn't make headlines—scandals do.

How Should I Respond?

When someone uses hasty generalization against prosperity teaching, I like to respond in this way:

- I understand you've seen examples of abuse, and I agree those are wrong and tragic. But you're taking a few examples and using them to make a sweeping claim about everyone who teaches biblical prosperity.
- That's like saying, "I knew a Baptist pastor who fell into sin, therefore all Baptist doctrine is false."
- We both know that's not sound reasoning. Let's judge prosperity teaching the same way we judge any doctrine—by Scripture, not by individual failures.
- Show me from the Bible why Deuteronomy 8:18 or 2 Corinthians 9 shouldn't be taught, and I'll listen. But don't ask me to reject Scripture because of someone's failure.

FALLACY 4: GUILT BY ASSOCIATION

This is very similar to what you've just read. Guilt by association is a logical error that attempts to discredit an argument or position by linking it to a disliked person, group, or movement, regardless of the actual merits of the argument itself. As one logic resource explains, this fallacy occurs when someone argues "that because two things share (or are implied to share) some property, they are the same."[42]

The fallacy works through implied reasoning: "Person X believes Y. Person X is bad. Therefore, Y must be false." But this reasoning is fundamentally flawed because the truth or errancy of an idea has nothing to do with who else happens to believe it.

Listen to how this fallacy shows up in attacks on biblical prosperity:

- "That televangelist from the 1980s who had a scandal taught prosperity, so anyone who teaches prosperity today must also be corrupt."
- "Certain cult leaders have talked about financial blessing; therefore, prosperity teaching is cultish."
- "This controversial figure teaches about sowing and reaping; so if you teach the same thing, you must be just like them."
- "Prosperity teaching is associated with the Word of Faith movement, and I don't like that movement; therefore, prosperity teaching is false."

Critics never engage with what Scripture says. They simply link prosperity teaching to someone or something unpopular, then declare guilt by association.

Each teaching must stand or fall on its own biblical merits. The fact that someone you dislike believes something doesn't make that thing false. Hitler was a vegetarian, but that doesn't make all vegetarians evil. False teachers quote Scripture, but that doesn't make Scripture false. Bad people sometimes tell the truth, and that doesn't make truth evil.

Association is not argumentation. Linking two things doesn't prove anything about either one. You must examine the actual content of what's being taught and compare it to Scripture. As 1 John 4:1 says:

> *Beloved, believe not every spirit, but try the spirits whether they are of God: because many false prophets are gone out into the world.*

We try (test) by Scripture, not by association. This fallacy would invalidate all of Christian doctrine if applied consistently. Consider this: the Crusaders killed in the name of Christ; therefore Christianity is violent. Slave owners quoted the Bible; therefore, Scripture supports slavery. Cultists claim to follow Jesus; therefore, Jesus must be a cult leader. We immediately recognize the absurdity when the fallacy is applied to doctrines we hold dear. Why accept it when applied to prosperity teaching?

Judge the message, not the messenger's associations. Paul wrote:

> *Some indeed preach Christ even of envy and strife; and some also of good will... What then? notwithstanding, every way, whether in pretence, or in truth, Christ is preached; and I therein do rejoice, yea, and will rejoice* (Philippians 1:15,18).

Paul separated the message from the messenger's motives. We must do the same.

How Should I Respond?

When someone uses guilt by association against prosperity teaching, respond like this:

- I understand that you have concerns about certain people who have taught on prosperity, but we need to separate the message from the messenger.
- The question is not, "Who else believes this?" but "Is this biblical?"
- Show me from Scripture why these verses are wrong, and I will listen.
- But I cannot reject what the Bible teaches simply because someone you dislike also teaches it. That would be guilt by association, and that is not sound reasoning.

FALLACY 5: APPEAL TO TRADITION

The appeal to tradition fallacy occurs when someone argues that a claim must be true (or false) simply because it has always been believed that way—or because most people believe it—rather than providing actual evidence or biblical support.[43]

"But we've always done it this way!" is never a good argument. This fallacy assumes that tradition or majority opinion equals truth. But as history repeatedly demonstrates, the majority can be wrong, and long-held traditions can be unbiblical.

You have probably heard these arguments many times:

- "Our denomination has never emphasized prosperity theology, so I'm not comfortable with it."
- "The historic church didn't teach this; therefore, it is a false innovation."
- "This is a modern invention, not traditional Christianity."
- "The great theologians of the past didn't focus on prosperity, so neither should we."
- "Most evangelical scholars reject prosperity teaching, so it must be wrong."

The implied argument is simple: Tradition (or majority opinion) says no; therefore, the answer is no. But this reasoning bypasses the most important question: What does Scripture say?

First: Scripture, not tradition or majority opinion, is the final authority. Paul warned in Galatians 1:8: *"But though we, or an angel from heaven, preach any other gospel unto you than that which we have preached unto you, let him be accursed."*

Notice that even apostolic authority is subject to the gospel truth. How much more should human tradition be tested against Scripture? There was a time when the entire world (except eight people) rejected God's truth and perished in the flood.

There was a time when all Israel worshiped the golden calf except Moses, Aaron, and the Levites. Majority opinion was wrong. The fact that "everyone believes it" or "we've always done it this way" proves nothing about whether it is biblical or true.

The Reformers themselves broke with 1,500 years of tradition. Martin Luther stood against the selling of indulgences, the authority of the Pope, and numerous Catholic traditions. He was condemned by the majority. He went against what "the Church has always taught."

Yet we honor him for returning to Scripture. If tradition were the standard, Luther was a heretic in those areas. But if Scripture is the standard, Luther was a reformer. You cannot logically honor the Reformation and then condemn others for questioning tradition.

Every generation faces the temptation to make their understanding "the tradition." When the Pharisees did this, Jesus rebuked them. Mark 7:13 says, *"Making the word of God of none effect through your tradition, which ye have delivered...."*

They had elevated their interpretations and practices to the level of Scripture itself. The same thing happens today when we say, "We've never taught prosperity; therefore, it must be unbiblical."

Denominational traditions have divided the body of Christ. Baptists believe one thing about baptism; Presbyterians another. Pentecostals emphasize gifts of the Spirit; Cessationists reject them. Each denomination appeals to tradition. But tradition conflicts with tradition. Which tradition is right?

Jesus answered this question: *"Search the scriptures; for in them ye think ye have eternal life: and they are they which testify of me"* (John 5:39).

He did not say, "Search your traditions." Tradition must bow to Scripture. Jesus was not afraid to confront the Pharisees: *"...Full well ye reject the commandment of God, that ye may keep your own tradition"* (Mark 7:9).

When tradition conflicts with Scripture, Scripture wins. Always.

As mentioned in a previous chapter, *Sola Scriptura* is a Latin term that means, "by Scripture alone."[44] This was a foundational principle of the Reformation. Not Scripture plus tradition. Not Scripture interpreted by tradition. Scripture alone is the final authority.

As Paul wrote: *"All scripture is given by inspiration of God, and is profitable for doctrine, for reproof, for correction, for instruction in righteousness"* (2 Timothy 3:16).

God's ways are higher than our ways. The Word declares in Isaiah 55:8-9:

> *For my thoughts are not your thoughts, neither are your ways my ways, saith the Lord. For as the heavens are higher than the earth, so are my ways higher than your ways, and my thoughts than your thoughts.*

God may teach something through His Word that challenges our traditional understanding. Our response should be humility and submission to His Word, not defense of tradition.

How Should I Respond?

When someone appeals to tradition or popular opinion in order to refute prosperity teaching, you may want to respond like this:

- I respect tradition and the wisdom of church history, but tradition is not our final authority. Only Scripture is our final authority.
- The Reformers stood against 1,500 years of Catholic tradition when they believed in Sola Scriptura—by Scripture alone. If we honor the Reformation, we must be willing to test all teaching, including traditional teaching, against the Word of God.
- So let me ask: What does the Bible say about prosperity?
- If Scripture says it, then it does not matter whether tradition has emphasized it or not. Our question must always be: Is it biblical?

FALLACY 6: FALSE DILEMMA

Either/Or When More Options Exist

The false dilemma fallacy, also called the "either/or fallacy" or "false dichotomy," occurs when someone presents only two options as if they are the only possibilities, when in fact more options exist.

This fallacy forces an artificial choice between two positions, when the truth might involve both, neither, or a third option entirely.[45]

Listen to how critics use false dilemmas to attack biblical prosperity:

- "Either you care for the poor OR you preach prosperity. You cannot do both."
- "Either you embrace persecution OR you embrace prosperity. Choose one."
- "Either you trust God OR you expect financial return—but not both."
- "Either you are spiritual OR you focus on money. Pick a lane."
- "Either you preach the Cross OR you preach blessing. They are mutually exclusive."

Do you see the pattern? The critic presents two options as if they were the only two possibilities, forcing you to choose one or the other.

The false dilemma fallacy fails because Scripture holds many of these commands simultaneously. The Bible does not force us to choose between caring for the poor and experiencing prosperity. God commands both. He does not say, "Be generous or be blessed." He says: *"Give, and it shall be given unto you; good measure, pressed down, and shaken together, and running over…"* (Luke 6:38).

Giving and receiving are part of the same Kingdom cycle. Biblical prosperity includes generous giving. One of the primary purposes of prosperity is to enable greater generosity. Paul wrote: *"God is able to make all grace abound toward you; that ye, always having all sufficiency in all things, may abound to every good work"* (2 Corinthians 9:8).

Notice the sequence: God gives abundance so that we may abound in good works, including giving to those in need. Prosperity and generosity go together.

The Christian life is full of paradoxes, not contradictions. We die to live. We give to receive. We are weak, yet strong. We mourn, yet rejoice. We are poor, yet make many rich.

Biblical faith embraces these paradoxes without forcing false choices. The false dilemma is often a manipulation tactic. By forcing an artificial choice, critics back you into a corner where no matter which option you choose, you lose.

"Do you care about the poor or not?" If you say yes, they claim you should not teach prosperity. If you say no, they paint you as heartless.

However, the question itself is flawed because it assumes you must choose one or the other, when neither option may be correct.

How Should I Respond?

When someone presents a false dilemma against prosperity teaching, respond like this:

- You are presenting this as an either/or choice, but Scripture teaches both/and.
- We do not have to choose between caring for the poor and believing God wants to prosper His people. We can do both because God commands both.
- Paul taught that God gives us abundance so that we can abound in every good work, including generosity. Jesus promised blessing with persecution.
- These are not contradictions. They are the paradoxes of Kingdom living.
- So, instead of the false choice you've offered, I will trust God for provision AND give generously. I will pursue biblical prosperity AND care for those in need. Scripture does not force us to choose.

LUTHER, CALVIN, AND THE REFORMER DOUBLE STANDARD

The attacks against prosperity preachers are vicious and unrelenting. These theological lynch mobs are stirred up by people who sit on a throne of hypocrisy. Critics honor Luther and Calvin as heroes despite their documented moral and theological failures, yet they crucify contemporary pastors who simply teach biblical stewardship.

This double standard must be exposed. If we can extend grace to the Reformers while still affirming their contributions, why can't we evaluate prosperity teaching on biblical grounds without character assassination?

LUTHER'S ANTI-SEMITISM

In 1543, three years before his death, Martin Luther published a 65,000-word treatise titled, "On the Jews and Their Lies."[46] In it, Luther called Jews "a base, whoring people" and described the synagogue as "an incorrigible whore and an evil slut."[47] He laid out a seven-point plan:

1. Burn synagogues and schools
2. Raze and destroy Jewish homes
3. Confiscate prayer books and Talmudic writings
4. Forbid rabbis to teach on pain of death
5. Abolish safe-conduct on highways for Jews
6. Confiscate all Jewish silver and gold
7. Force Jews into labor or expel them forever

Luther concluded: "We are at fault in not slaying them."[48]

Four hundred years later, the Nazis displayed Luther's treatise at Nuremberg rallies. The city of Nuremberg presented a first edition to Julius Streicher, editor of *Der Stürmer*, who called it, "the most radically anti-Semitic tract ever published."[49]

On Kristallnacht (November 10, 1938, Luther's birthday), Martin Sasse published a compendium of Luther's writings with a print run of 100,000 copies, applauding the burning of synagogues.[50]

At the Nuremberg trials, Streicher defended himself: "Dr. Martin Luther would very probably sit in my place in the defendants' dock today, if this book had been taken into consideration by the Prosecution."[51]

Since the 1980s, Lutheran churches have formally denounced Luther's anti-Semitic writings. In 1998, the Lutheran Church of Bavaria stated: "It is imperative for the Lutheran Church, which knows itself to be indebted to the work and tradition of Martin Luther, to take seriously also his anti-Jewish utterances."[52]

LUTHER'S CANON PROBLEMS

Luther questioned the divine inspiration of four New Testament books, placing them at the end of his 1522 Bible translation without numbers, treating them like the Apocrypha.[53]

Luther called the book of James an "epistle of straw" that "does not seem to me to be the writing of an apostle."[54] He said it "sets up no doctrines" and should not be counted among "chief books which are supposed to lay the foundations of faith."[55]

When discussing the book of Jude, he called it "an extract or copy of St. Peter's second epistle" that "need not be counted among the chief books."[56]

Regarding the book of Revelation, he said: "About this book of the Revelation of John, I leave everyone free to hold his own opinions. I would not have anyone bound to my opinion or judgment."[57]

Of Hebrews, Luther, "Questioned its apostolic authorship and placed it with the disputed books."[58]

The Council of Trent (1546) formally reaffirmed the canonicity of these books in direct response to Luther's doubts.[59]

JOHN CALVIN: THE HONORED THEOLOGIAN

With Blood On His Hands

Michael Servetus was a Spanish physician who denied the Trinity. In 1546, Calvin wrote to his friend William Farel: "If [Servetus] comes here, if my authority is worth anything, I will never permit him to depart alive."[60]

On August 13, 1553, Servetus attended Calvin's church service in Geneva. He was arrested. Calvin drew up the articles of indictment and acted as prosecutor. When the Geneva Council sentenced Servetus to be burned at the stake, Calvin requested the "green wood" because it would burn more slowly and cause more suffering.[61]

Calvin's theology on heretics, from his commentary on Deuteronomy 13: "Those who would spare heretics and blasphemers are themselves blasphemers. God extinguishes all those affections by which our hearts are softened...we must expunge from memory our mutual humanity" when God's glory is at stake.[62]

More Executions in Calvin's Geneva

Between 1541 and 1546, there were 58 executions and 76 banishments.[63] In 1558-1559 alone, 414 prosecutions for moral offenses occurred in a population of 20,000.[64] Offenses included wearing wrong colors, banned hairstyles, and not naming children after Old Testament characters.[65]

In 1545, Calvin wrote about a plague conspiracy: "A conspiracy of men and women has lately been discovered, who, for the space of three years, had spread the plague through the city...After fifteen women have been burnt, some men have been punished by death."[66] They were accused of smearing door-locks with "poisonous ointment."

The largest witch trial in Protestant Geneva occurred in 1571 (seven years after Calvin's death), when 29 people were executed for allegedly causing the plague through witchcraft.[67] All were executed on the basis of Calvin's instructions.

THE DOUBLE STANDARD

What We Extend to Luther:

- "He was a man of his times."
- "Take the good, leave the bad."
- "His contributions outweigh his failures."
- "Judge him by his best work."

What Luther Actually Did:

- Wrote 65,000-word genocidal treatise.
- Produced writings that were used by Nazis to justify the Holocaust.
- Questioned biblical canon (James, Jude, Hebrews, Revelation).
- Called the book of James the "epistle of straw."

What We Extend to Calvin:

- "He didn't personally light the fire."
- "It was the city council's decision."
- "He was a product of his time."
- "We should focus on his theological legacy."

What Calvin Actually Did:

- Wrote he'd "never permit [Servetus] to depart alive."
- Prosecuted Servetus personally.

- Oversaw regime with 58 executions, 76 banishments.
- Taught that "those who spare heretics are themselves blasphemers."

What We Extend to Prosperity Teachers:

- "Greedy charlatan."
- "Heretic."
- "False teacher."
- "Leading people to hell."

What They Actually Teach:

- Deuteronomy 8:18 (God gives power to get wealth).
- Psalm 35:27 (God delights in prosperity of His servant).
- 2 Corinthians 9 (Sowing and reaping).
- Luke 6:38 (Give and it shall be given).
- Biblical stewardship and generosity.

If we honor Luther despite calling for Jewish genocide and questioning Scripture, and honor Calvin despite orchestrating false and superstitious executions, how can we condemn prosperity teachers as "worse heretics" for teaching what the Bible explicitly states about God's provision? The standard cannot be:

- "Luther can question James = Hero."
- "Calvin can burn innocent people alive = Giant of faith."
- "Pastor teaches Deuteronomy 8:18 = Damnable heretic."

When critics attack prosperity teaching, ask:

- "By what standard are you judging?"
- "Do you apply this standard to Luther and Calvin?"

- "If you honor them despite documented atrocities, why not evaluate prosperity teaching biblically?"
- "Are you being consistent, or showing favoritism based on tradition?"

The double standard exposes intellectual dishonesty. We honor the Reformers' contributions while acknowledging their failures. We must extend that same grace to contemporary teachers, evaluating all doctrine by Scripture, not by double standards.

FALLACY 7: RED HERRING

Diverting from the Real Issue

A red herring introduces an irrelevant point to distract from the actual topic under discussion. The term comes from the practice of using a smoked herring to throw hunting dogs off a scent.[68]

It looks like this:

- "We should focus on discipleship, not whether God wants His people prosperous."
- "The real issue is spiritual growth, not financial blessing."

Notice how these statements shift the conversation to secondary matters. These diversions avoid engaging the biblical texts. They change the subject from, "What does Scripture say?" to matters of personal preference or social concern. Both/and thinking applies here: we can discuss biblical prosperity *and* address world problems.

When religious leaders tried to trap Jesus with political questions about paying taxes (Matthew 22:17-21), He refused the diversion and addressed the real issue. Similarly, when they brought an adulteress to trap Him (John 8:3-11), He redirected to the actual question of sin and forgiveness.

The following are some other examples of red herrings:

"Look at those televangelists with private jets!" This comment typically refers to the *excesses of certain personalities* rather than engaging

with what Scripture actually says about blessing, provision, and covenant promises. It's possible to critique a preacher's lifestyle without proving anything about God's plan for His people to be blessed. (It's also possible that the jet is not an excess at all, but a very real need for the minister's travel schedule.) A minister's ministry choices do not prove his biblical position to be false.

"What about suffering believers in persecuted nations?" This is an emotional appeal that ignores context, spiritual warfare, and the fact that prosperity teaching is *huge* in Africa, Asia, and Latin America for the precise reason that people are experiencing breakthrough. We'll address more of these objections in detail later on in this book.

How Should I Respond?

- I notice that you have changed the subject from what Scripture teaches to a peripheral issue.
- Let's stay focused on the biblical question: Does God's Word teach that He gives His people power to get wealth to establish His covenant?
- Once we establish what the Bible says, we can discuss application.

FALLACY 8: EQUIVOCATION

Using Words in Multiple Senses

Equivocation uses a word with multiple meanings in different senses within the same argument to mislead.[69] It's the old bait-and-switch with terminology: "By prosperity you mean yachts and private jets; therefore, your teaching is materialistic."

Critics redefine "prosperity" as "carnal wealth" or "excessive luxury," then attack their own definition rather than the biblical concept or your definition. This creates confusion. It substitutes the critic's definition for the biblical one, then attacks the false definition.

How Should I Respond?

- You're using "prosperity" to mean excessive materialism, but that's not the biblical definition.
- Biblical prosperity is God's provision for His purposes, including spiritual, physical, and financial blessing that line up with His Word.
- If you want to critique biblical prosperity, critique what the Bible actually means, not a redefinition of it.

FALLACY 9: APPEAL TO AUTHORITY

Misapplied

This fallacy cites a respected person or expert rather than Scripture, treating human authority as if it were infallible.[70]

- "This respected theologian said prosperity theology is heresy, so it must be wrong."
- "Famous Pastor X doesn't teach this; therefore, it's false."
- "Seminary professors reject this, so you should, too."

Human authorities can err. Only Scripture is infallible. Even godly teachers have blind spots. "Church fathers" held various errors on numerous doctrines. Even Peter needed correction from Paul (Galatians 2:11-14 NKJV):

> *But when I saw that they were not straightforward about the truth of the gospel, I said to Peter before them all, "If you, being a Jew, live in the manner of Gentiles and not as the Jews, why do you compel Gentiles to live as Jews?"*

Authority comes from alignment with God's Word, not from academic credentials.

To the law and to the testimony: if they speak not according to this word, it is because there is no light in them (Isaiah 8:20).

How Should I Respond?

- I respect that theologian, but his words are not inspired Scripture.
- Show me from the Bible where Deuteronomy 8:18, 2 Corinthians 9, etc. is wrong, and I'll listen.
- But I cannot reject what Scripture clearly teaches just because a respected person says so.

FALLACY 10: BEGGING THE QUESTION

Circular Reasoning

This fallacy assumes the truth of what it's trying to prove, using the conclusion as a premise.[71]

- "Prosperity teaching is greedy because it focuses on money, and focusing on money is greedy."
- "God doesn't want us wealthy because prosperity teaching is false, and we know it's false because God doesn't want us wealthy."

The argument goes in circles without proving anything. It assumes the very point that needs biblical demonstration. Establish what Scripture says first, then evaluate teaching based on biblical evidence. Don't start with your conclusion and work backward: "The prosperity gospel distorts the true gospel."

But this assumes the "true gospel" excludes material provision, which is the very thing under debate. They're using their conclusion as their starting point. "Prosperity preachers are in it for the money."

How do you know their motives? "Because prosperity teaching is about greed."

Pure circularity! The theology is judged by assumed motives, and motives are assumed based on the theology.

"Jesus didn't teach prosperity." Based on what hermeneutic? One that's already excluded prosperity from the Kingdom message?

It's maddening because it feels like an argument, but it's just restating the assumption with extra steps.

How Should I Respond?

- You're assuming your conclusion is true and then using it to prove itself. That's called circular reasoning.
- Let's start instead with Scripture. What does the Bible actually say about God's desire to prosper His people? Then we can evaluate teaching accordingly.

FALLACY 11: SLIPPERY SLOPE

This fallacy argues that if A happens, then Z will inevitably happen through a series of steps, without proving the connection.[72]

- "If we teach prosperity, people will become greedy, then materialistic, then they'll abandon faith entirely."
- "Prosperity teaching leads to abuse, which leads to scandals, which destroys the Church."

This assumes a chain reaction without proving each link. The solution to abuse is proper teaching, not abandoning biblical doctrine: *"What shall we say then? Shall we continue in sin, that grace may abound? God forbid…"* (Romans 6:1-2).

Paul anticipated the abuse objection to his grace teaching, but didn't stop teaching grace. He taught proper application. Similarly, we teach biblical prosperity with guardrails: stewardship, generosity, integrity, the Cross in view, and accountability in practice.

How Should I Respond?

- You're suggesting a worst-case scenario without proving it will happen.
- Yes, prosperity teaching can be abused, just like grace can lead to a license to sin, faith can become presumption, and love can enable sin.
- The answer is biblical balance and proper teaching, not silence on what Scripture clearly affirms.

FALLACY 12: POISONING THE WELL

Oh man, this one is rampant, and it's rhetorically effective, which is why it keeps getting used. This fallacy presents negative information about someone before their argument is heard, biasing the audience against them.[73]

- "Before we discuss this doctrine, you should know that this prosperity preacher did this… (fill in the blank)."
- "Prosperity gospel is the same heresy that led to these scandals. Now let's examine the teaching."
- "I've sat with people who gave their life savings to these ministries and got nothing but guilt when it didn't work out. That's what I want you to hold in your mind as we go through this."

This predisposes listeners to reject teaching before examining biblical evidence. It's manipulative rather than intellectually honest.

"Judge not according to the appearance, but judge righteous judgment" (John 7:24). Righteous judgment requires examining the actual teaching, not prejudging based on labels or negative framing.

Jesus Himself was "poisoned" in advance. They said, *"Can there any good thing come out of Nazareth?"* (John 1:46). The prejudgment was wrong.

"That's prosperity gospel teaching." Just labeling something "prosperity gospel" has become a way to dismiss it without engagement. The term itself has been so poisoned that simply applying the label is treated as a refutation. No actual argument needed.

"He's a Word of Faith preacher." Same thing here. It's a thought-terminating label. Once someone hears "Word of Faith," they're primed to reject whatever comes next even if the person is about to quote Scripture directly.

How Should I Respond?

- I notice you're framing this negatively before we even look at Scripture. That's called poisoning the well.
- Let's set aside the prejudgments and examine what the Bible actually says. Then we can evaluate the teaching fairly.

RECOGNIZING FALLACIES IN THE WILD

Now you have the tool kit to enable you to detect these fallacies when you encounter them. When critics attack prosperity teaching, listen for these patterns:

- ***Ad Hominem:*** Attacking lifestyle instead of engaging Scripture
- ***Straw Man:*** Misrepresenting what's actually taught
- ***Hasty Generalization:*** One bad example proves all wrong
- ***Guilt by Association:*** Linking to disliked figures
- ***Appeal to Tradition:*** "We've never taught this"
- ***False Dilemma:*** Forcing either/or choices

- ***Red Herring:*** Changing the subject
- ***Equivocation:*** Redefining terms
- ***Appeal to Authority:*** "Experts say..."
- ***Begging the Question:*** Circular reasoning
- ***Slippery Slope:*** "This will lead to that"
- ***Poisoning the Well:*** Prejudging before examining

When you identify the fallacy, name it. Then redirect to Scripture.

The question is never, "Do I like this teacher?" or "Does my tradition affirm this?"

The question is always: "What does God's Word say?"

> *Sanctify them through thy truth: thy word is truth* (John 17:17).

REPENT OF COMPROMISE

Many Christians have compromised biblical truth to avoid criticism. They've watered down prosperity teaching, apologized for biblical texts, or remained silent when they should have spoken. If that describes you, take time now to repent.

> *For do I now persuade men, or God? or do I seek to please men? for if I yet pleased men, I should not be the servant of Christ* (Galatians 1:10).

You cannot serve both God and the critics. You cannot honor Scripture and tradition when they conflict. You cannot teach full-counsel truth while fearing man's opinion.

We must repent of:

Silence born of fear: *"For God hath not given us the spirit of fear; but of power, and of love, and of a sound mind"* (2 Timothy 1:7).

Compromise for acceptance: *"Woe unto you, when all men shall speak well of you! for so did their fathers to the false prophets"* (Luke 6:26).

Envy toward those who prosper: *"Let not thine heart envy sinners: but be thou in the fear of the Lord all the day long"* (Proverbs 23:17).

Unbelief in God's provision: *"But without faith it is impossible to please him…"* (Hebrews 11:6).

As you defend and proclaim biblical prosperity, maintain these guardrails:

Keep the Cross central: *"But God forbid that I should glory, save in the cross of our Lord Jesus Christ…"* (Galatians 6:14).

Prosperity serves redemptive purposes, not selfish ambition.

Emphasize stewardship: *"Moreover it is required in stewards, that a man be found faithful"* (1 Corinthians 4:2).

Faithful management precedes greater blessing.

Model generosity: *"I have shewed you all things, how that so labouring ye ought to support the weak, and to remember the words of the Lord Jesus, how he said, It is more blessed to give than to receive"* (Acts 20:35).

Acknowledge trials and don't promise problem-free living: Jesus said, *"…In the world ye shall have tribulation: but be of good cheer; I have overcome the world"* (John 16:33).

Maintain accountability: *"Obey them that have the rule over you, and submit yourselves…"* (Hebrews 13:17).

Financial transparency and submission to oversight protects against abuse.

EXPECT OPPOSITION

Jesus gave us this warning: "*If ye were of the world, the world would love his own: but because ye are not of the world, but I have chosen you out of the world, therefore the world hateth you*" (John 15:19).

Paul added: "*Yea, and all that will live godly in Christ Jesus shall suffer persecution*" (2 Timothy 3:12).

When you teach biblical prosperity faithfully, expect:

- Critics to misrepresent your position
- Peers to distance themselves
- Social media attacks
- Accusations of greed and heresy
- Institutional pressure to conform

Remember that the Bible says:

> *Blessed are ye, when men shall revile you, and persecute you, and shall say all manner of evil against you falsely, for my sake. Rejoice, and be exceeding glad: for great is your reward in heaven: for so persecuted they the prophets which were before you* (Matthew 5:11-12).

Your greatest apologetic tool is consistency. When critics use fallacious reasoning, point it out. When they apply double standards, expose them. When they appeal to tradition over Scripture, redirect to the Word.

Ask these questions:

- Can you show me from Scripture where this teaching is wrong?
- Are you applying the same standard you use for other doctrines?
- If you honor Luther and Calvin despite their failures, why not evaluate my teaching biblically?

- Which specific biblical text are you rejecting, and by what authority?

Don't let them control the conversation. Insist on biblical engagement, not character assassination.

Pray this prayer:

Father, I repent of fear, compromise, envy, and unbelief. I receive Your Word that You delight in my prosperity and give me power to get wealth for the purpose of establishing Your covenant. I commit to teach biblical stewardship faithfully, regardless of the cost.

I will not bow to fallacious arguments or double standards. I will test all teaching by Scripture, including my own. I will walk in integrity, model generosity, and maintain accountability. I will keep the Cross central and acknowledge both blessing and trial.

When critics attack, help me to respond with truth and grace. When the pressure comes, strengthen me to stand on Your Word. When prosperity manifests, cause me to give generously and point others to You.

I refuse to be ashamed of what You have clearly revealed. I will defend biblical prosperity not for personal gain, but because Your Word deserves defense.

Make me a faithful steward of truth. Give me boldness to proclaim it without hesitation and the wisdom to apply it in every situation. Let my life demonstrate how Your desire to prosper Your people is neither greed nor heresy, but rather Your good pleasure.

In Jesus' name, I pray. Amen.

You've been equipped. You know the fallacies. You understand the double standards. You have biblical responses ready. You've been called to defend truth, not popular opinion.

> *Be on your guard; stand firm in the faith; be courageous; be strong* (1 Corinthians 16:13 NIV).

The battle for biblical prosperity is not about money. It's about whether Scripture alone is our authority, or whether tradition, popular opinion, and fallacious reasoning will dictate doctrine. Stand on the Word. Defend it with clarity. Live it with integrity. And watch God vindicate His own truth.

> *So shall my word be that goeth forth out of my mouth: it shall not return unto me void, but it shall accomplish that which I please, and it shall prosper in the thing whereto I sent it* (Isaiah 55:11).

The Word will prosper. The question is: Will you?

PART FIVE

COUNTING THE COST

14

THE AMERICAN GOSPEL

Thank God for the "American Gospel." The question that arises in my mind is just how did this issue become so divisive? How did *prosperity* become a dirty word in large portions of the Church?

The actual statistics tell a different story from the cultural pundits. Consider this: In 2024, Americans gave $592.5 billion to charitable causes. Individual Americans alone contributed $392.45 billion, more than the GDP of 140 other nations.[74] According to *The Philanthropy Roundtable,* Americans give seven times more than Europeans and twice as much as Canadians.[75]

The United States, comprising less than 5 percent of the world's population, sends out approximately 135,000 international missionaries, more than any other nation on earth.[76] American Christians fund the translation of Scripture into languages spoken by billions. American prosperity has built hospitals in nations where healthcare was a luxury, drilled wells in villages dying of thirst, and established schools where illiteracy was the norm.

When earthquakes level cities, American relief arrives first. When famine stalks entire regions, American grain ships break the horizon. When epidemics threaten to decimate populations, American medical teams land before the dust settles. When unreached people groups need Bible translation, American funding makes it possible. This is not merely American exceptionalism—this is the fruit of American prosperity applied to Kingdom purposes.

The United States leads the world, by an extraordinary margin, in medical innovation. From 1992 to 2004, 36 percent of all new molecular entities (life-saving drugs) were developed in the United States.[77] American universities contributed patents underpinning 50 percent of FDA-approved drugs from 2020 to 2024, with 87 percent of those academic breakthroughs coming from American institutions.[78] The medical devices, surgical techniques, cancer treatments, and vaccines that have extended human life expectancy globally were overwhelmingly pioneered on American soil, funded by American prosperity, developed in American laboratories.

American prosperity has been, without question, the single greatest engine for gospel advancement in human history.

That sentence deserves to be read again. American prosperity—the very thing now slandered as "greedy," dismissed as "materialistic," and attacked as "unbiblical"—has accomplished more for the Great Commission than any other economic system in the annals of Christianity.

While emperors built cathedrals and monks copied manuscripts, American prosperity has translated Bibles, sent missionaries, built seminaries, established media networks, and funded humanitarian relief on a scale that would have been incomprehensible to previous generations.

Yet despite this unprecedented fruit, fruit so abundant it cannot be ignored, so extensive it reaches every corner of the globe, "American Christianity" and "prosperity" have become epithets. Documentaries such as *The American Gospel* paint prosperity teaching as exploitation. Academic elites sneer at "the prosperity gospel" as if it were a con game rather than a biblical conviction. Evangelical leaders distance themselves from anything that smacks of wealth or success, terrified of being labeled "greedy" or "materialistic" or, Heaven forbid, "capitalistic."

Words that appear throughout Scripture like prosperity, blessing, abundance, increase, and wealth have been weaponized. Capitalism, the economic system that has lifted more people out of poverty than any ideology in history, is now treated as synonymous with exploitation.

Success is viewed with suspicion. Entrepreneurship is dismissed as selfishness. The accumulation of resources for Kingdom purposes is reframed as the hoarding of wealth for personal gain.

And the Church, incredibly, has internalized this propaganda.

We have wealth-shamed our congregations into poverty mindsets. We have trained believers to apologize for blessing. We have elevated the "struggling pastor" and the "poor prophet" as the gold standard of spirituality, as if financial lack proves devotion and material provision proves compromise. We have created an environment where discussing biblical prosperity is dangerous, where teaching on financial blessing is radioactive, where any mention of God's desire to prosper His people is immediately met with accusations of "preaching greed." This is tragic. And it is a lie.

The tragedy is not merely theological. The tragedy is practical. When the Church rejects biblical prosperity, missions funding collapses. When we paint prosperity as evil, we cripple the very mechanism God designed to advance His purposes on earth.

The stakes here are not abstract or theoretical. The stakes are millions of souls who will never hear the gospel because the Church has been convinced that the money needed to reach them, or any effort to attain it, is somehow tainted.

This chapter will dismantle that lie. We will trace the Protestant roots of American prosperity and show how the Reformation unleashed economic freedom that changed the world. We will examine the fruit of capitalism and demonstrate that free markets, far from being exploitative, have produced the most dramatic improvements in human welfare in history.

We will expose the Marxist propaganda that has infiltrated evangelical thought and show how class warfare categories have been weaponized against prosperity preachers. We will document how American prosperity funds global missions and prove that without it, billions will remain unreached. And we will reveal why this understanding of biblical prosperity is exploding globally, not because it's a Western invention, but because it's a biblical truth whose time has come.

PROSPERITY PROPAGANDA

But first, we must name the enemy. This attack on prosperity is not accidental. It is not organic. It is not a grassroots theological concern arising from careful biblical exegesis. It is ideological warfare designed to destroy the economic foundation of gospel advancement. None of this would be very successful if it weren't for the multitudes of "useful innocents" who attack God's people, thinking they are doing service to God (see John 16:2).

Without American prosperity, millions would be in hell. The world would be darker, sicker, hungrier, and more lost. Bible translation would stall. Medical missions would cease. Humanitarian relief would dry up.

The technology that enables global gospel proclamation would not exist. The publishing houses that print Christian literature would stop their presses. The seminaries that train pastors would close. The media networks that broadcast the gospel would go dark. Many curse the roots of prosperity preaching while standing on the very foundation it built, much like the modern liberal who denounces the West's Judeo-Christian heritage while freely enjoying the liberties that heritage secured.

Thank God for the "American Gospel." This seems all too obvious. We should be celebrating the "American Gospel," not denigrating it. What has happened? Is this venomous campaign against prosperity and all those who preach it merely a reaction to a few bad apples, or is there more to it?

To understand why prosperity has become radioactive in the Church, you must first understand the ideological framework that weaponized it. This is ideological warfare, and the Church has been conscripted as an unwitting soldier in a conflict most believers don't even know they're fighting.

BOURGEOISIE, PROLETARIAT, AND THE ZERO-SUM GAME

Karl Marx divided the world into two classes locked in eternal conflict: the bourgeoisie (those who own the means of production) and the proletariat (the workers who are exploited by them). In Marxist thought, all wealth is the result of exploitation. If you are prosperous, it is because you have extracted value from someone else's labor. If you are poor, it is because someone else has stolen the fruit of your work. There is no such thing as mutual benefit, voluntary exchange, or value creation. There is only exploitation and resistance, oppressor and oppressed, thief and victim.

This is a zero-sum worldview. For you to have more, someone else must have less. For you to rise, someone else must be pushed down. Profit is theft. Success is oppression. Wealth is violence.[79]

Under this interpretive grid, capitalism is not an economic system but a moral atrocity. Private property is not a right but a crime. Entrepreneurship is not innovation but exploitation. Anyone who defends these things, anyone who teaches that prosperity is achievable or desirable, is not simply mistaken, they are complicit in systemic evil.

This is the lens through which millions of people, including millions of Christians, now interpret the world.

THE INFILTRATION: FROM LATIN AMERICA TO THE AMERICAN CHURCH

Marxism did not storm the gates of the Church. It infiltrated slowly, subtly, cloaked in compassion and concern for the poor. The primary vehicle was liberation theology, a movement that emerged in Latin America in the 1960s and explicitly fused Christian language with Marxist class analysis.

Liberation theology developed within the Catholic Church in Latin America in the 1960s as a reaction to poverty and social injustice in the region. The term was coined in 1971 by Peruvian priest Gustavo Gutiérrez, who wrote one of the movement's defining books, *A Theology of Liberation.*[80]

But liberation theology was more than a Latin American phenomenon. According to Ion Mihai Pacepa, a former Romanian general and one of the highest-ranking Soviet defectors, the birth of liberation theology was part of a 1960 super-secret "Party-State Dezinformatsiya Program" approved by the KGB chairman and designed to take secret control of the World Council of Churches and convert liberation theology into a South American revolutionary tool.[81]

Whether you accept Pacepa's claims about Soviet origins or not, the Marxist character of liberation theology is undeniable. Leonardo Boff, one of its most influential theologians, stated explicitly: "What we propose is not to put theology into Marxism, but to put Marxism (historical materialism) into theology."[82]

Gutiérrez himself said that Marxism presents the best analysis of the oppression/liberation conflict in terms of class struggle, and that the liberation theologian must be committed to Marxism at least as an "analytical tool."[83]

The Vatican recognized the danger when, in 1984, Cardinal Ratzinger (later Pope Benedict XVI) criticized liberation theology's "uncritical" use of Marxist ideas, warning that "certain forms of liberation theology which use, in an insufficiently critical manner, concepts borrowed from various currents of Marxist thought" were "damaging to the faith" and a "deviation" from true Christian faith.[84]

But the infiltration continued. Liberation theology influenced black liberation theology, feminist liberation theology, and eventually the broader "social justice" movement that now dominates progressive Christianity. The language has shifted.

- *Bourgeoisie* became *the privileged.*
- *Proletariat* became *the marginalized.*
- *Class struggle* became *systemic oppression.*

But the framework remained Marxist: a zero-sum conflict between oppressor and oppressed, with wealth itself as evidence of exploitation. President Barack Hussein Obama and his previous pastor, Jeremiah Wright were champions of these ideas and helped to normalize them.

CLASS WARFARE IN THE PULPIT

Once Marxist categories are adopted, the application to prosperity teaching becomes inevitable. If all wealth is exploitation, then a prosperous pastor must be exploiting his congregation. If profit is theft, then a church with resources must be stealing from its people. If success is oppression, then anyone teaching believers to expect blessing must be complicit in a con game.

The attack on prosperity preachers mirrors classic Marxist class warfare rhetoric. They are painted as bourgeoisie profiteers "fleecing the flock," "preying on the poor," "getting rich off the backs of struggling believers."

The assumption is never questioned: Could these pastors be prospering because they're teaching biblical principles that actually work? Could their congregations be giving generously not because they're being manipulated, but because they're experiencing breakthrough and want to sow into what's blessing them? Could the prosperity itself be evidence that God honors His Word?

Not under a Marxist framework. Those questions cannot even be asked. The verdict is predetermined. Prosperity equals exploitation. End of discussion.

Notice the language used by critics. They don't say, "I disagree with this interpretation of Scripture." They say, "These con artists are stealing from vulnerable people." They don't engage theologically. They indict morally. Because in Marxist thought, this isn't a theological disagreement. It's a crime against the oppressed.

WEALTH-SHAMING: THE CHURCH'S INTERNALIZED OPPRESSION

The most insidious aspect of this propaganda campaign is not the external attack. It's the internal capitulation.

The Church has internalized wealth-shaming to such a degree that even believers who don't consciously embrace Marxism feel guilty about blessing.

The "poor prophet" has been romanticized. Poverty is treated as proof of authenticity, as if financial struggle sanctifies and material provision compromises. Pastors brag about how little they make, how simply they live, how sacrificially they serve, all to prove they're not "in it for the money." Believers apologize for being blessed, downplay their success, hide their increase, terrified of being judged as "greedy" or "worldly" or (God forbid) advocates of the "prosperity gospel."

Modesty has been elevated to doctrine. There's an unspoken rule: A good Christian lives simply. Translation: A good Christian lives poorly. You can have enough to survive, but not enough to thrive. You can meet your needs, but not exceed them. You can be comfortable, but not abundant. If you do experience significant blessing, you'd better keep quiet about it, give most of it away immediately, and certainly never, ever teach that God wants to bless others the same way.

This has created a generation of believers who are prosperity-paralyzed. They know the Bible talks about blessing, but they're afraid to expect it. They see God's promises of increase, but they spiritualize them into irrelevance. They experience breakthrough, but they attribute it to luck or hard work, never to *covenant faithfulness.* They have resources, but they feel guilty about them rather than stewarding them for Kingdom purposes.

The result? Churches remain chronically under-resourced. Missions go unfunded. Believers live beneath their covenant privileges. And the Great Commission stalls because the people who should be supporting it have been convinced that the money needed to fund it is somehow tainted.

THE DEVASTATING IRONY

Here is where the hypocrisy becomes impossible to ignore. Many of the loudest critics of prosperity teaching live in extraordinary affluence.

They own homes worth hundreds of thousands or even millions of dollars. They drive late-model cars. They send their children to private schools or prestigious universities. They travel internationally for conferences and speaking engagements. They publish books through major publishers and collect royalties. They build platforms on social media, monetize content, and benefit from every advantage that Western capitalism provides. And yet they rail against "prosperity preachers."

They benefit from American prosperity while attacking its theological foundation. They enjoy the fruit of capitalism while condemning those who teach that biblical principles align with free-market economics. They live in the top 1 percent of global wealth while accusing others of greed ($60,000 or more a year). They use technology invented by capitalist innovation, consume products created by free-market competition, and enjoy security provided by property rights, all while insisting that prosperity teaching is un-Christian.

The cognitive dissonance is staggering.

If prosperity is evil, why aren't these critics living in intentional poverty? If wealth corrupts, why haven't they divested themselves of their assets? If teaching people to expect financial blessing is exploitation, why are they charging for books, conferences, and speaking engagements? If American prosperity is the problem, why haven't they relocated to socialist countries where equality of outcome is enforced?

The answer, of course, is that they don't actually believe prosperity is wrong. They believe teaching about prosperity is wrong. They don't object to having wealth. They object to others having the audacity to teach that God wants His people blessed. They're perfectly comfortable with their own abundance. They just don't want you to expect the same.

This is Pharisaism at its finest. They lay heavy burdens on others that they themselves refuse to bear. They shut the Kingdom of Heaven in people's faces, neither entering themselves nor allowing others to enter. They travel land and sea to make converts, only to make them twice as much children of hell as themselves (see Matthew 23).

Here's another dirty, unspoken little secret: *Everyone* wants to prosper. Worse yet, *everyone* wants their children to prosper! Shocking? I know!

These prosperity Pharisees don't realize they've been duped and that they're being used in an ongoing propaganda campaign to keep people from receiving, enjoying, and using God's blessings here on earth.

This is the question that must be asked: When did Marxist class analysis become the lens through which evangelicals interpret Scripture?

When did "bourgeoisie" and "proletariat" replace "blessed" and "in need"? When did "privilege" and "oppression" become more important categories than "faithfulness" and "disobedience"? When did "systemic injustice" become a more urgent concern than personal sin? When did the redistribution of wealth become synonymous with biblical justice?

And most importantly, when did we start judging the validity of biblical teaching by these socialistic and Marxist principles rather than Scripture alone?

The Bible never says, "If it leads to wealth, it must be false." But Marxism does. The Bible never says, "Material blessing proves exploitation." But Marxism does. The Bible never says, "Success is oppression." But Marxism does.

So when evangelicals attack prosperity teaching using Marxist categories, they're not being biblical. They're being Marxist. They've adopted an atheistic, materialistic, revolutionary ideology and baptized it with Christian language. They've done it so thoroughly that they don't even recognize the source of their objections.

They're captives to an unbiblical ideology.

The tragedy is that believers who would never identify as Marxist, who would vehemently reject socialism, who consider themselves theologically conservative, have nevertheless internalized Marxist assumptions about wealth. They've been discipled by culture rather than by Scripture. They've allowed documentaries, blog posts, YouTube videos, and seminary professors to shape their view of prosperity more than the Word of God.

As a result, they're unable to receive what God wants to give them. You can never have what you continually criticize. They're suspicious of blessing, skeptical of increase, and paralyzed by guilt whenever they experience financial breakthrough. They've been taught to see prosperity as a problem rather than a promise, as evidence of compromise rather than covenant faithfulness.

THE STAKES

Let's be brutally honest about what's at stake here.

If the Church embraces Marxist assumptions about wealth, missions funding collapses. If believers are taught that prosperity equals exploitation, they won't pursue it. If they don't pursue it, they won't attain it. If they don't attain it, they won't steward it for Kingdom purposes. If they don't steward resources for Kingdom purposes, the Great Commission doesn't get funded.

This is not hypothetical. This is happening right now.

Western churches are declining. Giving is down. Missions agencies are cutting staff and closing field offices. Bible translation projects are stalling. Church plants are being postponed.

Humanitarian efforts are being scaled back. Why? Not because there isn't enough money in the world. Not even because there isn't enough money among believers. But because believers have been taught that accumulating resources is greedy, that expecting blessing is presumptuous, and that prosperity teaching is heresy.

Meanwhile, pastors in Africa, Latin America, and Asia are boldly teaching biblical prosperity and watching their churches explode with growth, generosity, and missionary sending. They're not embarrassed by blessing. They're not apologizing for increase. They're not paralyzed by Marxist guilt. They're simply believing God's Word and watching Him honor it.

The Western Church, drunk on Marxist propaganda, looks at these movements and condemns them as "prosperity gospel."

Never mind the fruit. Never mind the changed lives, the funded missions, the explosive church growth, the radical generosity. If it looks prosperous, it must be wrong.

This is how Marxism kills the gospel. Not by attacking it directly, but by poisoning the well, making believers suspicious of the very resources God wants to use to advance His Kingdom.

The propaganda campaign has been devastatingly effective. Until the Church wakes up to what's happened, until we recognize that we've been discipled by Marx rather than by Jesus on the issue of wealth, we will continue to underperform, underfund, and underreach the world that desperately needs the gospel we claim to believe.

15

CAPITALISM

THE CHILD OF REVIVAL

To understand American prosperity, you must first understand what came before it. You must understand the grinding, suffocating, generation-crushing poverty that defined the medieval world. You must understand how the Catholic Church and the feudal system conspired to keep the masses trapped in economic servitude. You must also understand how the Protestant Reformation shattered that system and unleashed the economic freedom that would eventually produce American prosperity.

THE REFORMATION AND CAPITALISM: HOW THE REFORMATION UNLEASHED ECONOMIC FREEDOM

This is where capitalism was born. This is where work became worship, where property became a right, and where individuals were freed to create, innovate, and prosper without permission from lords or priests.

MEDIEVAL FEUDALISM

For roughly a thousand years, from approximately AD 500 to AD 1500, Europe operated under a system called feudalism. It was a hierarchical structure with the king at the top, followed by nobles and bishops, then knights and lower clergy, and finally, at the very bottom, the peasants and serfs who comprised approximately 90 percent of the population.[85]

The feudal system was based on land ownership and control. The king granted large estates (called fiefs) to nobles and bishops in exchange for military support and loyalty. These lords then subdivided their lands to vassals, who promised service in return. At the bottom were the serfs, peasants bound to the land, forced to work it in exchange for "protection" and the right to survival.

The serfs had no property rights. They owned nothing. The land they worked belonged to the lord. The crops they grew belonged to the lord. Even they themselves, in a very real sense, belonged to the lord.

Serfs were required to give 30 to 50 percent of their crops to their lords, pay additional taxes and fees, and provide unpaid labor on the lord's land multiple days per week.[86] They could not leave the manor without permission. They could not marry without permission. They could not pursue a trade without permission. They were trapped in a cycle of poverty with virtually no social mobility.

Most peasants were dead before they reached 30 years of age. They worked six days a week, dawn to dusk, often barely producing enough food to survive. Disease, famine, and oppression were constant companions. The feudal lords exercised not just economic power but judicial power as well, controlling local courts and imposing fines and taxes for minor infractions. The wealth generated from these practices was used to fund military campaigns, fortify castles, and secure additional lands, creating an entrenched system that benefited the elite and further impoverished the lower classes.

This was by design. Feudalism was a control mechanism. Keep people poor, keep them dependent, keep them compliant.

The Catholic Church was not an innocent bystander in this system. The Church was one of the wealthiest institutions in medieval Europe, and it played an essential role in maintaining feudal exploitation.

Bishops received a mandatory tithe of 10 percent from all people in their diocese, making some of them extraordinarily wealthy.[87] The Church owned extensive lands and operated under the same feudal structure as secular lords, with peasants working church lands under the same oppressive conditions.

Church officials, bishops, and abbots acted as advisors to kings and lords, wielding significant influence in political affairs. The Church provided theological justification for the feudal hierarchy, teaching that this was God's ordained social order, that poverty in this life would be rewarded in the next, and that the suffering of the poor was a form of penance.

According to historian Christine Caldwell Ames, the Church was asserting its authority during this period "through a variety of interlocked media that included inquisition, a new and inescapable authority over all souls and bodies."[88] The function of all this control was to increase the surplus labor extracted from the peasantry through intensive management of both the production process and the reproduction of labor.

The Church provided feudal exploitation with legitimacy. According to its doctrines, lords were not simply extracting the products of peasant labor by force (although the threat of force was always there); they were collecting what God had mandated that the peasants hand over to the lords. Ecclesiastical institutions led the way in systematizing the management of their lands by moving their peasants from scattered settlements into larger villages where they could be more easily monitored and controlled.

There was a stunning contradiction at the heart of medieval Catholicism. Monks and nuns took vows of poverty, renouncing worldly wealth as a sign of spiritual devotion. But church hierarchy lived in opulence. Cardinals and bishops accumulated vast estates. The Vatican itself was a monument to wealth and power. The message was clear: poverty for the masses, prosperity for the elite. Suffering for the peasants, luxury for the priests.

This was the world into which Martin Luther was born. And this was the world the Protestant Reformation would shatter.

THE REFORMATION REVIVAL

On October 31, 1517, Martin Luther nailed his 95 Theses to the door of the Castle Church in Wittenberg, Germany. He was challenging the sale of indulgences, the practice of paying money to reduce time in purgatory. But Luther's challenge went far deeper than a single corrupt practice. He was challenging the entire theological framework that had justified feudal economics and clerical control.

Luther's central breakthrough was the doctrine of the priesthood of all believers. The Catholic Church taught that priests were spiritual mediators between God and man, that only clergy had true vocations or callings from God, and that "spiritual" work (prayer, contemplation, ministry) was superior to "secular" work (farming, trade, manual labor). This created a two-tiered system: sacred work done by clergy, and common work done by everyone else.

Luther demolished this distinction. He taught that all believers are priests before God, that every Christian has direct access to God through Christ, and that all honest labor is a calling from God. As historian Gene Edward Veith notes, "For Luther, a person's vocation was equated as his calling, but all callings were of equal spiritual dignity."

This was revolutionary. Luther wrote: "The whole world could be filled with the service of God, not just the churches, but the home, the kitchen, the cellar, the workshop and the fields."[89]

A farmer plowing his field was serving God just as truly as a priest celebrating Mass. A mother raising children was fulfilling a divine calling just as noble as a monk in a monastery. A merchant conducting honest trade was engaged in holy work just as sacred as a bishop administering a diocese.

Luther's doctrine of vocation stressed the spiritual and moral value of economic activity. He believed that God works through ordinary human beings to care for His creation. In our various callings as spouse, parent, church member, citizen, and worker, we are to live out our faith. This teaching affirmed manual labor and gave dignity to work that the medieval system had treated as mere drudgery.

WORK AS WORSHIP

If Luther planted the seeds, John Calvin cultivated them into a full theological framework for economic freedom.

Calvin took Luther's concept of vocation and expanded it. He taught that work itself was an act of worship, that success in one's calling could be a sign of God's blessing, and that stewardship of resources was a sacred responsibility. Calvin had little patience for the Catholic teaching that the contemplative life was superior to the life of labor. He argued that all types of work are equal if they are offerings to God, that a person's skill is a gift from God and should be treated as such, and that Christians should work diligently in whatever vocation they pursue.

Calvin's theology laid the groundwork for what Max Weber would later call the "Protestant work ethic."[90] Weber's famous book, *The Protestant Ethic and the Spirit of Capitalism*, argued that Protestant values of discipline, delayed gratification, reinvestment, and stewardship created the cultural conditions necessary for capitalism to flourish. Protestants worked hard not to earn salvation (which they believed was by grace alone through faith alone) but as grateful stewardship in response to God's grace.

The Protestant work ethic encouraged several key practices: working diligently in a chosen occupation with an attitude of service to God, viewing work as a calling and avoiding placing greater spiritual dignity on one job than another, working to achieve maximum productivity and profit, reinvesting profits back into one's business or productive endeavors, and associating success in one's work with the faithfulness of stewardship.[91]

This was not "work to get rich." This was "work as worship," and "God blesses faithful stewardship."

Calvin, though wrong in many other areas, was right when he taught that all occupations had dignity and value.[92] Prior to the Reformation, "calling" or vocation was largely restricted to ecclesiastical callings. You had a calling from God if you became a priest or a nun. But if you were a farmer, merchant, craftsman, or laborer? That was just work, not calling. Calvin revolutionized this understanding. He taught that any area of work (farming, teaching, governing, business) could be a valid calling from God, every bit as sacred as serving as a minister. This was a radical change in worldview that would ultimately alter economies, cultures, and countless human lives.

IF WORK IS HOLY, ITS FRUIT IS HOLY

Here is the theological principle that unlocks everything: If God calls you to your work, then your work is holy. If your work is holy, then the fruit of your work is holy. If the fruit of your work is holy, then wealth produced through faithful labor is not corrupt. It is grace multiplied.

This directly challenged the medieval Catholic framework that treated poverty as a virtue and wealth (for laypeople) as spiritually dangerous.

The Reformers said: No, work is part of the creation mandate. God commanded Adam and Eve to subdue the earth, to have dominion, to multiply and fill creation (Genesis 1:28). Labor is not the curse. Toilsome, frustrating labor is the curse (Genesis 3:17-19). But meaningful, productive work that serves God and neighbor is a blessing.

The eighth commandment, "You shall not steal," assumes private property. You cannot steal what no one owns. Property rights are thus biblical. If property rights are biblical, then individuals have the right to own, exchange, and profit from their labor and resources.

The Puritans, who brought Calvinist theology to America, carried these ideas with them.[93] They believed laziness was a sin not because it hurt the economy but because it failed to reflect the character of God.[94]

Industry and thrift were not just social virtues but spiritual disciplines. They worked diligently six days and rested on the seventh, honoring both the commandment to labor and the commandment to rest.

THE SACRED COD

In these early days of colonial New England, the settlers faced a hard truth quickly. Spiritual vision alone would not keep them alive. Before universities, before cathedrals, before political institutions, they needed provision. And along the Massachusetts coast, the Atlantic cod became that provision.

The waters were so full of fish that the colonists could catch enormous quantities with basic equipment. They salted and dried the cod, fed their families, traded it across the Atlantic, and used it to build commerce with Europe and the Caribbean. That single resource funded homes, roads, churches, schools, and eventually entire cities. The cod trade did not distract from faith, it financed it.

So central was this industry to the survival and prosperity of the colonies that a carved wooden cod was later placed in the Massachusetts State House as a symbol of the source that sustained them. It was acknowledgment that without prosperity, ideals collapse.

The pattern is consistent.

Even at America's founding, before pulpits rose and laws were written, before revival fires spread inland, the fish sustained the vision. Provision made the mission possible.

Fish come first.

In a nutshell, the Reformation produced a revival that gave birth to capitalism and to America.

REVIVAL MEETS ECONOMIC FREEDOM

The American colonies became the testing ground for this theology. The Puritans combined biblical anthropology (humans are creative image-bearers of God) with economic freedom (rule of law, limited government, protection of property rights) and produced unprecedented flourishing.

As Benjamin Hart argues in *Faith and Freedom*, America's founding and its economic freedom were rooted in Christian faith and Christian prosperity.[95] The nation was not a theocracy, but its institutions were built on a Christian worldview that affirmed the dignity of individuals, the importance of property rights, the necessity of rule of law, and the value of free exchange.

This synthesis produced something the world had never seen: a society where ordinary people could own land, start businesses, pursue vocations, accumulate wealth, and pass it on to their children without needing permission from lords or priests. Economic mobility became possible. Innovation was rewarded. Hard work paid off. The result was an explosion of productivity, prosperity, and human flourishing.

CHRISTIAN CAPITALISM VERSUS SOCIALISM

The Protestant vision of work, calling, stewardship, and economic freedom gave birth to capitalism. But what is capitalism, and how does it differ from other economic systems?

Capitalism is an economic system based on private property, voluntary exchange, free markets, and the profit motive. Under capitalism, individuals are free to work, save, invest, create, buy, sell, and compete without coercive interference from government or church. Prices are determined by supply and demand. Incentives align with productivity.

Innovation is rewarded. Those who serve customers best and produce value most efficiently prosper.

Contrast this with socialism or collectivism. Under socialism, property is controlled by the state, exchange is regulated or forbidden, markets are replaced by central planning, and profit is condemned as exploitation. The state decides what should be produced, who should produce it, how it should be distributed, and who deserves what. Incentives are destroyed. Innovation is stifled. Those who produce more are punished, and those who produce less are subsidized. The result, inevitably, is poverty, stagnation, and oppression.

One system assumes humans are creative image-bearers of God meant to flourish through freedom. The other assumes humans are parasites to be controlled by an elite who know better. Which one sounds more biblical?

Capitalism is not perfect because humans are not perfect. Greed, corruption, and exploitation can occur under any system. But capitalism does not create greed. Greed is a sin-nature issue that exists under every economic system. What capitalism does is create the conditions where voluntary exchange, mutual benefit, and value creation are rewarded, where innovation serves others and is compensated, and where prosperity can be widely distributed rather than hoarded by elites.

This is simply biblical truth applied to economic life. Genesis 1:28 (NKJV) gives humanity the creation mandate: *"...Be fruitful and multiply, fill the earth and subdue it; have dominion over the fish of the sea, over the birds of the air, and over every living thing that moves on the earth."*

God created humans to work, to create, to innovate, to build, to steward, to multiply. This calling was given before the Fall. Productive work is not a result of sin. It is part of God's design for humanity.

The Fall made work toilsome and frustrating (see Genesis 3:17-19). But redemption through Christ restores our ability to work meaningfully and fruitfully. The parables of the talents (see Matthew 25:14-30) and the minas (see Luke 19:11-27) commend those who multiply what they are given and condemn those who bury their resources out of fear. God rewards faithful stewardship and productivity.

The early Church practiced voluntary generosity, not forced redistribution. Acts 2 and Acts 4 describe believers sharing possessions and selling property to meet needs, but this was never commanded or coerced. It was a free expression of love within the community.

Even in this context, private property was respected. Peter tells Ananias in Acts 5:4: *"Whiles it remained, was it not thine own? and after it was sold, was it not in thine own power?"*

Property rights were assumed, even in the most generous community in Christian history.

The Protestant Reformers did not invent these truths. They rediscovered them. They went back to Scripture and found what had been buried under centuries of tradition, clerical control, and feudal oppression. When they unleashed these truths, they unleashed economic freedom that changed the world.

FROM FEUDAL POVERTY TO AMERICAN PROSPERITY

The pattern is clear. Medieval feudalism kept people trapped in poverty through control of land, labor, and theology. The Catholic Church provided ideological cover for this exploitation while accumulating its own wealth. The Protestant Reformation shattered this system by restoring the dignity of all work, affirming private property, and teaching that faithful labor is worship.

These ideas crossed the Atlantic with the Puritans and other Protestant settlers. Combined with political freedom, rule of law, and protection of property rights, they created the conditions for American prosperity. It was not prosperity for a tiny elite but prosperity that could be widely shared. It was prosperity that rewarded innovation, hard work, and value creation. It was prosperity that funded churches, missions, humanitarian work, and the advancement of the gospel.

This is not arbitrary American exceptionalism. This is biblical truth applied systematically, producing fruit that testifies to its divine origin.

Thank God for the Reformation. Thank God for the Protestant work ethic. Thank God for the theological framework that gave birth to capitalism and economic freedom. Thank God that America became the proving ground for these principles, producing prosperity that has blessed not just Americans, but the entire world.

16

COMBATING CHRISTIAN SOCIALISM

Theology without fruit is just theory. Ideas without impact are just words. So, let's continue to examine the fruit, and then we will look thoroughly at the scriptural root.

Let us look at what Protestant theology and economic freedom actually produced when combined in the American experiment. What happens when people are free to work, create, own, exchange, and prosper without coercive interference? The results are measurable and they have changed the world.

THE MIRACLE OF MARKET COORDINATION

In 1958, economist Leonard Read published a brief essay titled *I, Pencil.* It has become a classic illustration of how free markets coordinate human activity in ways that central planning never could.[96]

The essay is written from the perspective of a simple wooden pencil, explaining its own creation. The pencil observes that no single person on earth knows how to make a pencil from scratch. Think about it.

To make a pencil, you need wood from trees, which requires saws and trucks and rope. You need graphite from mines, which requires mining equipment and transportation. You need metal for the ferrule (the band that holds the eraser), which requires ore extraction, smelting, and metalworking. You need rubber for the eraser, which comes from rubber trees processed through complex chemical procedures. You need paint and lacquer and glue, each with their own supply chains stretching across continents.

Thousands of people are involved in producing a single pencil. Loggers in Oregon. Miners in Sri Lanka. Rubber workers in Malaysia. Factory workers in China. Truck drivers in Ohio. None of them know each other. None of them are coordinating with each other. Yet somehow, pencils exist. Millions of them. Cheap, available, accessible to anyone who wants one.

How? Through the price system and voluntary exchange. Each person in the chain responds to price signals, pursuing their own self-interest, and through what Adam Smith called "the invisible hand," their individual actions coordinate to produce pencils. No central planner designed this. No government agency mandated it. It emerged spontaneously from Christian freedom.

This is how God designed human society to function. Not through coercion and central control, but through voluntary cooperation enabled by freedom. The pencil is a testimony to the image of God in humanity. We are creators. We solve problems. We innovate. We coordinate. When we are free to do so, we produce abundance that blesses millions.

A CREATIVE EXPLOSION

The United States Constitution, Article I, Section 8, grants Congress the power "to promote the Progress of Science and useful Arts, by securing for limited Times to Authors and Inventors the exclusive Right to their respective Writings and Discoveries."[97] This provision led to the Patent Act of 1790, which created a market-based incentive for innovation by protecting inventors' rights to profit from their creations. The results have been staggering.

In 2022, the United States Patent and Trademark Office received approximately 669,000 patent applications and granted 374,006 patents.[98]

The biotechnology sector accounted for 15 percent of all patent applications. The pharmaceutical sector filed approximately 50,000 patents. Medical devices accounted for 40,000 patents. Electrical engineering, which includes semiconductors, telecommunications, and computer technology, received 25 percent of all applications.

But the numbers tell only part of the story. What matters is what these patents represent: life-saving drugs, medical breakthroughs, technological advances that have transformed human existence.

From 1992 to 2004, 36 percent of all new molecular entities (new drugs) were developed in the United States. The United Kingdom was second at only 10.4 percent.[99] When examining drugs with patents, 43.7 percent had their earliest patent filed by inventors in the United States.

American universities contributed patents underpinning 50 percent of FDA-approved drugs from 2020 to 2024, with 87 percent of those academic breakthroughs coming from American institutions.[100]

Think about what this means in human terms. The polio vaccine that saved millions of lives? American innovation. The antibiotics that transformed medicine? Largely American innovation. Cancer treatments, surgical techniques, diagnostic tools, medical devices that extend and improve human life? Overwhelmingly developed in America, funded by American prosperity, created by people who were free to innovate and profit from their discoveries.

The United States ranks first in the number of new drugs and medical devices gaining regulatory approval. America ranks first by a wide margin in Nobel prizes in chemistry or medicine per capita.[101] The US ranks second in scientific impact as measured by citations. America's innovative health care sector is by far the largest in the world.

This is not an accident. This is the fruit of freedom combined with prosperity. When people have the time, resources, and incentive to pursue innovation, when they are rewarded for success rather than punished for it, when they can own the fruits of their intellectual labor, they create things that change the world. God understands this more than we do.

CAPITALISM'S MORAL SUPERIORITY

Thomas Sowell, one of the greatest living economists and a champion of free markets, has spent decades documenting how capitalism lifts people out of poverty and creates human flourishing. His arguments are not merely economic. They are moral. Sowell writes:

> *No government of the left has done as much for the poor as capitalism has. Even when it comes to the redistribution of income, the left talks the talk but the free market walks the walk. What do the poor most need? They need to stop being poor. And how can that be done, on a mass scale, except by an economy that creates vastly more wealth?*[102]

This is the question that destroys all socialist arguments and cuts to heart of the anti-prosperity crowd. The poor do not need redistribution. They need wealth creation and wealth creation happens under capitalism, not socialism.

Sowell continues:

> *It was Thomas Edison who brought us electricity, not the Sierra Club. It was the Wright brothers who got us off the ground, not the Federal Aviation Administration. It was Henry Ford who ended the isolation of millions of Americans by making the automobile affordable, not Ralph Nader. Those who have helped the poor the most have not been those who have gone around loudly expressing "compassion" for the poor, but those who found ways to*

> *make industry more productive and distribution more efficient, so that the poor of today can afford things that the affluent of yesterday could only dream about.*[103]

Read that again. The "poor of today can afford things that the affluent of yesterday could only dream about." This is a documented fact. Most officially "poor" Americans today have big screen TVs, thousand-dollar cell phones, microwave ovens, and their own cars. Half of all poor households have air conditioning.[104] Items that did not even exist a century ago are now common in households below the poverty line.

How did this happen? Not through government programs. Not through wealth redistribution. It was through capitalism creating so much abundance that even those at the bottom of the economic ladder have access to goods and services that would have been considered luxury items in previous generations. Keep in mind, this is all the result of a revival!

Sowell also addresses the moral accusation often leveled against capitalism: "I have never understood why it is 'greed' to want to keep the money you have earned but not greed to want to take somebody else's money."[105]

Exactly. Under capitalism, you prosper by serving others, by creating value, by solving problems. Under socialism, you prosper by using political power to take from others. Which system is actually greedy?

Milton Friedman, another towering figure in free-market economics, made similar arguments. He demonstrated that free markets maximize both freedom and prosperity, that economic freedom and political freedom are inseparable, and that controlled economies maximize neither wealth nor liberty.

Friedman showed that when governments intervene in markets, they create distortions, inefficiencies, and unintended consequences that hurt the very people the interventions are supposedly designed to help.[106]

The moral case for capitalism is simple because it respects human dignity by treating people as free agents capable of making their own decisions.

Capitalism rewards productivity and service to others, allows people to keep the fruits of their labor, creates conditions where innovation and risk-taking are possible, and capitalism generates more wealth for more people than any system in history.

THE GLOBAL IMPACT

American prosperity has not just benefited Americans. It has changed the world.

Consider medicine. American pharmaceutical companies and research institutions have developed treatments that have saved hundreds of millions of lives globally. The medical devices invented in America, the surgical techniques pioneered in American hospitals, the vaccines developed in American laboratories have been distributed worldwide. Life expectancy globally has increased dramatically in the past century, and American medical innovation has been the primary driver.

Consider agriculture. American agricultural innovation, mechanization, and efficiency have fed billions. The Green Revolution that prevented mass starvation in Asia and Africa was largely driven by American agricultural research. Norman Borlaug, an American agronomist, is credited with saving over one billion lives through his development of high-yield, disease-resistant wheat varieties.[107]

Consider technology. The computer, the internet, the smartphone, GPS, and countless software applications that have transformed human communication, commerce, and access to information were all developed primarily in America. These technologies have empowered billions of people, created economic opportunities where none existed, and connected the world in ways previous generations could not have imagined.

Consider transportation. The airplane revolutionized global travel and trade. American aerospace innovation has made international travel accessible to the masses, not just the elite. This has enabled not just commerce, but cultural exchange, education, and yes, missionary activity on a scale that would have been impossible without aviation technology.

What funded all this innovation? The "American Gospel." Who discovered these breakthroughs? People with time and resources to research, to experiment, to fail, and to try again. Where did it happen? Overwhelmingly in free societies, particularly America, where property rights were protected, where innovators could profit from success, and where failure did not mean starvation.

WHY NOW?

Why has prosperity preaching become such a prominent subject in our time? Why is it that we didn't hear much about this in previous generations? First, we need to acknowledge that it does not matter what has been taught historically. What matters is what the Word of God says.

However, here is a truth that is often overlooked: innovation requires margin. You cannot innovate when you are focused entirely on survival. You cannot research when you are laboring from dawn to dusk just to produce enough food to eat. You cannot experiment when failure means your family starves.

Prosperity creates the conditions for innovation by providing time, resources, and the safety to take risks. When basic needs are met, when there is surplus, when people have security, then human creativity can flourish.

This is why other economies produce little innovation. The peasants under feudalism, working six days a week just to survive, had neither the time nor the resources to invent new tools or techniques. Even if they had ideas, they had no incentive to innovate because they did not own the fruits of their labor. Everything they produced beyond survival belonged to the feudal lord.

But in a free-market economy where property rights are protected, where individuals can keep what they produce, where success is rewarded, innovation explodes. The promise of profit, the opportunity to improve one's condition, the freedom to pursue ideas without needing permission from authorities, all these factors combine to unleash human creativity.

This is Maslow's hierarchy applied economically. When physiological needs (food, shelter) are barely met, all energy goes toward meeting those needs. When those needs are met with surplus, people can pursue higher callings: learning, creating, innovating, serving, worshiping, and digging deeper into God's Word.

The American prosperity revival gave masses of people what only elites once had: leisure for study, reflection, creativity. This is why American innovation has been so productive and why we see an explosion of revelation concerning the scriptural truths surrounding prosperity.

It's not because Americans are genetically superior, it's because Americans have lived in conditions of freedom and prosperity that allow human creativity to flourish.

HE IS THE GOD OF INCREASE

This is not "secular" success disconnected from God. This is the image of God manifested through human creativity.

Genesis 1 tells us that God created the heavens and the earth. God spoke, and things came into existence. God designed, organized, and declared His creation good. Then God created humans in His image and gave them a mandate: be fruitful, multiply, fill the earth, subdue it, and have dominion.

We are most like God when we are creating. When humans solve problems, design solutions, innovate tools, build systems, produce value, and prosper, they are displaying the image of God. This is what we were created to do. Not to merely survive or consume, but to create, to add value, to improve, to solve, to build.

Capitalism rewards this because it is born from Christian ideals. Socialism punishes it.

Under capitalism, the innovator who creates something useful is rewarded with profit, which enables further innovation.

Under socialism, the innovator who produces more than others is viewed with suspicion, taxed heavily, or even punished for making others look bad or for creating inequality.

Which system honors the image of God in humanity? Which system treats humans as the creative beings God designed them to be?

God has created a system that, when followed, produces a flourishing human society. This does not mean capitalism is perfect. Sin corrupts every human system. But capitalism works with human nature (including our fallen nature) in ways that actually produce profitable outcomes. It channels self-interest toward serving others. It rewards productivity. It creates conditions where mutual benefit is possible through voluntary exchange.

Socialism, by contrast, works against human nature. It assumes people will work just as hard when the fruits of their labor are taken from them. It assumes central planners know better than millions of individuals making decisions for themselves. It assumes that coercion will produce better outcomes than freedom. History has proven these assumptions catastrophically wrong—every single time.

THE POVERTY OF CONTROLLED ECONOMIES

If you want to see the fruit of economic freedom, compare free nations to controlled economies. Compare South Korea to North Korea. Same people, same culture, same history. One chose freedom; one chose socialism. South Korea, though moving in the wrong direction, has historically been prosperous, innovative, and a global economic powerhouse. Why? Because of a powerful revival that hit that nation. North Korea is impoverished and isolated, a humanitarian disaster where people literally starve.

Compare West Germany to East Germany before the fall of the Berlin Wall. Same people, same culture, divided by an economic system. The West flourished. The East stagnated.

Compare the United States to Venezuela. Venezuela, once one of the wealthiest nations in Latin America, embraced socialism. The result? Economic collapse, hyperinflation, starvation, and millions fleeing the country. The United States, built on capitalist principles, remains the wealthiest and most innovative nation on Earth.

The pattern is consistent across history and geography. Free markets produce prosperity. Controlled economies produce poverty. Capitalism lifts people up. Socialism pushes them down. These are not theories. These are documented outcomes repeated across decades and continents.

Thomas Sowell said it perfectly, "Socialism in general has a record of failure so blatant that only an intellectual could ignore or evade it."[108]

I must emphasize again—those who criticize the "American Gospel" would likely agree with every economic argument we've made thus far when applied to nations. They'll defend capitalism, property rights, and free enterprise with passion, but the moment they step inside the church, something short-circuits.

It's as though a switch flips in their minds, and suddenly they begin to parrot the same socialist rhetoric they once condemned, attacking prosperity preachers with the very arguments Marx used against capitalists. It's a strange double standard, a kind of theological schizophrenia, that borders on madness.

The intellectuals who rail against capitalism while enjoying its fruits are no different from the modern critics of the prosperity gospel. Both groups dine at the table they purport to despise. They lecture against excess from behind the safety of abundance. They condemn the blessings of others while quietly living in the overflow of the very principles they denounce.

These religious moralists, who preach asceticism from air-conditioned sanctuaries, are the theological cousins of socialist professors who sip over-priced lattes from corporate coffee shops while condemning free markets. In both cases, hypocrisy dresses itself as virtue. Their criticism isn't born of purity. It's born of privilege sustained by the prosperity they pretend to reject. It would be laughable if the stakes were not so high.

WHAT PROSPERITY ENABLES

Let us return to the big picture. What does prosperity actually enable?

- Prosperity enables parents to feed, clothe, educate, and raise children without constant anxiety about survival.
- Prosperity enables individuals to pursue callings and vocations that match their gifts and passions.
- Prosperity enables churches to build facilities, fund programs, support pastors, and send missionaries.
- Prosperity enables businesses to hire workers, create jobs, and serve customers.
- Prosperity enables communities to build hospitals, schools, libraries, and infrastructure.
- Prosperity enables nations to defend themselves, help other nations, and promote human flourishing globally.

"Personal freedom and economic freedom are indivisible. You can't have one without the other. You can't lose one without losing the other."[109]

—Margaret Thatcher

Prosperity is not the enemy of the gospel. Prosperity is the fuel for gospel advancement.

Thank God for the revival of the Protestant work ethic that restored the dignity of labor. Thank God for the free-market principles that protect property and reward innovation. Thank God for American capitalism that has demonstrated on a massive scale what happens when people are free to work, create, and prosper. The fruit speaks for itself.

17

THE SHOCKING ECONOMICS OF EVANGELISM

Here is where theology meets reality. Here is where the rubber meets the road. Here is where we answer the question: So what? Why does any of this matter? Why should we care about Protestant work ethic, economic freedom, and American prosperity?

Because missions cost money. Because the Great Commission requires resources. Because reaching the world with the gospel is not just an ethereal endeavor but a logistical, financial, and organizational challenge that demands massive funding.

American prosperity has provided that funding on a scale unprecedented in Christian history.

THE STATISTICAL REALITY

Let's begin with the numbers.

The United States sends approximately 135,000 international missionaries, more than any other nation on earth. Brazil is second with 40,000 missionaries. South Korea is third with 35,000. The Philippines sends 25,000.[110] But America alone sends more missionaries than those next three countries combined.

In 2024, Americans gave $592.5 billion to charitable causes. Of this, individuals alone contributed $392.45 billion. Religion received

23 percent of all charitable giving, approximately $136 billion.[111] Even accounting for the fact that much religious giving goes to congregational operations rather than missions, the amount directed toward evangelism, missions, Bible translation, and humanitarian work from American Christians far exceeds what the rest of the world combined contributes.

According to missions researchers, American Christians provide the overwhelming majority of global missionary funding. While exact percentages vary by source and methodology, conservative estimates suggest that US churches and individuals fund 60 to 70 percent of all Protestant missionary activity worldwide.[112] When you include Catholic missions funding, American Christians still account for the majority of global missions resources.

Consider what this means practically. The Bible translators working to bring Scripture to unreached language groups are largely funded by American Christians. The church planters establishing congregations in restricted-access nations are supported by American giving. The medical missionaries providing healthcare in regions with no other access to treatment are backed by American prosperity. The humanitarian organizations drilling wells, building schools, and providing disaster relief are resourced primarily through American donations.

Without American prosperity channeled into Kingdom purposes, the modern missions movement would collapse.

PROSPERITY ENABLES GENEROSITY

The connection is straightforward. Prosperity produces surplus. Surplus enables generosity. Generosity funds missions.

You cannot give what you do not have. A church living hand-to-mouth, barely able to pay its pastor and keep the lights on, cannot send missionaries. A believer who is struggling to feed his family cannot support Bible translation. A congregation trapped in poverty theology, viewing financial struggle as a badge of spirituality, will be hampered in their ability to fund the Great Commission.

But when believers prosper, when they experience increase, when they have margin beyond their needs, they can give generously. American Christians, benefiting from the most prosperous economic system in history, have given more generously than any group of believers in any era.

Second Corinthians 8:14 (ESV) says, *"your abundance at the present time should supply their need. . . ."*

Paul assumed that abundance would exist among believers. He expected surplus. He taught that those who have more should support those who have less, not out of coercion, but out of love and partnership in the gospel. Then he proceeded to promise blessings to those who give.

Paul was not embarrassed to talk about money. He collected offerings. He organized relief funds. He commended generous churches and challenged stingy ones. He understood that the spread of the gospel required resources, and he mobilized believers to provide those resources.

American prosperity has enabled this on a scale Paul never could have imagined. Millions of believers with surplus income directing billions of dollars toward gospel advancement. This is what happens when prosperity is embraced rather than rejected, stewarded rather than squandered, multiplied rather than hidden.

WHY MISSIONS ORGANIZATIONS ARE HEADQUARTERED IN AMERICA

There is a reason most major Christian organizations are based in the United States. It is not just because Americans are more spiritual or more committed. It is because the economic infrastructure exists to sustain these organizations.

Wycliffe Bible Translators, the largest Bible translation organization in the world, is headquartered in Orlando, Florida. Cru (formerly Campus Crusade for Christ), one of the largest evangelistic organizations in history, is based in Orlando as well. Youth With A Mission (YWAM), a massive missions-sending organization, has its international headquarters in Colorado. Samaritan's Purse, the humanitarian relief organization, operates out of North Carolina. The Billy Graham Evangelistic Association is in North Carolina. Compassion International is in Colorado. World Vision's US headquarters is in Washington State.

Why? Because these organizations need funding, and the funding is in America. They need donors, and American Christians give more than any other group worldwide. They need infrastructure, technology, logistics, and professional expertise, all of which are abundant in America.

This is not just about money. It is about the entire ecosystem that prosperity creates. When a nation is prosperous, it has:

- Educational institutions that train leaders.
- Communication infrastructure that enables global coordination.
- Transportation systems that move people and resources efficiently.
- Legal frameworks that protect organizations and enable fundraising.
- A culture of philanthropy that celebrates generosity.
- Technology platforms that facilitate connections between donors and needs.

All of this exists in abundance in the United States because of prosperity. And all of this is leveraged for Kingdom purposes by organizations committed to the Great Commission.

CHRISTIAN MEDIA

Why is Christian publishing dominated by American companies? Why are Christian radio and television primarily an American innovation? Why are Christian websites, apps, and digital platforms largely developed in America?

Again, the answer is prosperity. Publishing requires capital. Radio and television require technology and funding. Digital platforms require expertise and investment. America has all of these in abundance.

The Bible you read was likely published by an American company or an international company with significant American operations. Zondervan, Destiny Image, Harrison House, Thomas Nelson, Tyndale House, Crossway, B&H Publishing, NavPress, and dozens of other Christian publishers are based in the US. The study resources, commentaries, devotionals, and theological works that shape global Christianity are largely produced in America and distributed worldwide.

Christian radio reaches billions. Christian television broadcasts to every continent. Christian websites provide discipleship resources in hundreds of languages. Christian apps equip believers with Scripture, worship music, and teaching. Where did all this come from? Primarily from American innovation funded by American prosperity.

Even critics of American Christianity benefit from resources created by American prosperity. The seminary professor in Europe who writes against the prosperity gospel likely studied from American textbooks, uses American Bible software, and publishes through companies that exist because of American economic strength. The African pastor who preaches against "American materialism" (though there are not many of them because the African Church is exploding right now with a revelation of prosperity) probably trained at an institution funded by American donors and travels to conferences sponsored by American organizations.

The system works even when people do not acknowledge it.

PROSPERITY PROVIDES TIME

Here is a dimension that is often overlooked. Prosperity creates time. When you are not laboring 16 hours a day just to survive, you have time to study. When your basic needs are met with margin, you have mental and emotional capacity to engage with complex ideas. When you have resources, you can access education, books, and tools that deepen understanding.

Western Christians, particularly American Christians, have had unprecedented access to biblical scholarship. Seminaries, Bible colleges, online courses, podcasts, books, commentaries, study Bibles, biblical languages tools, all of this is widely available because of prosperity.

This has produced a generation of believers who can engage Scripture at a level of depth that would have been impossible for previous generations. The medieval peasant, even if he could read (which most could not), had no access to a Bible in his language. The Reformation believer might have had access to Scripture, but commentaries and study tools were rare and expensive.

Even believers in the 19th century had limited resources compared to what is available today.

American prosperity has democratized biblical education. What once required years in a monastery or access to a university library can now be accessed on a smartphone. Sermons from the best preachers in history are available for free online. Theological debates can be followed in real-time on social media. Believers in remote villages can access Bible teaching through apps and websites.

Who funded the development of this technology? Who created these platforms? Who provides the content? Largely, American Christians leveraging prosperity for Kingdom advancement.

Abraham was blessed so he could be a blessing (see Genesis 12:2-3). God prospered Abraham materially so Abraham's household could be a channel of blessing to the nations. Solomon's wealth enabled him to build the temple, establish Israel's influence, and bring the knowledge of the true God to surrounding nations (1 Kings 10:1-13). The Queen of Sheba came to Jerusalem because of reports of Solomon's wisdom and wealth, and she left having encountered the God of Israel.

The churches Paul planted supported his missionary journeys. The Philippian church sent financial support to Paul multiple times (see Philippians 4:15-18 ESV). Paul commended them for their partnership in the gospel and called their gift *"a fragrant offering, a sacrifice acceptable and pleasing to God."* He thanked God for their generosity because it enabled his ministry to continue.

Throughout church history, the pattern has held. Wealthy believers and prosperous churches have funded missions, built institutions, supported ministers, and advanced the gospel.

William Carey's missionary work was funded by British Christians. Hudson Taylor's China Inland Mission was sustained by donations from believers across Europe and the USA. The modern missions movement has been financed primarily by prosperous Western Christians.

This is how God designed it. Prosperity is not the problem. Prosperity, stewarded for Kingdom purposes, is the solution.

WHAT IF THE CHURCH FULLY EMBRACED BIBLICAL PROSPERITY?

Imagine if every American Christian truly embraced biblical prosperity—not greed, not materialism, not the accumulation of wealth for personal comfort and luxury. Rather, what if there were a wholehearted acceptance of true biblical prosperity: increase received as blessing from God, stewarded with wisdom, and directed toward Kingdom advancement?

Imagine if believers stopped apologizing for blessing and started aggressively pursuing it so they could give more, fund more, send more. Imagine if churches stopped preaching poverty theology and started teaching believers how to prosper biblically so that the missions budget could multiply. Imagine if entrepreneurs saw their businesses as Kingdom funding mechanisms rather than merely personal income sources.

The Great Commission could be completed in our generation. There is enough wealth among American Christians right now to translate the Bible into every remaining language, send missionaries to every unreached people group, plant churches in every city, and provide humanitarian aid to every region in need.

The problem is not the lack of resources. The problem is lack of vision, lack of teaching, and lack of willingness to embrace what God has provided.

Religiously affiliated Americans together earn nearly $5 trillion annually.[113] If they gave even 10 percent to Kingdom work, that would be $500 billion per year directed toward gospel advancement. Currently, Christians give approximately 2.5 percent of their income,[114] and only a tiny fraction of that goes to unreached people groups.[115]

This is not a resource problem. This is a theology problem. The Church has been discipled by poverty theology rather than biblical prosperity teaching. As a result, the Great Commission is underfunded, missionaries are undersupported, and billions remain unreached.

The next generation is watching. If we teach them that prosperity teaching is heresy, if we instill guilt about blessing, if we romanticize poverty as spirituality, they will not become the generous funders of missions. They will become consumers of resources rather than producers and distributors of them.

If, however, we teach them biblical prosperity, if we show them how God blesses faithful stewardship, if we model generosity from abundance, if we celebrate what God provides and direct it toward eternal purposes, they will become the most generous, most missions-focused generation in Christian history.

The future of global missions hangs in the balance, and that future depends, in large part, on whether the American Church embraces or rejects biblical prosperity.

THANK GOD FOR THE AMERICAN PROSPERITY GOSPEL

American prosperity, channeled through generous believers committed to the Great Commission, has been God's primary means of funding gospel advancement for the past century. This is not nationalism. This is acknowledgment of what God has done through a nation that, despite its flaws and sins, has operated on economic principles that align with Scripture and have produced abundance that has been leveraged for Kingdom purposes.

We should not be embarrassed by this; instead, we should be grateful. We should be faithful stewards, and we should teach the next generation to be the same.

Thank God for the "American Gospel." Without it, the world would be lost.

18

THE QUESTION NO ONE IS ASKING

If prosperity teaching is the American heresy that critics claim it is, why is it exploding in the Global South? Why are the fastest-growing churches in Africa, Latin America, and Asia boldly preaching biblical prosperity while Western churches that mock it are declining?[116]

The critics have no answer for this. They cannot explain why believers who have actually experienced poverty are the ones most enthusiastically embracing prosperity teaching, while comfortable Western evangelicals who have never missed a meal are the ones condemning it.

Those who know poverty firsthand recognize that it is not a virtue. Those who have lived without options understand that prosperity creates opportunities to serve God and others. Those who have watched their children go hungry are not embarrassed to believe God for provision. They are desperate for it, and when they discover that Scripture promises it, they receive it with joy.

Church history demonstrates a consistent pattern. Each generation faces unique challenges and discovers the biblical truths necessary to address those challenges. The early Church fought for the Trinity, the deity of Christ, and the canon of Scripture. The Reformation era rediscovered justification by faith and the authority of Scripture. The Holiness movement emphasized sanctification and holy living. The Pentecostal movement restored the baptism of the Holy Spirit and spiritual gifts.

Now, in our generation, biblical prosperity is being recovered. Not because it is new revelation, but because previous generations lacked the capacity to fully explore it.

As I've stated, for most of human history, believers were simply trying to survive. The medieval peasant working dawn to dusk had neither time nor resources to study what Scripture says about financial blessing. The Reformation believer, while freed theologically, still lived in an agrarian economy with limited mobility.

But American prosperity created something unprecedented: masses of people with education, access to Scripture, time to study, and freedom to apply what they learned. For the first time in history, ordinary believers could engage Scripture at depth.

The same reason for American innovation is the same reason for the explosion of this revelation. They could compare passages, study original languages, access commentaries, and think critically about what the Bible actually says versus what tradition had taught.

When they looked honestly at Scripture, they found promises of blessing, increase, abundance, and prosperity woven throughout both Testaments. These promises are part of the normal Christian experience, apart from persecution, for those walking in obedience and faith.

SURVIVOR'S GUILT

Visit a thriving church in Nigeria, Kenya, Brazil, or South Korea, and you will find believers who are unapologetic about expecting God's blessing. They pray for provision without shame. They have not inherited the Western neurosis that confuses humility with self-contempt.

In the West, many Christians suffer from a form of *spiritual survivor's guilt.* They live in nations built on biblical work ethic, covenant generosity, and free enterprise—and yet they feel unworthy of it. They subconsciously apologize for the fruit of faith, diligence, and divine favor. Like survivors of a tragedy who cannot enjoy life while others suffer, affluent believers often resent their own prosperity and feel as though attacking it might ease their conscience.

This guilt manifests as virtue signaling: crafting sermons against, "health and wealth," being suspicious of other's success, criticizing "name it and claim it theology" and the glorification of lack. It's not holiness, it's psychological penance. Having prospered under biblical principles, they now despise those same principles when preached by others.

They mistake the comfort of their civilization for moral compromise and the hardship of others for righteousness. In doing so, they rewrite the gospel of grace into a gospel of guilt, a theology where abundance must be hidden and prosperity treated as a sin.

Not so with those in Africa and other poverty-stricken nations. Why? Because they have lived the alternative. They know what poverty produces: limited options, constant anxiety, inability to help others, watching children suffer, powerlessness to change circumstances. They do not romanticize it. They do not spiritualize it. They recognize it as a condition to escape, not a badge of honor to wear.

When these believers discover that the God they serve promises to supply all their needs according to His riches in glory, that He takes pleasure in the prosperity of His servants, that He gives power to get wealth so His covenant may be established, they believe it. No apology. No qualification. No embarrassment. Just faith.

The fruit is undeniable. Churches in the Global South are growing explosively. They are sending missionaries. They are building schools and clinics. They are establishing businesses. They are lifting entire communities out of poverty. They are demonstrating what happens when biblical prosperity teaching is received and applied without the filter of Western skepticism.

Meanwhile, Western churches that mock prosperity teaching are declining, closing, and becoming culturally irrelevant. The contrast should make us pause and ask some questions.

The Church stands at a crossroads. The decision we make about prosperity will determine the trajectory of gospel advancement for the next generation.

If the Church embraces biblical prosperity as Scripture teaches it, the results are predictable. Believers will pursue excellence in their work, not as workaholics, but as faithful stewards. They will expect God to bless their obedience and faithfulness. They will receive increase without guilt. They will give generously from abundance rather than scarcity.

Churches will be well-resourced, able to fund ambitious missions initiatives. Entrepreneurship will be celebrated as a Kingdom calling. Believers will start businesses, create jobs, generate wealth, and then direct it toward eternal purposes.

If the Church rejects biblical prosperity and continues down the road of poverty theology, the results are equally predictable. Believers will apologize for blessing and hide their increase. They will live beneath their potential, constrained by guilt and low expectations.

Churches will remain chronically under-resourced, unable to fund significant ministry. The next generation will be taught that expecting provision is presumptuous and that financial struggle proves spirituality.

Missions funding will decline as the generation that built it dies off and is not replaced. Millions will remain unreached, not because reaching them is impossible, but because the Church refused to embrace the prosperity necessary to fund it.

CRITICS DEPEND ON WHAT THEY CONDEMN

Here is the part that no one wants to acknowledge. The Western evangelical establishment that attacks prosperity teaching depends entirely on the prosperity created by the principles they condemn.

The seminary that trains pastors to preach against prosperity operates on tuition income, endowments, and donations from people who prospered under the "American Gospel." The publishing house that prints books criticizing prosperity gospel is a for-profit business leveraging free-market principles. The conference that gathers speakers to denounce materialism charges registration fees, sells books, or generates revenue through offerings.

Everyone benefits from prosperity. The only question is whether we will be honest about it and teach others how to biblically steward it, or whether we will pretend it is suspect while quietly depending on it.

When believers prosper biblically, several things happen:

First, their families are secure. Children are fed, clothed, and educated. The constant anxiety about survival is removed.

Second, they have margin to serve. Time and resources become available for ministry, volunteering, and discipleship.

Third, they can give generously. Churches are funded, missionaries are sent, the poor are served.

Fourth, they become testimonies. Their lives demonstrate that God keeps His promises, that obedience leads to blessing, that faith works.

This is what the world should see when they look at the Church: not poverty, not struggle, not barely-getting-by, but rather abundance managed wisely, generosity flowing freely, and provision testifying to God's faithfulness.

The Church must reclaim biblical prosperity from those who have manipulated it and those who have slandered it. We must teach it clearly, model it openly, and defend it boldly.

We must call out the Marxist assumptions that have infiltrated our theology. We must reject the poverty mindset that limits God and cripples believers.

This does not mean embracing greed, materialism, or the love of money. Those are sins under any economic system. It means joyfully accepting what Scripture actually teaches: that God delights in prospering His servants, that He gives power to get wealth, that obedience and faithfulness lead to blessing, and that increase is meant to be stewarded for His glory and purposes.

The next generation is watching. If we hand them poverty theology, we hand them a debilitated gospel. If we give them biblical prosperity teaching, we give them the full counsel of God and the resources to complete the Great Commission. This is not a minor disagreement between equally valid interpretations. This is a battle for the future of gospel advancement.

If prosperity theology wins, missions will be funded, the gospel will advance, and the Great Commission can be completed. If poverty theology wins, missions will be starved, the gospel will stall, and billions will die without hearing the name of Jesus.

You have a choice to make today. Will you believe what God says about prosperity or will you believe what Marxists say about wealth? Will you embrace Scripture or surrender to propaganda? Will you pursue biblical prosperity so you can give generously, or will you accept a poverty mindset and watch missions collapse?

The future of global evangelization depends on how the Church answers these questions. The answer cannot be delayed. The world is waiting. Time is running out—God is waiting to see if His people will trust Him enough to believe what He promises and receive what He offers.

Thank God for the "American Gospel." May we have the courage to preach it, live it, and pass it on to the next generation who will complete what we have begun.

PART SIX

THE WEALTH TRANSFER

19

FISHERS OF MEN

In previous chapters, we unpacked the revelation of *fish come first.* From the very beginning, Jesus didn't call His disciples with a sermon. He called them with a financial miracle. Luke 5 and John 21 both open with a supernatural catch of fish, which in their world meant sudden income, sudden provision, and sudden stability.

Fishing wasn't a hobby, it was their business. Peter, Andrew, James, and John operated in a commercial trade that involved employees, equipment, and Roman-issued fishing licenses.

When Jesus filled their nets, God stepped into their economy before He stepped into their theology.

God revealed Himself as the One who provides, the One who commands increase, and the One who breaks the fear of lack. God called them through a financial breakthrough.

Why? He called them through a financial breakthrough because that miracle revealed three things they needed to know before they could follow Him:

1. *His character as Provider:* He is Jehovah Jireh, and lack has no authority in His presence.
2. *His dominion over resources:* The fish obeyed Him. The Creator commands the economy of creation.
3. *His intention to break their fear of lack:* Before He asked them to leave their nets, He proved He could fill them.

This is the pattern: provision precedes the call. Yet even with those miracles in front of them, the disciples struggled to follow Him fully. Scripture shows that fear held them back.

Jesus named the two great enemies of discipleship: 1) the cares of this world; and 2) the deceitfulness of riches. These pressures kept them tied to their nets, always drifting back to the familiar because they worried about provision more than they trusted His call.

Their greatest failures weren't caused by storms, demons, or persecution. Mark 6 says they were terrified in the middle of the sea because they *"considered not the miracle of the loaves"* and fishes (see Mark 6:52). They forgot the financial miracle that Jesus had just performed. When believers forget how God has provided, fear always returns, and obedience always collapses.

Here is the insight you cannot afford to miss: When believers forget God's provision, fear returns and obedience collapses.

The enemy's strategy has not changed. He doesn't need to stop God from providing. He only needs to make you forget that He already has. *If he can disconnect your memory from the miracle, he can dominate your future with fear.*

This is why we testify. This is why we remember. This is why Scripture commands us to rehearse what God has done.

Jesus dealt with their fear by dealing with their finances. *Fish came first* because He was teaching them that the God who fills your net can care for every area of your life.

MEN AS FISH?

When Jesus declared, "*Follow Me, and I will make you fishers of men*" (Matthew 4:19 NKJV), He was not simply referring to evangelism. He was embedding Kingdom economics into the call itself.

Think about what that phrase actually requires. If you are going to fish for something, the thing you're fishing for must behave like a fish. If Jesus is making us fishers of men, then God must, in some spiritual and economic sense, make men function like fish in the lives of His people.

DOMINION OVER FISH

Before we can fully understand what it means for humans to function prophetically like fish, we need to go back to Genesis 1 where the language of dominion first appears.

Look closely at what the Bible says in Genesis 1:26 when God created mankind:

> *And God said, Let us make man in our image, after our likeness: and let them have dominion over the fish of the sea, and over the fowl of the air, and over the cattle, and over all the earth, and over every creeping thing that creepeth upon the earth.*

Notice the order. Fish are listed first (*fish come first*). Before the fowl. Before the cattle. Before every creeping thing. Before *"all the earth."* Man's dominion mandate begins with fish. This is not accidental.

In Scripture, the order of listing often reveals priority. Before man had dominion over land, animals, or even over the earth itself, God gave him authority over the fish of the sea. The first arena of human dominion was aquatic, the realm that would come to symbolize economic provision throughout the Bible.

Now look at what God said two days earlier in the creation account in Genesis 1:22: *"And God blessed them, saying, Be fruitful, and multiply, and fill the waters in the seas…."*

This is the first time the phrase *"be fruitful and multiply"* appears in Scripture and it is spoken over fish. The blessing of multiplication was first pronounced over the creatures that would later represent provision, supply, and economic breakthrough. Before that blessing was given to mankind, it was given to fish.

Do you see the pattern? Prosperity and multiplication are tied directly to the fish blessing. And dominion over fish is the first dominion mankind received. When Jesus tells Peter to cast his net and become a fisher of men, He is reaching all the way back to Genesis. He is restoring what Adam lost: dominion over the realm of provision.

PEOPLE FUNCTION PROPHETICALLY LIKE FISH

Here is the principle that will change how you understand Kingdom economics: Any role fish played in Scripture, we will play in the life of God's people.

If Jesus makes us fishers of men, then God makes people like fish. Not in a *dehumanizing* sense but in a *functional* sense. Just as God used fish to supply, direct, and fund His servants in the Old and New Testaments, He now uses people. This means:

- *We become carriers of provision:* God deposits resources in people and then draws those people into your life.
- *God draws them into your net:* Just as fish were supernaturally directed into Peter's net, God directs people as clients, partners, employers, investors, givers toward those He wants to bless.
- *God uses them to advance His purposes in your life:* Provision is not random. It is relational. The wealth of the Kingdom moves through covenant connections.

Think about your own testimony. How many times has breakthrough come through a person? A phone call. A referral. A contract. An unexpected gift. A door opened by someone you barely knew. That wasn't luck. That was God making humans like fish drawing them into your net by His hand. You should also seek to be that for others in your personal life.

EXAMPLES OF PEOPLE OPERATING PROPHETICALLY LIKE FISH

God has always advanced His purposes through covenant connections and He still does it today. Jesus' own ministry was supernaturally funded by people God assigned to Him. Luke records Joanna, Susanna, and *many other women* who provided for Him out of their substance (see Luke 8:1-3). These were covenant-aligned partners God brought into His life at the right moment.

Paul had the same testimony. Lydia, a seller of purple, opened her home and her purse to the gospel and immediately became a key supporter of the Philippian church (see Acts 16:14-15, 40), later participating in Paul's ongoing ministry partnership (see Philippians 4:15). Scripture is full of these divine alignments:

- *The Shunammite woman* built a room for Elisha and supplied him continually (see 2 Kings 4:8-10).
- *Barzillai the Gileadite* brought provision to David in his time of need (see 2 Samuel 17:27-29).
- *The early Church* thrived because believers sold their property, houses, and lands and *"laid the resources at the apostles"* feet (see Acts 4:34-35).

When God gives you an assignment, He also gives you people. Covenant connections are one of His primary channels of increase. Let's trace this pattern through Scripture so you can see how consistently God works this way.

THE COIN IN THE FISH'S MOUTH: MATTHEW 17

When the temple tax was due, Jesus didn't send Peter to the treasury. He sent him to the sea.

> *Notwithstanding, lest we should offend them, go thou to the sea, and cast an hook, and take up the fish that first cometh up; and when thou hast opened his mouth, thou shalt find a piece of money: that take, and give unto them for me and thee* (Matthew 17:27).

The coin Peter found was a *stater*, a Greek silver coin worth four drachmas, which was exactly enough to pay the temple tax for two people. God provided the precise amount needed through a fish.

In Jesus' day, God used a literal fish to deliver money. Today, God uses people in the same way. Your provision may come through a person whose "mouth" opens a conversation, offers a contract, arranges a recommendation—and suddenly, the exact resource you needed is delivered. The principle hasn't changed, just the delivery system.

RAVENS SENT TO SUPPLY ELIJAH: 1 KINGS 17

When Elijah was hiding by the brook Cherith during the famine, God didn't drop manna from Heaven, he deployed ravens.

> *And the ravens brought him bread and flesh in the morning, and bread and flesh in the evening; and he drank of the brook* (1 Kings 17:6).

Ravens are unclean birds and scavengers, but they became the delivery agents for God's provision. God will use the most unlikely sources to supply His servants.

Today, God still sends *"ravens."* They may not have feathers, but they still carry resources: the client you didn't expect, the connection that made no sense, the person from a completely different world who shows up with exactly what you need.

God is not limited by your network. He has access to people you've never met!

THE WEALTH OF THE WICKED REDISTRIBUTED: JOB 27

Job understood something that many believers have forgotten: the wicked do not get to keep what they accumulate.

> *This is the portion of a wicked man with God, and the heritage of oppressors, which they shall receive of the Almighty. ... Though he heap up silver as the dust, and prepare raiment as the clay; he may prepare it, but the just shall put it on, and the innocent shall divide the silver* (Job 27:13, 16-17).

Read that again: *"he may prepare it, but the just shall put it on."* The wicked gather; the righteous inherit.

This is a biblical principle woven throughout Scripture. The sinner labors, but his labor ultimately funds the Kingdom. The wealth he heaps up is laid up, stored, and reserved for those who walk uprightly before God.

GOOD MEASURE, PRESSED DOWN, SHAKEN TOGETHER: LUKE 6:38

I have shown you this principle using fish, birds, and certain men. But I want you to realize that God may move on the heart of *anyone,* at *anytime.* When you give of yourself for the sake of ministry, there is an abundant return of provision released toward you:

> *Give, and it shall be given unto you; good measure, pressed down, and shaken together, and running over, shall men give into your bosom...* (Luke 6:38).

The Bible does specify from whom it will be *"given unto you,"* it only specifies that it will abundant! The Greek word translated *bosom* in Luke 6:38 is *kolpos,* which literally refers to the fold of a garment at the chest that first-century people used as a pocket or purse to carry goods and money. When Jesus said that men would, "give into your bosom," He was describing a literal overflowing pocket, purse, or wallet.

This is what it means for us to function like fish. The world is full of people accumulating resources that do not belong to them eternally. And God, in His sovereignty, redirects that wealth into the hands of His people through business deals, inheritances, opportunities, and divine appointments. We dive deeper into this in a moment.

Fish come first because finances come first in the training of a disciple.

And if you will receive it: the men and women around you are swimming in a sea of resource and God is directing some of them into your net. This is all true, but you still have to guard your heart. Covenant connections are not an excuse for covetousness or envy.

- Exodus 20:17 warns: "*Thou shalt not covet....*"
- Proverbs 14:30 reminds us that "*A sound heart is the life of the flesh, but envy is the rottenness of the bones.*" You are not to be eyeing what someone else has or fantasizing about their bank account.
- Psalm 75:6-7 tells us to keep our trust in God alone, remembering that "*promotion cometh neither from the east, nor from the west...but God is the judge....*"

As you walk in obedience, you allow Him—in His timing and His way—to move resources toward your assignment. Increase comes by faith, not by fixation.

THE WEALTH TRANSFER PROVEN

Some believers flinch at the phrase *wealth transfer*. It sounds too bold. Too presumptuous.

Maybe even greedy. Many take a fatalistic view because they fear appearing this way. They say, "If God wants me to have it, He'll give it to me." As mentioned previously, that sounds humble, but it is quietly dangerous. What if the wealth transfer is accessible only to those who prepare for it? Scripture shows that God releases provision in response to faith, obedience, and expectation—not passivity.

The first step in being prepared is knowing God's will because you cannot act on a promise you doubt.

From Genesis to Revelation, Scripture consistently speaks of a divine redistribution or a transfer of resources from the hands of the wicked into the hands of the righteous. It speaks so strongly in this regard that it could be considered a reasonable covenant expectation. And if you are going to walk in the fullness of what God has prepared for you, you must build your faith on what the Word actually says.

Let's let Scripture speak for itself.

Solomon, the wisest and wealthiest man of his era, observed something deeply troubling:

> *There is an evil which I have seen under the sun, as an error which proceedeth from the ruler: Folly is set in great dignity, and the rich sit in low place. I have seen servants upon horses, and princes walking as servants upon the earth* (Ecclesiastes 10:5-7).

Solomon saw an inversion. He saw people who should have been in places of authority and wealth walking in poverty and servitude while fools and sinners sat in positions of power.

He called it an *"evil"* under the sun. This was not God's design. This was disorder. And what Solomon identified as a grievous error is exactly what God intends to correct through the principle of wealth transfer.

Just a few chapters earlier, Solomon revealed the mechanism:

> *For God giveth to a man that is good in his sight wisdom, and knowledge, and joy: but to the sinner he giveth travail, to gather*

> *and to heap up, that he may give to him that is good before God…* (Ecclesiastes 2:26).

Read that carefully. The sinner is given travail, labor, toil, exhausting work in order to gather and heap up. But for what purpose? *"That he may give to him that is good before God."*

The wicked gather; the righteous receive. The sinner doesn't know it, but he is working for the Kingdom. His accumulation has an assignment and that assignment is transfer.

Now here is perhaps the most direct wealth transfer promise in Scripture, found in Proverbs 13:22: *"A good man leaveth an inheritance to his children's children: and the wealth of the sinner is laid up for the just."*

Notice two things:

First, a good man thinks generationally. He doesn't just provide for his children; he leaves an inheritance for his grandchildren. Biblical prosperity is multigenerational.

Second, the wealth of the sinner is laid up for the just. Laid up means stored, reserved, set aside. The sinner may possess it temporarily, but it has a destination… it is for the just. I dare you to declare it: "The wealth of the sinner is laid up for me."

20

THE RHYTHM OF KINGDOM ECONOMICS

As previously mentioned, there is no shortage of money in the world; there is no shortage of resources in the world. God's creation is abundantly supplied with everything necessary to not only sustain His people, but also to allow them to prosper.

The Old Testament prophets understood this:

> *Then thou shalt see, and flow together, and thine heart shall fear, and be enlarged; because the abundance of the sea shall be converted unto thee, the forces of the Gentiles shall come unto thee* (Isaiah 60:5).

And again:

> *But ye shall be named the Priests of the Lord: men shall call you the Ministers of our God: ye shall eat the riches of the Gentiles, and in their glory shall ye boast yourselves* (Isaiah 61:6).

God's people are called to be priests, but they are not called to be poor. They will eat the riches of the Gentiles. They will partake of the wealth of the nations. This is end-time economy. This is Kingdom finance.

When God was preparing to rebuild His temple through Zerubbabel, He spoke through the prophet Haggai:

> *And I will shake all nations, and the desire of all nations shall come: and I will fill this house with glory, saith the Lord of hosts. The silver is mine, and the gold is mine, saith the Lord of hosts* (Haggai 2:7-8).

God shakes the nations. And when He shakes, wealth moves.

The silver belongs to Him. The gold belongs to Him and He decides who holds it. When the earth is shaken, resources are released and God directs them toward His purposes and His people.

The apostle James delivers one of the most severe warnings in the New Testament, found in James 5:1-3:

> *Go to now, ye rich men, weep and howl for your miseries that shall come upon you. Your riches are corrupted, and your garments are motheaten. Your gold and silver is cankered; and the rust of them shall be a witness against you, and shall eat your flesh as it were fire. Ye have heaped treasure together for the last days.*

James is speaking to ungodly rich people whose wealth will testify against them on the day of judgment. They have heaped up earthly treasure when they should have been heaping up treasure in Heaven. But notice the timing: *"Ye have heaped treasure together for the last days."*

In the last days, there will be an unprecedented concentration of wealth in the hands of the wicked. But that concentration is the setup for the transfer. What they have gathered, they will not keep. What they have hoarded, the righteous will inherit. James continues:

> *Behold, the hire of the labourers who have reaped down your fields, which is of you kept back by fraud, crieth: and the cries of*

> *them which have reaped are entered into the ears of the Lord of sabaoth* (James 5:4).

God hears the cries of those who have been defrauded. He hears the laborers who were cheated. And He will answer not only with judgment on the oppressors, but also with restoration to the oppressed. This is the wealth transfer. It is a correction. It is justice. And it is coming.

Now we know where the wealth is: it's in the hands of the wicked. But where is it supposed to be? According to Scripture, that wealth belongs in the hands of the righteous: *"Wealth and riches shall be in his house: and his righteousness endureth for ever"* (Psalm 112:3).

The psalmist is describing the blessed one who fears the Lord and delights in His commandments. And what does he say about that? Wealth and riches shall be in his house. Not in someone else's house. Not in the sinner's account. Not hoarded by the ungodly. In his house.

God is not against wealth. God is against the wrong people controlling it.

When resources are in the hands of the wicked, they fund wickedness, exploitation, idolatry, perversion, and the advancement of darkness. When those same resources are transferred into the hands of the righteous, they fund the Kingdom, evangelism, discipleship, mercy, justice, and the building of God's house.

The wealth of the world is currently misallocated. But God is the God of order, and He has every intention of setting His house in order.

THE EXODUS PATTERN

If you want to see wealth transfer in action, look no further than the Exodus. When Israel left Egypt after 430 years of slavery, they did not leave empty-handed:

> *He brought them forth also with silver and gold: and there was not one feeble person among their tribes. Egypt was glad when they departed: for the fear of them fell upon them* (Psalm 105:37-38).

They left laden. Loaded down. Carrying more than they came in with. Every tribe. Every family. Not one feeble among them. This was reparations—not like what the Marxists are demanding today; this was divine reparations. There were four centuries of unpaid labor, and God collected on their behalf.

But here's the question: Why did God transfer the wealth of Egypt to His people?

Was it so they could build bigger tents? Buy nicer sandals? Impress the surrounding nations?

The answer is found in Exodus 25:1,8): *"And the Lord spake unto Moses, saying, Speak unto the children of Israel, that they bring me an offering.... And let them make me a sanctuary; that I may dwell among them."*

The wealth of Egypt funded the Tabernacle. God transferred silver and gold out of the treasure houses of Pharaoh so that His people could build His dwelling place. The wealth had a purpose and that purpose was the manifest presence of God.

The wealth transfer must never be about self-indulgence. It is about an assignment. God releases resources to His people so that His purposes can be funded, His house can be built, and His glory can dwell among them. Psalm 105:44-45 confirms it: *"And gave them the lands of the heathen: and they inherited the labour of the people; that they might observe his statutes, and keep his laws. Praise ye the Lord."*

They inherited what others had labored for so that they could serve God.

- The wealth was for obedience.
- The transfer was for a testimony.
- The resources were for righteousness.

THIS IS YOUR INHERITANCE

If you are in Christ, you are a child of Abraham. The covenant promises belong to you. The sinner is laboring right now, gathering and heaping up not knowing that his accumulation has your name on it. The wealth of the nations is being shaken loose. The gold and silver belong to the Lord, and God is looking for righteous stewards who will use what He releases to build His Kingdom, bless their families, and establish His purposes on earth.

God will make men as fish. Are you ready to be a fisher of men? The wealth transfer does not fall on those who shrug their shoulders. It falls on those who align with His will, speak His Word, sow their seed, steward with integrity, and expect His covenant promises to manifest.

If fear convinces you to stand still, you will watch what God intended for you pass to someone else.

But if you prepare in faith, you will be in position when God moves.

POWER TO GET WEALTH?

If wealth transfer is real—and Scripture makes clear that it is—God hasn't asked you to sit back and wait for money to fall from the sky. He has given you something far more powerful: He has given you the power to get wealth.

This is one of the most important financial verses in the entire Bible, and yet many believers have never meditated on its implications:

> *But thou shalt remember the Lord thy God: for it is he that giveth thee power to get wealth, that he may establish his covenant which he sware unto thy fathers, as it is this day* (Deuteronomy 8:18).

Let's break this apart:

First, God gives power. Not suggestions. Not good wishes. Not vague spiritual encouragement. Power. The Hebrew word is *koach* and it means strength, ability, force, capacity. God deposits into His covenant people a supernatural ability to generate, attract, and accumulate wealth.

Second, this power is specifically for wealth. Not poverty. Not survival. Not "just enough to get by." The text doesn't say that God gives you power to endure lack. It doesn't say He gives you power to be content with nothing. It says He gives you the power to get wealth. If God only wanted you to survive, He would have said so. But He didn't. He spoke of *wealth*, and He gave you the power to obtain it.

Third, wealth is covenantal. Look at the purpose clause: *"that he may establish his covenant which he sware unto thy fathers."*

This wealth is not disconnected from covenant. When God made promises to Abraham, Isaac, and Jacob, those promises included material blessing, land, increase, and abundance. And God gives you the power to get wealth so that His covenant can be established, made visible, made manifest, and made undeniable on earth.

When you prosper, the covenant is on display. When you walk in abundance, the promises of God are proven. When your household flourishes, the world sees that the God of Abraham keeps His word.

Fourth, if God gives the power, then wealth acquisition is obedience, not greed. This is where religious thinking has crippled so many believers. They've been told that wanting wealth is carnal. That pursuing increase is worldly. That financial ambition disqualifies you from spiritual maturity.

If God Himself gave you the power to get wealth, then using that power is not greed. It is stewardship. It is alignment with His purpose. It is doing what He equipped you to do.

The question is not, "Is it okay to pursue wealth?" The question is, "Am I using the power God gave me, or am I burying it in the ground?"

WHERE IS THIS POWER LOCATED?

Now that you know that God has given you the power to get wealth, the next question is critical: Where is it? The apostle Paul answers this in his letter to the Ephesians:

> *Now unto him that is able to do exceeding abundantly above all that we ask or think, according to the power that worketh in us...* (Ephesians 3:20).

Catch that phrase: *"according to the power that worketh in us."* Not around us. Not above us. Not floating somewhere in the atmosphere, waiting for the right prayer to pull it down—*in us.*

God has placed the engine of prosperity inside the believer. This is a game changer. You are not waiting on God to do something external. You are carrying something internal. You have the power to create, to build, to increase, to prosper, and it is already within you by the Spirit of God as you walk in Christ.

This is why two believers can be in the same city, the same economy, and the same industry and one will thrive while the other barely survives. The difference is not location. The difference is revelation and activation. The power is in you. The questions are: Have you accessed it? Have you cultivated it? Have you released it?

God has already done His part. He has deposited *koach*—strength, ability, and capacity—into your spirit. Now it's your turn to steward what He's given.

- You are *not* powerless.
- You are *not* dependent on the economy.
- You are *not* subject to the whims of the world system.

- You carry covenant power to generate wealth, and it is working in you right now.

PROSPERITY REQUIRES ACTION

Understanding wealth transfer is one thing. Believing God has given you power to get wealth is another. But here's where it gets practical: Are you ready to move your money?

When Israel left Egypt laden with silver and gold, that wealth did not magically appear in their tents. They had to take it. Exodus 12:35-36 says:

> *And the children of Israel did according to the word of Moses; and they borrowed of the Egyptians jewels of silver, and jewels of gold, and raiment: And the Lord gave the people favour in the sight of the Egyptians, so that they lent unto them such things as they required. And they spoiled the Egyptians.*

Notice the language: *they spoiled the Egyptians.* The Hebrew word for *spoiled* is *natsal.* It means to strip, to plunder, or to deliver by force. God gave them favor, but they had to go to the Egyptians. They had to ask. They had to receive what was handed to them and carry it out. Faith required action.

And it didn't stop there. After they crossed the Red Sea and arrived at Sinai, God gave Moses instructions for building the Tabernacle. And what did He require?

> *Speak unto the children of Israel, that they bring me an offering: of every man that giveth it willingly with his heart ye shall take my offering* (Exodus 25:2).

The same people who had just received the wealth of Egypt were now being asked to give it back—not to Egypt, but to God. The silver and gold that had been transferred into their hands was now to be transferred into the work of God's house.

This is the rhythm of Kingdom economics: receive and release.

You cannot hoard what God transfers to you. Wealth comes to you so that it can move through you toward God's purposes, toward His house, toward His Kingdom agenda on earth. Faith always moves resources toward God's purpose. If your money isn't moving, your faith isn't working. And yes, along the way you will find yourself driving something nice and living somewhere beautiful—that's okay, that's just what happens when God can trust you with His resources.

Prosperity is not accumulation for accumulation's sake. It is stewardship in motion: receiving from God, giving to God, and trusting Him to multiply what passes through your hands.

So let me ask you again:

- Are you ready to move your money?
- Are you ready to give when He says give?
- Are you ready to invest when He says invest?
- Are you ready to sow when your flesh says hoard?

The wealth that is coming to the body of Christ in these last days will not rest in the hands of the stingy. It will flow to those who understand that *blessed to be a blessing* is not a slogan, it is a way of life.

THE MULTIPLICATION OF LOAVES AND FISH

Before Jesus fed the 5,000, He asked Philip a financial question. John 6:5 records; *"Whence shall we buy bread, that these may eat?"*

He involved His disciples in the economic impossibility of the situation before He revealed His supernatural provision. Then He took what they had, five loaves and two fish, and multiplied it. The miracle required something to be placed in His hands first.

As we've already seen, Jesus didn't call Peter with a sermon. He called him with a catch. Before Peter would leave everything to follow Christ, Jesus filled his nets to breaking and his boats to sinking. The financial miracle preceded the call to ministry. When the temple tax was due, Jesus sent Peter fishing not for fish, but for money. The tax was paid through an economic miracle.

And notice: this miracle was connected to Peter's vocation. God used what Peter knew how to do and sanctified it for supernatural provision.

After the resurrection, when the disciples had gone back to fishing and had caught nothing, Jesus appeared on the shore and directed them to cast on the other side. One hundred fifty-three fish later, they were having breakfast with the risen Lord, and Peter was being restored and recommissioned. Again, the financial breakthrough came first.

Why does God do this? Because He will not entrust you with true riches until you have passed the money test.

Jesus says it plainly, recorded in Luke 16:10-11 (NIV):

> *Whoever can be trusted with very little can also be trusted with much, and whoever is dishonest with very little will also be dishonest with much. So if you have not been trustworthy in handling worldly wealth, who will trust you with true riches?*

Money is the test. It is *"very little."* It is *"worldly wealth."* But how you handle it determines whether God can trust you with true riches like spiritual authority, Kingdom influence, and eternal reward. This is why God involves finances before He releases the greater things. He is watching. He is weighing. He is asking:

- Can I trust you with more?
- Will you steward what I give you or squander it?
- Will you move it toward My purposes?
- Will you hoard it for your own use?

The miracles of provision that marked Jesus' ministry were not random displays of power. They were tests and invitations. Every net full of fish, every coin in a fish's mouth, every basket of leftovers was God saying, "I am able. Now will you trust Me with what you have?"

- If you want to see the miraculous, start by being faithful with the material.
- If you want true riches, pass the money test.
- If you want wealth transfer, prove that you can handle wealth.

God is not looking for perfect people. He is looking for faithful stewards, men and women who will receive what He gives, release it when He says, and trust Him for the multiplication. That's the kind of believer Heaven backs. That's the kind of steward who inherits the wealth of the sinner. That's the kind of disciple who sees *fish come first* and knows it's just the beginning.

21

MIDDLE NO MORE

THE LIE OF THE MIDDLE CLASS

It's time to break free from the middle-class mentality that limits you. In those rare ministries that do talk about God's will concerning prosperity, most deal with a poverty mentality; however, few hit on what afflicts most in the American Church—*the curse of the middle class!*

The middle class is not a blessing. It's a holding pattern. You're not crashing, but you're not climbing either. You're circling the runway, burning fuel, going nowhere and somehow convinced that this is normal. That this is success. That this is the "American Dream." It's not. It's a debt-induced illusion. And it's time to wake up.

THE GREAT FACADE

Walk through any middle-class neighborhood today, scroll through Instagram, or even glance at the new SUVs lined up in school pickup zones, and you'll think everyone's doing just fine. The homes are updated, the wardrobes are polished, the kids have iPhones, and the vacations look lavish. But there's a harsh truth behind this illusion—most of it is financed.

The cars are leased. The furniture is on credit. The vacations went on Visa. The house belongs to the bank for the next thirty (or even

50) years. And the lifestyle that looks so put-together is held up by a scaffolding of monthly payments, minimum balances, and quiet desperation. Debt has become the framework propping up a lifestyle that was once attainable with just a single, stable income.

What used to be achieved through hard work, savings, and delayed gratification is now manufactured through borrowing. We don't own our lifestyles anymore, we rent them from lenders. And every month, we pay interest for the privilege of looking like we've made it. But looking blessed and being blessed are not the same thing.

Here's what the world won't tell you: the middle class is fast becoming an illusion.

In 1971, about 61 percent of American adults lived in middle-income households. By 2021, that number had dropped to 50 percent.[117]

Fewer people are in the middle class than ever before. But here's the more troubling statistics:

In 1970, middle-income households controlled about 62 percent of all household income in America—but by 2020, that share had fallen to just 42 percent.[118]

So not only are fewer people in the middle class, but the people who are still there have less economic power than previous generations did. The people still in it have less purchasing power, less savings, less margin, and less upward mobility than their parents and grandparents had.

You're working harder to stay in the same place. And the system calls that "stability."

THE MOBILITY MYTH

Here's something that may shock you. Statistically, if you're in the middle class, you are less likely to break into wealth than someone starting from the bottom.

Those growing up in the middle-class (50th percentile) have taken the largest hit in upward mobility. Within this bracket, individuals born in 1980 have only a 45 percent chance of outearning their parents at age 30, compared to 93 percent for those born in 1940.[119]

Did you catch that? If you were born in 1940 and grew up middle class, you had a 93 percent chance of doing better than your parents. If you were born in 1980? Only 45 percent. The ladder is broken. And the middle rung is where people get stuck.

The middle class creates a dangerous comfort zone. You're not desperate enough to take risks. You're not hungry enough to demand personal change. You have just enough to lose that you play it safe and just little enough to gain that you never break free.

The poor often have more upward mobility because they know they need a breakthrough. They have nothing to lose and everything to gain. But the middle class has been sedated by stuff (stuff they don't even own) into thinking they're okay.

You're not okay. You're stuck.

Just since the 1980s, the wealthy have reduced their debt ratio while the rest of America has increased theirs to the point where the average household now owes more than they earn in a year. The rich got richer by owing less. The middle class got poorer by owing more. And the system kept telling everyone they were doing fine. This is not prosperity. This is bondage with a nicer view. A gilded cage is still a cage.

THE SECONDHAND MENTALITY

Here's what I want you to see: the middle class has trained believers to accept a secondhand life. We've confused access with ownership. You have access to a nice car, but the bank owns it. You have access to a beautiful home, but the lender holds the deed. You have access to designer clothes, but the credit card company holds the balance.

We're not building wealth. We're renting a lifestyle and somewhere along the way, we started calling that *being blessed.*

But the Bible doesn't define blessing as "the ability to borrow." Deuteronomy 28:12 says the blessed will lend to many nations and borrow from none. That's the standard. That's the goal. Anything less is not the fullness of what God promised.

- It's time to break the secondhand mentality.
- It's time to stop accepting borrowed success as real success.
- It's time to stop settling for *looking* blessed and start *being* blessed.

God didn't call you to rent your life from Visa or Mastercard. He called you to own your future debt-free, fear-free, and fully funded for your Kingdom assignment. Now let me show you why this matters spiritually.

The middle-class mindset can lull you into complacency, leaving you just comfortable enough to keep you from praying bold, desperate prayers, but not equipped with enough abundance to fully pursue His calling without limitation.

You can pay your bills (barely), so you don't cry out for breakthrough. You have a retirement account (underfunded), so you don't seek God for supernatural provision. You're *surviving*, not *thriving*.

The enemy doesn't need to destroy you, he just needs to sedate you—and debt is his anesthesia.

When you're numb, you don't fight. When you're comfortable, you don't contend. When you're managing, you stop believing for miracles. But God didn't save you to manage. He saved you to dominate. He saved you to take territory. He saved you to fund the Kingdom, bless your children's children, and leave an inheritance that outlasts your life.

You can't do that from the middle.

MIDDLE NO MORE

So here's the declaration of this chapter:

- No more settling.
- No more being satisfied with "enough."

- No more letting debt numb me into thinking "I'm okay."
- No more renting my life from lenders.
- No more secondhand blessings.
- I am middle no more!

You were created for dominion and dominion doesn't live in the middle. In the course of this book, I have shown you and will continue to reveal to you what God requires before He can release wealth into your hands:

- ***Passing the money test***. If you fail this test, you cannot be promoted to the higher things of the Spirit.
- ***Applying practical, debt-destroying strategies***. Refusing financial instruction keeps you broke, but using these strategies can change your financial situation almost immediately.
- ***Training the next generation*** so your children don't end up serving another master through debt.

It's time to break out of the middle. It's time to pass the money test. It's time to step into the prosperity God has always intended for His people.

Let's start with the money test.

THE MONEY TEST

If you want to understand why so many believers are stuck—anointed but broke, called but limited—you need to understand what Jesus taught in Luke 16. This is one of the most important financial passages in the entire New Testament, and yet most Christians have never been taught what it actually means.

Jesus is speaking directly to His disciples in Luke 16:10-12 when He lays out a principle that should stop every one of us in our tracks:

> *He that is faithful in **that which is least** is faithful also in much: and he that is unjust in the least is unjust also in much. If therefore ye have not been faithful in the **unrighteous mammon**, who will commit to your trust the **true riches**? And if ye have not been faithful in that which is another man's, who shall give you that which is your own?*

There it is. The elementary test. Money is *"that which is least...."*

Notice what Jesus calls money: that which is *least*, not that which is *most*. Not the ultimate measure of your spirituality. Not the thing that matters above all else. He calls it least, the entry-level exam or the quiz you take before you're allowed into the real classroom.

Think of it this way: money is elementary school, and true riches are graduate school. You don't get to skip grades in God's Kingdom.

You don't get to bypass the fundamentals and jump straight to the advanced courses. If you can't pass arithmetic, you don't get to do calculus. If you can't handle dollars, you don't get to handle destiny. God has established an order, and that order requires mastery of the basics before promotion to the next level.

Here's the uncomfortable truth that many in the body of Christ need to hear: we are trying to operate in graduate-level anointing while failing elementary-level stewardship.

- We want to cast out devils, but we can't cast out debt.
- We want to heal the sick, but our finances are on life support.
- We want to see signs, wonders, and miracles, but we don't even have control of our own spending.
- We want authority over demons in the spiritual realm, but we haven't exercised authority over our credit cards in the natural realm.

God is showing us the path to promotion, and that path runs straight through our wallets!

WHAT ARE THE TRUE RICHES?

Jesus draws a clear contrast between *"unrighteous mammon"* and *"true riches." This* raises an important question: what exactly are the true riches He's referring to?

True riches are not money. True riches are what money qualifies you for. They include spiritual authority, anointing, peace. They are Kingdom influence, the capacity to shape culture, communities, and even nations for God's purposes. The operation of the gifts of the Spirit. They also include eternal rewards, treasure laid up in Heaven that cannot be stolen, corrupted, or lost. These are the things that matter. These are the things that last. These are the things God wants to give you.

But He often will not release them until you pass the money test.

This is because how you handle the temporary reveals how you'll handle the eternal. How you steward the material reveals how you'll steward the spiritual. Your faithfulness in the seen realm determines your authority in the unseen realm. If God can't trust you with a paycheck, He can't trust you with a city. If you mismanage your household budget, how will you manage the resources required for revival? If you're careless with the little He's already given, why would He entrust you with more?

This is the principle Jesus is teaching. Money is the proving ground. It's the test that determines whether you're ready for what God really wants to give you.

YOUR MONEY AND YOUR ANOINTING

I want you to seriously consider this next question, because it may be the most important financial principle you've ever encountered: what if your handling of money determines, to some extent, the amount of anointing God can release through your life? If this is even partly true, then we need to seriously consider the ramifications.

This is Jesus preaching, not some "prosperity pimp." He's the One who said, from the passage in Luke 16:10-12 that we just looked at: *"If therefore ye have not been faithful in the unrighteous mammon, who will commit to your trust the true riches?"*

The word *commit* in that verse means to entrust, to deposit, to hand over for safekeeping. God has true riches He wants to commit to you: spiritual authority, Kingdom influence, anointing, (non-salvific) eternal reward, but He's waiting to see how you handle the preliminary test.

Think about it from God's perspective for a moment. He has a generation to reach. He has cities to transform. He has nations to disciple. He has a bride to prepare for His Son's return. And He's looking for people He can trust with the resources and authority to get it done.

So He watches. He observes. He tests. Not because He's harsh or stingy, but because He's wise. A loving father doesn't give car keys to a child who hasn't learned to ride a bicycle. A wise employer doesn't hand the company credit card to someone who can't manage their personal account. And a sovereign God doesn't release unlimited anointing to someone who hasn't proven faithful with limited resources.

This test is God's way of *preparing you for* what He's already *prepared for you.* Pass the test, and promotion follows. Fail the test, and you stay in the same grade, praying the same prayers, believing for the same breakthroughs, wondering why nothing ever seems to change.

THE BOTTLENECK IN THE BODY OF CHRIST

Let me speak candidly for a moment about what I've observed in the body of Christ over the years. The Church is full of gifted people who are financially broke. We have prophets who can't pay their light bills. We have pastors who preach about God's provision on Sunday and lie awake worrying about money on Monday. And I'm not saying this to shame anyone. I'm saying it because this is the bottleneck that's holding back everything else.

This is one reason why revival tarries. This is one of the reasons why the harvest is delayed. This is why the wealth of the sinner is still sitting in the sinner's bank account instead of funding Kingdom work. God is waiting for a generation that will get this area right. He's looking for people who will treat money as the test it is—not as an end in itself, but as a qualifier for something far greater.

He's looking for people who will master the elementary so they can be trusted with the advanced. He's looking for people who will stop making excuses, stop blaming the economy, stop waiting for a lottery ticket or an inheritance, and start being faithful with what they already have.

That's who God promotes. That's who receives the true riches. That's who breaks out of the middle.

TWO MASTERS, ONE CHOICE

Jesus concludes this teaching with a statement that should settle the matter for every believer. Luke 16:13 says: *"No servant can serve two masters: for either he will hate the one, and love the other; or else he will hold to the one, and despise the other. Ye cannot serve God and mammon."*

This verse in the New International Version says it this way: *"No one can serve two masters. Either you will hate the one and love the other, or you will be devoted to the one and despise the other. You cannot serve both God and money."*

You cannot serve both God and money. Either money serves you, or you serve money. Either you master your finances, or your finances master you. Either you tell your dollars where to go, or you spend your life wondering where they went.

There is no neutral ground on this issue, and there is no "middle class" in God's Kingdom economy. There are stewards who pass the test and receive promotion, and there are those who remain stuck because they never took the test seriously.

The elementary test is sitting on your desk right now. It's in your bank account. It's in your spending habits. It's in your debt load. It's in your giving patterns. It's in the way you handle the *"least"* that God has already entrusted to you. Every purchase, every payment, every financial decision is part of the exam. And God does not grade on a curve; He grades on faithfulness.

Pass this test, and God will commit to your trust the true riches: the spiritual authority, the Kingdom influence, the anointing, and the (non-salvific) eternal reward that He's been waiting to release.

These things I'm talking about are not salvific or central to your salvation, but they are important for Kingdom advancement and leading others to salvation.

Fail this test, and you'll remain stuck in the middle: anointed but limited, called but constrained, believing for breakthrough but never quite breaking through.

The good news is that it's an open-book test. The principles are right there in Scripture. The strategies are available to anyone willing to learn. And God Himself is cheering for you to pass.

So let's keep going.

Now, let's talk about what may have been holding you back from even taking the test seriously.

22

PROSPERITY IS NOT INSTANT

As we have seen, one of the enemy's most effective deceptions in the body of Christ has been the idea that poverty is somehow spiritual. Somewhere along the way, believers started confusing lack with humility and financial hardship with holiness.

Poverty is not a badge of honor. It's a consequence of refusing wisdom. And shame accompanies it. Not shame that God puts on you, but shame that naturally results from living beneath your created potential. When you were designed for dominion but you are living in lack, something is wrong. When you were called to fund the Kingdom and you live in a free society, but you can't fund your own household, something is misaligned. That misalignment isn't because God has abandoned you. It's because, somewhere along the way, instruction was refused, reproof was rejected, or wisdom was ignored.

FOUR TYPES WHO MISS THE BLESSING

Over the years, I've observed that there are four types of people who never seem to break through financially, no matter how many sermons they hear or books they read. These aren't bad people. Many of them love God sincerely. But they have internal barriers that prevent them from receiving what God is trying to teach them about stewardship and prosperity.

The first type is the undecided: These are the people who agree with everything they hear but never actually commit to anything. They nod along during the sermon, highlight passages in their Bible, maybe even say *Amen* at the right moments. But when it's time to make a concrete decision, they hesitate.

They're waiting for a sign. They're waiting for the "right time." They're waiting until they feel more ready. And while they wait, nothing changes. James 1:8 describes this person: *"A double minded man is unstable in all his ways."*

Instability in your mind produces instability in your finances. You cannot waffle your way into wealth. At some point, you have to decide that you're going to get this area of your life right and then act on that decision.

The second type is the unteachable: This is the person Proverbs 13:18 is directly addressing—the one who refuses instruction. They already know everything. They've heard this before. They don't need another budget sermon or another stewardship class because they've "tried all that" and it didn't work.

What they don't realize is that their unwillingness to receive correction is the very thing that is blocking their breakthrough. Proverbs 12:1 says, *"Whoso loveth instruction loveth knowledge: but he that hateth reproof is brutish."*

That's strong language. God takes teachability seriously. If you want His blessing, you have to want His teaching even when it confronts areas you'd rather not examine.

The third type is the unfocused: These believers have good intentions but no follow-through. They get excited about a new financial strategy for about two weeks, then something else grabs their attention and the budget gets abandoned.

They start the debt snowball, make three payments, then forget about it when life gets busy. They set goals in January that are forgotten by March. Proverbs 24:30-34 paints a picture of this person:

> *I went by the field of the slothful, and by the vineyard of the man void of understanding; and, lo, it was all grown over with thorns, and nettles had covered the face thereof.... So shall thy poverty come as one that travelleth; and thy want as an armed man.*

Lack of focus leads to lack of fruit. Prosperity requires sustained attention over time, not bursts of enthusiasm followed by neglect.

The fourth type is the unexpectant: This might be the saddest category of all. These are believers who have been disappointed so many times that they've stopped expecting anything to change. They pray about their finances, but they don't really believe anything will happen. They hear teaching on prosperity, but in the back of their mind they're thinking, *That's nice for other people, but it probably won't work for me.*

Hope deferred has made their heart sick (see Proverbs 13:12), and that sickness has infected their faith. But here's what Matthew 9:29 says, "*...According to your faith be it unto you.*"

If you expect nothing, nothing is exactly what you'll receive. Expectation is the atmosphere in which miracles happen. You have to believe that God's principles will actually work for you—in your situation, with your income—starting now.

Which of these four categories describes you? Be honest. You can't fix what you won't face. And the good news is that all four of these barriers can be overcome. The *undecided* can decide today. The *unteachable* can humble themselves and receive instruction. The *unfocused* can develop discipline. The *unexpectant* can stir up their faith and start believing again. None of these conditions are permanent unless you choose to let them be.

TRUST THE PROCESS

Now, having said all that, I need to balance it with an equally important truth: prosperity is not instant. Just because you've decided to get your finances right doesn't mean you'll be debt-free by Friday, although I've seen God do stranger things on many occasions. In fact, I encourage you to believe for instant miracles while at the same time walking in patience (Hebrews 6:12). Just because you've humbled yourself to receive instruction, it doesn't mean a check is arriving in tomorrow's mail. God's Kingdom operates on process—not magic. Understanding this will save you from discouragement when the breakthrough doesn't happen as quickly as you'd like it to.

Consider David. In 1 Samuel 16, the prophet Samuel came to Jesse's house and anointed the youngest son, a teenager tending sheep, to be the next king of Israel. David received a genuine anointing from God. The Spirit of the Lord came upon him from that day forward. The calling was real. The promise was authentic. The destiny was set.

But David didn't sit on the throne until he was 30 years old. That's roughly 13 years between the anointing and the assignment. Thirteen years between the promise and the palace. Thirteen years of running from Saul, hiding in caves, leading a ragtag band of men who were in debt and discontent. Thirteen years learning to trust God in obscurity before he could lead a nation in prominence.

Why does God work this way? The reason is that anointing alone isn't enough.

- You need character to sustain what calling initiates.
- You need wisdom to steward what faith obtains.
- You need process to prepare you for the position.

If David had been crowned king at 17, he wouldn't have been ready. The cave experiences, the wilderness seasons, and the years of warfare and waiting shaped him into the king that Israel needed.

The same is true for your financial breakthrough. God may have anointed you for prosperity, but He's not going to skip the process that prepares you to steward it. Perhaps you are in the cave right now. You're in the in-between season; you've received the promise, but you haven't seen the fulfillment yet. Don't despise the process. Don't look for short-cuts. Don't fall for get-rich-quick schemes that promise to bypass the years of faithful stewardship God is using to shape you.

The process isn't punishment, it's preparation. Trust it.

EXCELLING IN THE GRACE OF GIVING

There's one more piece we need to address before we move into practical strategies, and it might be the most important of all. Everything we've discussed—passing the elementary test, overcoming internal barriers, trusting the process—leads to this: you are being prepared to give.

Biblical prosperity has never been about accumulation for its own sake. And this is where many believers miss it. They want the wealth transfer, but they haven't developed the heart of a giver. They want the abundance, but they're still holding their current resources with a closed fist. And God, in His wisdom, will not pour new wine into old wineskins.

In 2 Corinthians 8, Paul writes to the Corinthian church about the offering being collected for the suffering believers in Jerusalem. But before he makes his appeal, he points them to an unexpected example, the churches of Macedonia:

> *Moreover, brethren, we do you to wit of the grace of God bestowed on the churches of Macedonia; how that in a great trial of affliction the abundance of their joy and their deep poverty abounded unto the riches of their liberality. For to their power,*

> *I bear record, yea, and beyond their power they were willing of themselves; praying us with much intreaty that we would receive the gift, and take upon them the fellowship of the ministering to the saints* (2 Corinthians 8:1-4).

Look at what Paul is describing. These Macedonian believers were in *"deep poverty"* and *"great trial of affliction."* By every natural measure, they were the last people who should have been giving. They were the ones who should have been receiving. But instead, they begged Paul for the opportunity to participate in the offering. They gave beyond their ability. They gave out of their lack. And Paul calls this *"the grace of God bestowed"* on them.

Generosity is a grace. It's not just a discipline or a duty, it's a spiritual gift, and it's as powerful as prophecy or the working of miracles. And like every other grace, it can be grown and developed. That's why Paul goes on to tell the Corinthians:

> *Therefore, as ye abound in every thing, in faith, and utterance, and knowledge, and in all diligence, and in your love to us, see that ye abound in this grace also* (2 Corinthians 8:7).

The Corinthians were excelling in faith, in speech, in knowledge, in diligence, in love. They were spiritually mature in many areas. But Paul challenged them to excel in *"this grace also,"* the grace of giving.

In other words, generosity isn't automatic. It's something you learn to abound in. It's something you grow in. It's something you must intentionally develop.

This is why the practical strategies we're about to discuss matter so much. Getting out of debt isn't just about improving your credit score or reducing your stress. It's about freeing up resources so you can excel in the grace of giving. Building wealth is about having something to give when God prompts you.

The goal of biblical prosperity is not a bigger house, it's a bigger offering (though you will get both). It's not a fatter retirement account, it's a fatter harvest for the Kingdom. When you truly get this, you'll stop looking for harvests and start looking for seeds.

You're not just trying to escape the "middle" for your own sake. You're positioning yourself to become a conduit of blessing that can change your family, your church, your city, and your generation. You're preparing to participate in the wealth transfer that Scripture promises—not as a recipient only, but as a distributor of God's resources wherever they're needed most.

So let's get practical. Let's talk about the specific strategies that will move you from where you are to where God is calling you to be. It's time to master the money so the money stops mastering you.

MASTER DEBT OR DEBT WILL MASTER YOU

Everything we've covered so far has been building to this moment. We've exposed the illusion of the middle class. We've examined the elementary test that determines your promotion. We've identified the internal barriers that keep people stuck. We've established that prosperity is a process, not a lottery. And we've seen that the ultimate goal is excelling in the grace of giving so that you can participate in God's end-time wealth transfer.

I want to be very clear about something: you cannot spiritualize or meditate your way out of debt. Faith without works is dead, and that principle applies to your finances just as much as it applies to anything else. Yes, God is your Provider. Yes, He can and will do miracles. Yes, the wealth of the sinner is laid up for the just. But God has also given you wisdom, principles, and practical strategies, and He expects you to use them.

Think about it this way. If you were sick, you would pray for healing. But you would also go to the doctor, take the medicine, and follow the treatment plan. Generally speaking, unless God told you otherwise, you wouldn't refuse medical care and say, "I'm just trusting God." That's not faith, that's foolishness. The same logic applies to your financial health. Pray for provision, absolutely. Believe God for breakthrough, without question. But also make a budget. Also cut unnecessary spending. Also attack your debt with a plan.

Faith and practicality are not enemies, they're partners.

The apostle James addressed this exact issue when he wrote:

> *What doth it profit, my brethren, though a man say he hath faith, and have not works? can faith save him? If a brother or sister be naked, and destitute of daily food, and one of you say unto them, Depart in peace, be ye warmed and filled; notwithstanding ye give them not those things which are needful to the body; what doth it profit?* (James 2:14-16)

James is saying that faith must be accompanied by corresponding action. Believing for financial freedom while refusing to change your financial behavior is like telling a hungry person to be filled without giving them food. It sounds spiritual, but it accomplishes nothing.

Debt is not going to leave your life until you force it out. It's not going to pack its bags and move on because you attended a prosperity conference. It's not going to release its grip because you gave a big offering. Those things have their place, but they are not substitutes for discipline, strategy, and sustained effort over time. You have to fight for your freedom. You have to be intentional. You have to make a plan and work the plan until the plan works.

Proverbs 22:7 states it plainly: *"The rich ruleth over the poor, and the borrower is servant to the lender."*

Notice the word *servant*. In the Hebrew, it's the word *ebed*—the same word used for a slave or bondservant. When you owe money, you are in bondage to the one you owe. Your labor, your income, or your future earnings don't fully belong to you. A portion of everything you make is already claimed by someone else.

You work, but the fruit of your work flows to Mastercard, to Sallie Mae, to the mortgage company, and to the car dealership. You're generating wealth, but it's building someone else's kingdom instead of yours.

This is why getting out of debt is not optional for the believer who wants to walk in their full calling. As long as you're in bondage to lenders, you cannot fully serve God. Your resources are divided. Your options are limited. Your ability to respond to Kingdom opportunities is constrained. When God says "Give," you have to check with your creditors first. When God says "Go," you have to calculate whether you can afford it. Debt puts a middleman between you and obedience and that middleman doesn't care about your calling.

But here's the good news, debt can be defeated. It's not invincible. It's not permanent. It's not your destiny. Millions of people have climbed out of debt using proven strategies, and you can too. It will require sacrifice. It will require discipline. It will require saying "no" to what you want, so you can say "yes" to what matters more.

But, it can be done. On the other side of that process, there is a freedom you may have never experienced, the freedom to give generously, save wisely, and respond instantly when God speaks.

The strategies I'm about to share with you are not theories. These are battle-tested, practically proven methods that have helped countless people break the chains of debt and step into financial freedom. Some of them will seem simple, maybe too simple.

Don't mistake simplicity for ineffectiveness. The basics work. The fundamentals win.

If you will commit to applying these strategies consistently over time, you will see results. So grab a pen. Take notes. Turn to the next chapter and get ready to fight for your freedom!

23

TEN DEBT-DESTROYING STRATEGIES

Over the years, I have studied every possible debt-destroying strategy I could get my hands on. I've collected them, used them, and shared far and wide the ones that worked.

Financial teachers, counselors, and advisors have been recommending variations of these strategies for generations. Some have become so popular that they've been given catchy names and built into entire systems. That's fine. Truth doesn't need to be novel to be powerful, and wisdom doesn't require a trademark to transform your life.

What makes these strategies *Kingdom* strategies is not their novelty, it's their biblical foundation. Long before any modern financial guru put pen to paper, God's Word was teaching these principles. The concepts of budgeting, saving, systematic debt elimination, and wise stewardship are woven throughout Scripture from the storehouse of Joseph to the gleaning of Ruth to the faithful servants in Jesus' parables. We're not borrowing from the world, we're reclaiming what belongs to God's people.

STRATEGY 1

Establish Your Vision and Build Your Plan

Proverbs 29:18 declares: "*Where there is no vision, the people perish....*"

The Hebrew word translated *perish* means to cast off restraint and to become undisciplined. Without a clear financial vision, you will spend impulsively and wonder where the money went.

Start by tracking every expenditure for thirty days: Don't judge it; just document it. You cannot redirect your resources until you see where they're actually going. This is the financial equivalent of Haggai 1:5: *"Consider your ways."*

Then, create a written budget and a plan that tells every dollar where to go before the month begins: Habakkuk 2:2 instructs us to: *"Write the vision, and make it plain…."*

Every dollar has an assignment. Your budget is your written vision for your money. When it's clear and specific, you can run with it.

STRATEGY 2

Find Hidden Treasure in Your Current Spending

Before attacking debt aggressively, examine your existing expenses for waste. Many households have hundreds of dollars leaking out monthly through such items as forgotten subscriptions or services that they could get cheaper elsewhere.

Review every recurring charge. Cancel what you don't use. Call your insurance, cell phone, and Internet providers and ask for better rates. This is key! Often, if you just talk to these companies, you can get better pricing. Get competitor quotes and use them as leverage. Look into refinancing if rates have dropped.

Search for unclaimed money—old savings bonds, state-held property, unredeemed rewards. Every dollar you find is a dollar deployed against debt.

STRATEGY 3

Build a Storehouse Foundation

Set aside funds for emergency use only. This is the Storehouse Principle. You must prepare for the unexpected so that a flat tire doesn't become a financial catastrophe.

Joseph stored grain during times of plenty in order to survive famine. Your initial storehouse keeps common emergencies from derailing your progress.

I also encourage you to build what I call a giving reserve, a storehouse ready for the moment God speaks. He gives seed to the sower, and a sower always has seed in hand before the opportunity arrives. Start simple: keep $100 set apart in your wallet, not for bills, not for coffee, not for emergencies, this money has one job, and that's Spirit-directed giving above your tithe. When God nudges you, you're already ready. You move when He moves.

As you become savings-minded, make sure you're equally seed-minded.

While you're doing this, ***commit to adding no new debt to your life.*** You cannot escape a pit if you are still digging.

STRATEGY 4

Negotiate and Reclaim the Interest

Call every credit card company and request a lower interest rate. Explain that you're paying off debt and considering transferring to a competitor. This works more often than you'd expect. Even small reductions save real money.

Explore balance transfer opportunities—some cards offer promotional periods with zero percent interest for twelve to eighteen months. Move high-interest debt strategically, but read the terms and have a plan to eliminate the balance before rates increase. The goal is to stop the bleeding so more of your payment attacks principal instead of enriching lenders.

STRATEGY 5

The Jericho Method: One Wall at a Time

This is the heart of debt elimination. ***List all debts except your mortgage from smallest to largest balance.*** While making minimum payments on everything else, throw every extra dollar at the smallest debt until it's gone. Then apply the payment you were making to the next smallest debt. As each debt falls like the walls of Jericho, your payment will grow larger, and your momentum will increase.

Financial advisors such as Dave Ramsey and others have popularized this, and for good reason—it works! Take down one wall at a time, until they all fall.

STRATEGY 6

The Gleaning Principle: Every Small Amount Matters

Small amounts, consistently applied, add up to significant results.

- Apply tax refunds, work bonuses, garage sale proceeds, and found money directly to debt.
- Pick up overtime or side work temporarily.
- Sell items you don't need.

Individually these amounts seem small, but like Ruth's handfuls, they accumulate. Over a year, these "gleanings" can add thousands to your debt payoff while keeping you engaged in the fight.

STRATEGY 7

Redirect Your Tax Refund

If you consistently receive large tax refunds, you're lending the government your money interest-free all year. ***Consider adjusting your W-4 so that your withholdings match your actual liability.*** The extra money in each paycheck can be used to attack debt immediately, rather than waiting until April.

When refunds do come, resist spending them on something fun. Apply them directly to your Jericho Method. That refund could eliminate an entire small debt, or it could make a significant dent in a larger one.

STRATEGY 8

Eliminate Your Mortgage

Once consumer debt is gone, turn to your mortgage. This sounds impossible, but consider: you now have a fully loaded payment that was previously spread across multiple debts. The sum of all those payments is now free to be applied your mortgage.

Make extra principal payments monthly. Apply bonuses and tax refunds to the balance. What seemed like a 30-year sentence can often become seven to ten years with focused effort.

Imagine life with no mortgage! That freedom is achievable for anyone willing to work the plan.

STRATEGY 9

Break the Car Payment Cycle

The average car payment now exceeds $700 monthly, with loan terms stretching to six years. People finance vehicles they can't afford, watch them depreciate, then trade them in underwater, rolling negative equity into new loans.

Here's the principle: if you can't pay cash, you can't afford that car. Once out of debt, save for your next vehicle. Drive your current car while it's safe and reliable. Pay cash for quality used vehicles. You'll never have a car payment again, saving hundreds of thousands over your lifetime for Kingdom purposes.

STRATEGY 10

Use Artificial Intelligence

We're living in an unprecedented era where powerful tools are available to anyone with a smartphone or computer. The same technology that you may be using to read or listen to this book can become a valuable ally in your debt-elimination journey.

This isn't about replacing wisdom or discipline, it's about using every tool God has made available in your generation. I wrote about this extensively in my book, *Summoning the Demon: AI, Aliens and the Antichrist.* Ecclesiastes 10:10 says: *"If the iron be blunt, and he do not whet the edge, then must he put to more strength: but wisdom is profitable to direct."* A sharp tool makes the work easier. AI is a tool and a sharp one. Here's how to put it to work:

- Upload your bank statements to an AI assistant and ask it to categorize your spending and identify subscriptions you've forgotten about.
- Ask it to create a customized debt payoff plan using the Jericho Method with your specific balances and interest rates.
- Have it calculate exactly how much you will save by paying an extra $100 monthly toward your highest-interest debt.
- Request negotiation scripts before you call your credit card company to ask for a lower rate.
- Ask for side hustle ideas based on your specific skills and available hours.

- Use AI to compare insurance quotes, find better service providers, or analyze whether a balance transfer makes sense for your situation.
- The same technology that powers billion-dollar corporations is now available to help you break free from debt. Wisdom says use it. Ask questions, get strategies, run the numbers, and let AI do the heavy lifting on research and calculations while you focus on execution and discipline.
- Then do what I do: Ask it to explain it all to you as if you were a five-year-old. You have a tireless assistant helping you find every possible advantage.

TRAIN UP A CHILD

We have been discussing how to break free from the crippling power of debt. We have been exploring ways to eliminate that debt and master stewardship over our resources. This is vital information for our everyday lives if we want to fulfill the highest and best God has for us.

But everything we've discussed means very little if we don't pass it on. The goal should be generational freedom. The wealth transfer we've been discussing throughout this book isn't meant to stop with you. It's meant to flow through you to your children and your children's children.

Proverbs 22:6 is one of the most quoted verses in Christian parenting: *"Train up a child in the way he should go: and when he is old, he will not depart from it."*

We've built entire Sunday school curricula around this verse. We teach our kids Bible stories, memory verses, worship songs, and moral principles—and so we should. But here's what most of us have missed: look at the very next verse: *"The rich ruleth over the poor, and the borrower is servant to the lender"* (Proverbs 22:7).

These verses are connected. Solomon isn't randomly jumping from parenting to finance. He's telling us that training up a child includes teaching them about money, debt, and stewardship. The context of *"train up a child"* flows directly into the warning about borrowers becoming servants. Biblical parenting isn't complete without biblical financial education.

Think about what's actually happening in many Christian homes. We raise our children in church. We teach them to worship. We take them to youth group and summer camp. We pray over them and dedicate them to the Lord.

And then they turn 18, go off to college, and sign student loan documents that will enslave them for the next 20 years. They get their first credit card and max it out within months. They finance cars they can't afford. They buy houses with no money down. And suddenly, the child we trained up in the way they should go is serving the kingdom of darkness with their labor because the borrower is servant to the lender.

This isn't an exaggeration—it's an epidemic. Young believers who love Jesus and want to serve Him are financially paralyzed before they even start their adult lives. They feel as though they can't tithe because they are drowning in debt. They can't give to missions because they're barely making minimum payments.

They can't respond to God's call on their lives because they're chained to a desk paying off debt they accumulated before they knew any better. We failed to train them in the way they should go, financially. This has to change with this generation.

Start teaching your children about money as soon as they can count. Give them opportunities to earn, save, give, sow, and spend wisely. Let them see your budget. Talk openly about financial decisions. Explain why you're saying "no" to certain purchases. Demonstrate the Jericho Method as you eliminate your own debt. Show them what it looks like to live free.

When they're teenagers, involve them in family financial discussions. Teach them about interest and how it works for you when you save and against you when you borrow. Show them the math on what a car payment really costs over five years. Walk them through student loan calculations before they ever set foot on a college campus. Prepare them for the financial wolves waiting to devour them the moment they turn 18.

Deuteronomy 6:6-7 says:

> *And **these words**, which I command thee this day, shall be in thine heart: And thou shalt teach them diligently unto thy children, and shalt talk of them when thou sittest in thine house, and when thou walkest by the way, and when thou liest down, and when thou risest up.*

Financial stewardship is part of *"these words."* It is not separate from discipleship. Talk about it at dinner. Discuss it during car rides. Make it as normal as prayer and Bible reading.

The generation you're raising can be the first in a long time to start adulthood debt-free. They can be the generation that funds revival instead of funding banks. They can be the generation that walks in the wealth transfer because they were trained to steward it. But it starts with you:

- Decide that biblical parenting includes biblical financial education.
- Do the work to train them up in the way they should go.

BREAK OUT!

Over these past few chapters, you have learned that the middle class is a debt-induced illusion designed to keep you just comfortable enough so that you do not cry out for more, but never quite prosperous enough to fulfill your Kingdom assignment. We exposed the statistics: the middle class is shrinking, weakening, and being propped up by debt that previous generations never carried. We have been sedated into settling for less than what God has promised.

We examined the elementary test of Luke 16. Money is *"that which is least."* Passing the money test is elementary school. True riches are graduate school. Your handling of finances determines the anointing God can release through your life. We cannot keep failing the money test and expecting spiritual promotion.

We have identified the barriers—the *undecided,* the *unteachable,* the *unfocused,* and the *unexpectant*—and declared that none of these conditions are permanent. We have established that prosperity is a process, not a lottery, and that excelling in the grace of giving is the ultimate goal of biblical wealth.

Then we got practical with Kingdom strategies to destroy debt and finally, we committed to training the next generation, recognizing that Proverbs 22:6 and 22:7 are connected. Biblical parenting includes biblical finance.

Now stand up and declare this over your life:

I declare that I am middle no more.

I refuse to be numbed by debt into thinking I'm okay when I'm not free.

I accept the elementary test. I will be faithful with that which is least so God can trust me with true riches.

I am not undecided, unteachable, unfocused, or unexpectant. I receive instruction, and I expect breakthrough.

I commit to the process. I will use every strategy, every tool, and every opportunity to destroy debt and walk in financial freedom.

I will train up my children in the way they should go including the way they should handle money.

The wealth of the sinner is laid up for me.

I am preparing to receive it and steward it for Kingdom purpose.

I am not a borrower. I am not a servant to lenders.

I am a child of the King, and I will walk in the freedom He purchased for me.

I am middle no more.

In Jesus' name, amen!

PART SEVEN

SOWING AND REAPING— IT'S THE LAW!

24

WHAT ABOUT "SEED FAITH"?

Let's not pretend this isn't a controversial subject. The moment you mention *seed faith* in certain Christian circles, you can feel the temperature in the room change. Eyes roll. Arms cross. Defenses go up.

For some believers, the very phrase has become synonymous with manipulation, greed, and televangelists asking for money. They've seen the abuses. They've heard the stories. And they've decided that the entire concept must be rejected.

I understand the skepticism. There have been abuses. There have been preachers who twisted Scripture to fill their own pockets. There have been vulnerable people manipulated into giving money they couldn't afford to ministries that didn't steward it well. Those abuses are real, and they're grievous. But here's the question we must answer honestly: *Is seed-faith biblical or isn't it?*

If the principle of sowing financial seed and expecting a harvest is actually found in Scripture, then we don't get to throw it out just because some people have misused it. Consider this:

- We don't reject the doctrine of grace because some ministers have turned it into a license to sin.
- We don't abandon the gifts of the Spirit because some have operated in the flesh.
- And we don't discard a biblical financial principle because some preachers have abused it for personal gain.

The abuse of a truth doesn't invalidate the truth, it just means we need to understand it correctly.

So let's settle this. Not with opinions. Not with emotions. Not with reactions to what we've seen on television. Let's settle it with Scripture.

THE DOCTRINE OF JESUS

In Mark 4:2-3, Jesus begins teaching in parables. Let's take a look:

> *And he taught them many things by parables, and said unto them in his doctrine, Hearken; Behold, there went out a sower to sow....*

Verse 2 says something fascinating: Jesus *"said unto them in his doctrine."* Stop right there! This is *His* doctrine, His teaching. Not Baptist doctrine. Not Methodist doctrine. Not Pentecostal doctrine. This is what Jesus Himself thinks about Scripture.

The word *doctrine* simply means what an individual or group understands about Scripture, what they think about it. It's the lens by which we understand God's Word. So Mark 4 is revealing to us what goes through the mind of Jesus when He considers the promises of God. This is how He thinks.

And if we want the mind of Christ as Philippians 2:5 instructs, *"Let this mind be in you, which was also in Christ Jesus,"* then we need to understand how He thinks about everything: salvation, healing, provision, and yes, finances.

You have no doubt heard the parable of the sower Jesus told here in Mark 4. He describes a man who went out to sow, whose seed fell upon several different types of ground, which eventually bore a multiplied harvest. He explained this parable to His disciples, and He used it as a springboard to explain more about the how the Kingdom of God works. Then, He went on to ask His disciples this question: *"Know ye not this parable? and how then will ye know all parables?"*

In other words, this parable is the master key. If you don't understand this one, you won't understand any of them.

The seed and harvest principle isn't one teaching among many, it's the foundation for understanding everything Jesus taught.

The doctrine of Jesus is seed-based.

When Jesus thinks about salvation, He thinks about it through the lens of seed and harvest. When He thinks about the Kingdom of God, He uses seed and harvest language. When He thinks about faith, He compares it to a seed. And when He thinks about finances—giving and receiving, sowing and reaping—He applies the same principle.

This isn't a televangelist's gimmick. This is the doctrine of Jesus Christ.

PARABLES ARE PARALLELS

Before we go any further, we need to understand how parables work. A parable is nothing more than a parallel or a natural illustration that reveals spiritual truth. Jesus used earthly stories to communicate heavenly realities. And here's the key: whatever is true for the natural item in the parable is also true for the spiritual reality it represents.

When Jesus talks about a farmer sowing seed, He's not giving an agriculture lesson. He's revealing how the Kingdom operates. And whatever is true about natural seed—its power to reproduce, its need for good ground, its process of growth, its potential for multiplication—is also true for the spiritual realities He's teaching about.

This means that when Scripture applies seed-language to money, we're not forcing a connection. We're following the parallel that Jesus Himself established. And as we'll see throughout this chapter, Scripture repeatedly treats financial giving as seed with the potential for supernatural harvest.

THE POWER OF A SEED

Every farmer understands that a seed has power. You can hold a tiny seed in the palm of your hand—something so small it seems insignificant. Yet locked inside that seed is the potential to produce a harvest that weighs thousands of times more than the seed itself.

One kernel of corn can produce a stalk with multiple ears, each ear containing hundreds of kernels. One apple seed can become a tree that produces thousands of apples over its lifetime, each containing seeds of its own. The multiplication potential inside a single seed is staggering.

Seed faith isn't treating God like a genie in a bottle. It's reverencing His design.

God built reproduction and multiplication into the very nature of a seed. Genesis 1:11 records God's command:

> *...Let the earth bring forth grass, the herb yielding seed, and the fruit tree yielding fruit after his kind, whose seed is in itself....*

From the beginning, seed was created with the power to reproduce after its kind. This is the law of seedtime and harvest that God established before He ever created man.

Now here's what most believers have missed: Scripture doesn't limit seed power to agriculture. Throughout the Bible, God applies the seed principle to multiple spiritual realities. If we want to understand how the Kingdom operates, we need to recognize everything Scripture assigns to the seed.

FAITH IS A SEED

In Matthew 17:20, Jesus told His disciples: "*If ye have faith as a grain of mustard seed, ye shall say unto this mountain, Remove hence to yonder place; and it shall remove; and nothing shall be impossible unto you."*

Notice He didn't say "faith as big as a mustard seed." He said, *"faith as a grain of mustard seed."* He is comparing the nature of faith to the nature of a seed. A mustard seed is one of the smallest seeds, yet it grows into one of the largest garden plants. Faith operates the same way. It may start small, but it has the inherent power to grow and produce results far beyond its initial size.

Paul confirms this in 2 Thessalonians 1:3: *"...your faith groweth exceedingly...."*

Faith can grow. Faith can increase. Faith can multiply. Why? Because faith has a seed nature. It's designed to reproduce and expand.

THE KINGDOM OF GOD IS A SEED

In Mark 4:26-27, Jesus says, *"So is the kingdom of God, as if a man should cast seed into the ground; and should sleep, and rise night and day, and the seed should spring and grow up, he knoweth not how."*

The Kingdom of God operates like seed. When you plant Kingdom principles in your life, they don't produce instant, visible results. There's a process, a period when the seed is underground—invisible and seemingly inactive. But something is happening beneath the surface. The seed is germinating. Roots are forming. Life is stirring. And eventually, what was planted in hiddenness breaks through into visible manifestation.

This is critical to understand. God's ways are like seed not only in how they operate but in how they spread. When you begin operating by Kingdom principles in one area of your life, finances, for example, you will find those same principles begin to affect other areas: your relationships, your health, your thinking. The seed of the Kingdom, once planted, keeps reproducing.

CHRISTIANS ARE SEED

Galatians 3:29 declares: "*And if ye be Christ's, then are ye Abraham's seed, and heirs according to the promise.*"

You are seed. You carry the spiritual DNA of Abraham, the father of faith, the friend of God, the one to whom the promises were made. And just as God told Abraham (see Genesis 15:5) that his descendants would be as uncountable as the stars in the heavens, you are now part of that number.

If you are seed, then you have a seed nature. You were designed to be planted, to die to yourself, and to produce a harvest of righteousness that multiplies beyond your individual life. You're not meant to be hoarded or preserved in a jar. You're meant to be sown into the earth, into your community, your sphere of influence, your generation so that you can reproduce after your kind.

JESUS IS THE SEED

In John 12:24, Jesus makes a profound statement about Himself: "*Verily, verily, I say unto you, Except a corn of wheat fall into the ground and die, it abideth alone: but if it die, it bringeth forth much fruit.*"

Some Greeks had come wanting to see Jesus, and instead of granting them an audience, He gave them a revelation. He explained Himself through the lens of seed.

Jesus was the corn (the seed) of the wheat. He would fall into the ground and be buried in a tomb for three days. He would die. But His death would not be the end. It would be the planting.

And from that single seed, planted in the earth and resurrected by the power of God, would come a harvest of souls beyond numbering that continues to multiply 2,000 years later.

This is how Jesus thought about everything. When He considered His own mission, His own death, His own purpose, He saw it through the grid of seed and harvest. This is His doctrine.

MONEY IS A SEED

Now we arrive at the point that makes everyone uncomfortable—but Scripture is clear. In 2 Corinthians 9:6, Paul writes, and I quote from the Living Bible for clarity: *"But remember this—if you give little, you will get little. A farmer who plants just a few seeds will get only a small crop, but if he plants much, he will reap much."*

Paul is talking about financial giving. The entire context of 2 Corinthians 8 and 9 is a collection being taken for the poor saints in Jerusalem. Paul is receiving an offering, and he applies seed-and-harvest language directly to it. Give little, get little. Plant much, reap much.

A few verses later, in 2 Corinthians 9:10, Paul goes even further: *"Now he that ministereth seed to the sower both minister bread for your food, and multiply your seed sown, and increase the fruits of your righteousness."*

Look at the precision of that verse. God ministers seed to the sower—not to the hoarder, not to the consumer—but to the one who plants. And what does God do with the seed that is sown? He multiplies it.

The seed you keep doesn't multiply. The seed you eat doesn't multiply. Only the seed you sow enters the multiplication cycle.

This is why money has the potential for supernatural increase. It's not because of Wall Street strategies or investment portfolios. It's not because it's some sort of divine slot machine. It's because God designed financial seed to operate by the same law that governs every seed in His Kingdom. Sow it, and it can multiply. Hoard it, and it remains alone.

THE PRINCIPLE IS CONSISTENT

This seed principle isn't applied randomly throughout Scripture. It's applied consistently to the most important realities of the Kingdom. Faith is a seed. The Kingdom is a seed. Christians are seed. Jesus Himself is the seed. And money, when given according to Kingdom principles, functions as seed.

If someone rejects seed-faith teaching when it comes to money, they need to explain why Scripture applies seed language to finances just as clearly as it applies seed language to faith. You cannot accept Matthew 17:20 and reject 2 Corinthians 9:6. They operate by the same principle. They reflect the same doctrine. They come from the same God, the Lord of the Harvest.

This means that Christians should be *sowers*, but how many are merely *throwers?* There's a profound difference between the two, and understanding it will change how you approach every offering for the rest of your life.

A thrower is careless, random, disconnected from outcome. He drops something in a bucket the same way he'd toss a coin to a street performer, a momentary gesture with no thought of return, no expectation of harvest, no follow-up whatsoever. He's tipping God, not partnering with Him.

A sower is entirely different. A sower is intentional. A sower selects seed carefully, examines the ground, considers the timing, and plants with purpose. A sower doesn't throw seed into the wind and hope for the best. He places it in soil he's prepared, at a depth he's calculated, in a season he's discerned. And after the planting, the sower's work isn't finished. He waters. He watches. He protects. He tends what he's sown with the same intentionality he used when he planted it.

If money is seed then your giving should carry that same level of intentionality. What are you sowing for? Where are you planting? What harvest are you expecting? And after you've given, are you watering that seed with prayer, protecting it with faith, and tending it with expectation? Or did you throw an offering in a bucket, check the box, and never think about it again?

Throwing produces tips. Sowing produces harvests. We'll examine this more closely later, but for now, settle this in your spirit: God isn't looking for tippers. He's looking for sowers. And He's promised to multiply seed to the sower, not to the one who mindlessly throws and walks away.

SKEPTICS, HATERS, AND WATCHDOGS

If the seed principle is so clearly taught in Scripture—and it is—then why do so many sincere Christians reject it? Why does the mere mention of giving to receive trigger such strong negative reactions in certain circles? Why are there Bible-believing, Jesus-loving people who read the same passages we've examined and come away with completely different conclusions?

The answer is found in something Jesus said to His disciples in Mark 4:11. Think back to the parable of the sower we just examined. After teaching the parable of the sower to the multitudes, Jesus withdrew with His inner circle. When they were alone, the disciples asked Him about the parable. And His response reveals something crucial about how Kingdom truth operates:

> *And he said unto them, Unto you it is given to know the mystery of the kingdom of God: but unto them that are without, all these things are done in parables.*

The Amplified Bible makes it even clearer:

> *He said to them, "The mystery of the kingdom of God has been given to you [who have teachable hearts], but those who are*

outside [the unbelievers, the spiritually blind] get everything in parables (Mark 4:11 AMP).

You have to be able to see the principle before you can operate in it. You have to perceive the law of seedtime and harvest before you can benefit from it. And that seeing, that perceiving, comes through spiritual birth and the ongoing illumination of the Holy Spirit.

MANY CRITICS ARGUE FROM OUTSIDE

Many critics of seed-faith teaching are arguing from the outside. If you listen carefully to their arguments, you will notice they're not engaging with the actual Scriptures, they're reacting to the abuses they've witnessed. They're not wrestling with Genesis 8:22 or Mark 4:11 or 2 Corinthians 9:6, they're rejecting what they saw on television at 2 a.m. That's just cynicism. Many act as though cynicism is the tenth fruit of the Spirit, but I can assure you, it is not.

Hosea 4:6 says: *"My people are destroyed for lack of knowledge...."*

Not lack of sincerity. Not lack of effort. Not lack of desire. Lack of knowledge. God's people perish—cut off, silenced, brought to nothing—because they don't know what they need to know.

Some people are right in their hearts but wrong in their heads. They love God. They want to honor Him. They would never intentionally operate outside His will. But they've never received revelation of how His Kingdom economy functions.

They've also been propagandized against prosperity. So they work hard, give sporadically, pray desperately, and wonder why abundance never comes.

Meanwhile, other believers who may have no more sincerity or effort than the first group are experiencing supernatural provision. They give, and it comes back. They sow, and they reap. They operate by laws that the first group doesn't even know exist. The difference isn't favoritism. God shows no favoritism. The difference is knowledge.

How do you move from confusion to clarity, from skepticism to revelation?

First, you must be born again. Spiritual reality requires spiritual birth. If you've never surrendered your life to Jesus Christ, that's where you start. You cannot see the Kingdom until you've been born into it.

Second, you must ask for revelation. James 1:5 says: *"If any of you lack wisdom, let him ask of God, that giveth to all men liberally, and upbraideth not; and it shall be given him."* God doesn't mock people who come to Him with honest questions. He gives wisdom liberally to those who ask.

Third, you must approach Scripture with humility rather than defensiveness. If your theological grid won't allow certain passages to mean what they plainly say, your grid needs to change, not Scripture. Come to the Word asking, "What are You saying, Lord?" rather than "How do I make this fit what I already believe?"

Finally, you must be willing to act on what you receive. Revelation isn't given for information; revelation is given for transformation. When God shows you something about seedtime and harvest, He expects you to plant. When He illuminates the principle of giving and receiving, He expects you to give. Knowledge without application isn't really knowledge at all. It's just data.

THE LAW OF SEEDTIME AND HARVEST

Everything we've discussed so far, the seed nature of faith, the Kingdom, Christians, Jesus, and money rests on a foundation that God Himself established at the very beginning of human history after the flood. It's found in Genesis 8:22, and it's one of the most important verses in the Bible for understanding how God's economy operates:

> *While the earth remaineth, seedtime and harvest, and cold and heat, and summer and winter, and day and night shall not cease.*

Read that again slowly. God is making a covenant declaration—a promise that will remain in effect as long as the earth exists. And notice what He places in the same category as the rotation of seasons and the cycle of day and night: seedtime and harvest. It's not a cultural principle limited to an agricultural society.

It's a law as fixed and reliable as gravity, as certain as the sunrise. As long as this planet keeps spinning, the law of seedtime and harvest remains in effect. You can count on it the same way you count on summer following spring and morning following night.

A LAW, NOT A LOTTERY

Many believers have treated financial blessing like a lottery or a random, unpredictable, divine whim. They pray for provision the way someone buys a scratch-off ticket, hoping they'll be the lucky one who hits the jackpot. And when blessing doesn't come, they assume God said no or that it wasn't His will or that they must not have had enough faith. But seedtime and harvest isn't a lottery. It's a law. It's a principle that if faithfully practiced over time, will yield results.

A farmer doesn't plant corn and then wonder nervously whether the universe will randomly decide to give him a crop. He understands the law. He knows that seed plus soil plus time plus tending equals harvest. There's no mystery about it. There's no anxiety about whether it will work. He plants with confidence because he's operating according to established, unchanging principles.

The same should be true for the believer who understands Kingdom economics. You don't give and then anxiously hope that God will decide to bless you. You sow with confidence because you understand the law. Seedtime and harvest shall not cease.

YOU CANNOT HARVEST WHAT YOU HAVEN'T PLANTED

This brings us to a truth that should be obvious but somehow gets overlooked: you cannot reap a harvest from a field you never planted. Every farmer knows you can't sit on your front porch, thank God for the rain, praise Him for the sunshine, and expect corn to appear in your field if you never put seed in the ground.

It doesn't matter how sincere your gratitude is. It doesn't matter how many hours you spend in prayer. It doesn't matter how much faith you confess. If you don't plant, you won't harvest.

That's the law.

Yet this is exactly how many Christians approach their finances. They pray for abundance, but they never sow. If you want a harvest, you have to plant a seed. Period.

In addition to this, many believers have sown, sometimes sacrificially, sometimes over many years, but they've never *received* a harvest. And after enough disappointment, they gave up. They plowed their crops under. They decided the principle didn't work, or didn't work for them, or only worked for certain special people. They stopped sowing altogether, convinced that seed faith was a scam or that God had exempted them from the blessing.

But what they didn't understand was that the law of seedtime and harvest includes more than just planting. There's work to be done between the sowing and the reaping. There's tending required. There's watering, weeding, protecting, waiting. And most importantly, there's understanding.

Look at what Jesus says in Mark 4:24 (NKJV): *"Take heed what you hear. With the same measure you use, it will be measured to you; and to you who hear, more will be given."*

The word *hear* in this passage doesn't mean simply letting sound waves hit your eardrums. It means to understand, to comprehend, to grasp the meaning. Jesus is saying that the measure of your harvest is directly connected to the measure of your understanding.

Think about it this way. If I gave you a farm with everything you needed, equipment, seed, farmhands, fertile soil but you had no understanding of farming, your harvest would be minimal at best. You wouldn't know when to plant, how deep to sow, what to do about pests, or when to harvest. Your lack of knowledge would limit your results.

But if I gave you that same farm, and I also gave you a book on farming, access to weekly classes, and a mentor who walked you through every step, your harvest would increase every year. Why? Because your understanding increased. The farm didn't change. The seed didn't change. The soil didn't change. You changed. And as your knowledge grew, your harvest grew with it.

This is why some believers sow and reap while others sow and wonder what went wrong. It's not that God is playing favorites. It's that understanding determines outcome. The seed is the same. The law is the same. But the level of comprehension and therefore the level of tending is different.

THE PROCESS: BLADE, EAR, FULL CORN

There's another reason many give up too soon. They don't understand that harvest is a process, not an event:

> *And he said, So is the kingdom of God, as if a man should cast seed into the ground; and should sleep, and rise night and day, and the seed should spring and grow up, he knoweth not how. For the earth bringeth forth fruit of herself; first the blade, then the ear, after that the full corn in the ear* (Mark 4:26-28).

Notice the progression: first the blade, then the ear, after that the full corn. There are stages. There's development. There's a process that cannot be skipped or rushed. When a farmer plants corn, he doesn't go out the next morning expecting to find a fully mature stalk with ears ready for harvest. He knows there's a growth cycle.

First, a small green shoot breaks through the soil: the blade. It doesn't look like much. If you didn't know better, you might think nothing significant was happening. But the farmer isn't discouraged. He knows the blade is evidence that the seed is working. Life is emerging. The process has begun.

Then comes the ear. The stalk grows taller, and the structure that will hold the kernels begins to form. Still not harvest time, but progress is visible. The farmer continues to tend, water, and protect.

Finally, the full corn appears. The ear fills out. The kernels mature. And only then is it time to harvest. Many believers have sown financial seed, seen the blade, and have been discouraged because it wasn't the full corn. They expected instant, mature results and gave up when the process took longer than they wanted. They plowed under crops that were actually growing, just not as fast as they'd hoped.

The law of seedtime and harvest includes *time*. There's a season between planting and reaping that cannot be eliminated. If you sow today, you will not necessarily reap tomorrow. But if you stay faithful through the process, if you keep watering, keep believing, keep tending, the full corn will come.

THE HUNDREDFOLD REQUIRES HUMAN PARTICIPATION

Let me address something that trips up a lot of sincere believers. The hundredfold return is not a naturally occurring event. It requires human participation.

Think about an apple orchard with a hundred trees. Every year, those trees drop thousands of apples, and every apple contains seeds. If the hundredfold happened automatically, that orchard would become a forest within a few years, with millions of trees spreading in every direction. But that's not what happens. The apples fall, the seeds lie on the ground, and very few of them ever become trees.

That is because multiplication requires intervention. Someone has to pick up the seed, prepare the soil, plant intentionally, and nurture what's been planted. Without human participation, the potential remains unrealized.

The same is true in the Kingdom. God has established the law. He has made the multiplication available. But He has also assigned you a role. You have to sow intentionally. You have to tend what you've planted. You have to guard against the enemies that try to steal your harvest (and we'll talk about those enemies later). You have to participate in the process.

This is true partnership with God. He provides the law, the seed, the soil, and the growth. You provide the obedience, the intentionality, and the faithful tending. Together, the harvest comes.

That covenant is still in effect. The earth is still here. Seedtime and harvest have not ceased. The law that governed Isaac's hundredfold return in Genesis 26 is the same law available to you today. The principle that multiplied the widow's oil in 1 Kings 17 hasn't been revoked. The promise Jesus made in Mark 10:30 about a hundredfold return now in this time, still stands.

Will you sow or will you sit on your porch hoping for a harvest without a planting? Will you tend your seed or throw an offering in a bucket and forget about it? Will you stay faithful through the blade and the ear, or will you plow under your crop because the full corn didn't come fast enough?

25

SHOULD CHRISTIANS SOW FINANCIAL SEED AND EXPECT A HARVEST?

Let's dive a little deeper. We are now going to take a look at several biblical examples of seed faith. These are examples where someone's giving produced a harvest.

Some critics argue that seed faith is a modern invention, a clever fundraising technique cooked up by televangelists in the twentieth century. They claim it has no basis in Scripture and exists only to manipulate gullible believers into emptying their wallets. But here's the problem with that argument: the biblical record tells a completely different story.

From Genesis to the Epistles, we find example after example of God asking people to give something and then blessing them in return. It's a pattern established by God Himself, woven throughout the entire narrative of Scripture. The names change, the circumstances vary, but the principle remains constant: sow and reap, give and receive, plant and harvest. In fact, God often promises a blessing to encourage His people to give.

Let's walk through these examples together. As we do, watch for the pattern. Notice how consistently God honors those who give in faith. And ask yourself: *If this principle appears this many times across thousands of years of biblical history, can it really be dismissed as unbiblical?*

ABEL'S OFFERING

The very first offering recorded in Scripture demonstrates the seed-faith principle. Abel brought the firstborn of his flock to the Lord, and Genesis tells us that *"the Lord had respect unto Abel and to his offering"* (Genesis 4:4).

Notice two things. First, Abel brought his first and his best. He didn't wait to see how the rest of the flock turned out before deciding what to give God. He gave the firstborn, trusting that more would follow. Hebrews 11 calls this act faith. That's seed faith.

Second, God *"had respect"* to the offering. The Hebrew word suggests that God looked favorably upon it, that He regarded it with acceptance and pleasure. Abel's willingness to give his first and best moved the heart of God.

ABRAHAM'S TITHE TO MELCHIZEDEK

After Abraham (this was before God changed his name from Abram to Abraham) rescued Lot and defeated the coalition of kings, he encountered Melchizedek, the priest of the Most High God. And without being commanded, without any law requiring it, Abraham gave Melchizedek a tenth of everything (see Genesis 14:18-20).

This happened centuries before the Mosaic Law established tithing as a requirement. Abraham tithed voluntarily, from a heart of gratitude and recognition that his victory came from God. And what followed? Melchizedek blessed him, and God appeared to Abraham in Genesis 15:1 and made the covenant promise: *"I am thy shield, and thy exceeding great reward."*

We see this act of giving and the blessing that followed referred to again and again in the book of Hebrews as we discover that Jesus is the High Priest after the order of Melchizedek (Hebrews 5:6,10; 6:20; 7:1,11,15,17,21).

The only thing we know about Melchizedek is that he received tithes and released blessings. This is a powerful New Testament witness to the significance of sowing and reaping. *"Here mortal men receive tithes; but there he receives them, of whom it is witnessed that he lives"* (Hebrews 7:8 NKJV).

JACOB'S VOW AT BETHEL

Jacob, fleeing from Esau with nothing but the clothes on his back, had an encounter with God at Bethel. In response, he made a vow: *"...of all that thou shalt give me I will surely give the tenth unto thee"* (Genesis 28:22).

Notice the expectation in Jacob's vow. He had nothing. He was giving in advance, by faith, anticipating that God would bless him. And God did. Jacob went to Laban's house with nothing and returned 20 years later with enormous wealth: flocks, herds, servants, and family.

The principle—giving by faith, even before the blessing manifests—demonstrates trust in God's faithfulness and positions us for increase.

THE WIDOW OF ZAREPHATH

This might be the most dramatic seed-faith story in the Old Testament. A widow, in the middle of a famine, had enough flour and oil for one final meal for herself and her son. She was preparing to eat it and die. Then Elijah showed up and made an outrageous request: *"Make me a little cake first"* (see 1 Kings 17:8-16).

Think about that. A prophet of God, who had been eating well, asked a starving widow to give her last meal to him before feeding herself or her son. By any natural calculation, this was cruel and unreasonable. But Elijah attached a promise: *"The bin of flour shall not be used up, nor shall the jar of oil run dry..."* (1 Kings 17:14 NKJV).

The widow obeyed. She gave her last. And for the remainder of the famine (perhaps two to three years), her flour and oil never ran out.

One meal's worth of ingredients fed three people for years. That's not a hundredfold return. That's a thousandfold—or more!

God sometimes asks for our last precisely because He wants to prove His supernatural provision. When we obey, He multiplies beyond anything we could calculate. If this is true, how can we blame a preacher for suggesting that this may be the will of God for some?

THE SHUNAMMITE WOMAN

Here's an example that shows seed-faith blessing unfolding over years and through multiple circumstances. A wealthy woman in Shunem noticed that Elisha passed through regularly, so she built a room onto her house specifically for him. She sowed hospitality and provision into the prophet's life and, as a result, Elisha wanted to bless her. When he learned she had no son and her husband was old, he prophesied: *"About this season, next year, you shall embrace a son"* (2 Kings 4:16).

And it happened exactly as he said, but the story doesn't end there. Years later, the boy died suddenly. The woman sought out Elisha, and God used the prophet to raise her son from the dead. Then, during a seven-year famine, Elisha warned her to leave the region. When she returned, she appealed to the king for her land and possessions, and not only did she receive everything back, but the king ordered that she be given all the profits from her land during the years she was away. This amazing story is found in 2 Kings 4:8-37 and 2 Kings 8:1-6.

The act of sowing led to a son, a resurrection, preserved wealth, and years of back profits. The harvest kept multiplying.

ISAAC'S HUNDREDFOLD

In the middle of a famine, God told Isaac not to go to Egypt but to stay in Gerar. Isaac obeyed and sowed in that land during the famine year. The result?

> *He received in the same year an hundredfold: and the Lord blessed him* (Genesis 26:12).

This is the first explicit mention of hundredfold return in Scripture, and the context is crucial:

- It happened during famine.
- It happened in obedience to God's specific instruction.
- It happened because Isaac sowed when natural wisdom would have said to hoard.

The Philistines envied him. His wealth became so great that King Abimelech asked him to leave because *"thou art much mightier than we"* (Genesis 26:16). The act of sowing during difficult seasons can produce hundredfold returns that make even unbelievers take notice.

THE QUEEN OF SHEBA

When the Queen of Sheba visited Solomon, she didn't come empty-handed. She brought 120 talents of gold (roughly $200 million in today's value), along with spices and precious stones in quantities never seen before or since. Her gift was extravagant. And Solomon's response?

> *King Solomon gave unto the queen of Sheba all her desire, whatsoever she asked, beside that which Solomon gave her of his royal bounty...* (1 Kings 10:13).

She received everything she asked for plus whatever Solomon decided to give her from his own generosity. She came with a fortune and left with more than she brought (see 1 Kings 10:1-13).

Another example of how extravagant giving to those God has anointed opens the door to extravagant receiving—both what you ask for and what you didn't think to ask for.

DAVID'S OFFERING FOR THE TEMPLE

When David prepared materials for the temple Solomon would build, he didn't just give from the royal treasury. He gave *"of mine own proper good,"* his personal wealth, over and above what he'd already provided: gold, silver, and precious stones worth billions by modern estimates (see 1 Chronicles 29:1-20).

His example inspired the leaders of Israel to give willingly, and the total offering was staggering. David's prayer of gratitude reveals his understanding: *"...all things come from You, and of Your own we have given You"* (1 Chronicles 29:14 NKJV).

SOLOMON'S SACRIFICE AND GOD'S RESPONSE

At the beginning of his reign, Solomon went to Gibeon and offered a thousand burnt offerings on the altar. It was an extraordinary act of worship and generosity toward God.

That same night, God appeared to Solomon in a dream and said, *"Ask! What shall I give you?"* Solomon asked for wisdom, and God was so pleased that He gave Solomon not only wisdom but also riches and honor beyond any king before or after him (see 1 Kings 3:4-13 NKJV).

Worship through giving captures God's attention and opens the door for Him to offer blessings beyond what we've requested.

THE BOY WITH FIVE LOAVES AND TWO FISH

A boy in a crowd of thousands had a small lunch: five barley loaves and two small fish (see Mark 6:35-44; John 6:5-14).

When Jesus asked what food was available, Andrew brought the boy forward, though he doubted such a small amount could matter.

But the boy gave what he had (see John 6:9). Jesus blessed it, broke it, and multiplied it until 5,000 men (plus women and children) ate until they were full. And twelve baskets of fragments remained—much, much more than what the boy had started with.

No seed is too small for God to multiply. What matters is not the amount of what you give but your willingness to release it into His hands.

CORNELIUS: ALMS AS A MEMORIAL

Cornelius was a Roman centurion—his story begins in Acts 10:1-4. He was a Gentile, not yet a believer in the full New Testament sense. But he feared God, prayed continually, and *"gave much alms to the people."* Then an angel appeared to him and said something remarkable: *"Thy prayers and thine alms are come up for a memorial before God."*

His giving had ascended to Heaven and caught God's attention. The result? Peter was sent to his house, the gospel was preached, and Cornelius and his household became the first recorded Gentile converts, receiving the Holy Spirit and opening the door for the gospel to go to all nations.

Generous giving can rise before God as a memorial and can trigger divine visitation and breakthrough.

THE PROVERBS PATTERN

Throughout Proverbs, Solomon (writing under divine inspiration) establishes the giving-and-receiving pattern repeatedly:

> *Honour the Lord with thy substance, and with the firstfruits of all thine increase: so shall thy barns be filled with plenty, and thy presses shall burst out with new wine* (Proverbs 3:9-10).

> *There is one who scatters, yet increases more; and there is one who withholds more than is right, but it leads to poverty. The generous soul will be made rich, and he who waters will also be watered himself* (Proverbs 11:24-25 NKJV).

> *He who gives to the poor will never want, but he who shuts his eyes [from their need] will have many curses* (Proverbs 28:27 AMP).

The principle: generosity leads to increase; withholding leads to poverty. This is stated as proverbial wisdom, meaning it reflects how God's economy consistently operates.

THE MALACHI CHALLENGE

This is the only place in Scripture where God explicitly invites His people to test Him:

> *Bring ye all the tithes into the storehouse, that there may be meat in mine house, and prove me now herewith, saith the Lord of hosts, if I will not open you the windows of heaven, and pour you out a blessing, that there shall not be room enough to receive it* (Malachi 3:10).

God is so confident in the law of seedtime and harvest that He tells Israel to put Him to the test:

- Bring the tithe.
- See what I do.
- Watch the windows of Heaven open.
- Experience blessing you don't have room to contain.

God backs His promise of return with an open invitation to prove Him. He's that certain that the principle works.

JESUS' PROMISE OF MULTIPLIED RETURN

Jesus didn't speak vaguely about giving. He made a specific promise:

> *Give, and it shall be given unto you; good measure, pressed down, and shaken together, and running over, shall men give into your bosom. For with the same measure that ye mete withal it shall be measured to you again* (Luke 6:38).

The imagery here is of grain measurement. When you buy grain, you want the merchant to press it down, shake the container to settle it, and fill it until it overflows. You want maximum value.

Jesus says that's how God measures the return on your giving. Not stingy, not exact—but pressed down, shaken together, running over.

And notice: *"shall men give into your bosom."* God uses people as the delivery mechanism for your harvest. Because you're called to be fishers of men, He will make men as fish.

The measure you use becomes the measure used for your return. This is biblical.

PAUL'S TEACHING ON SOWING AND REAPING

The apostle Paul makes the seed-faith principle explicit:

> *But this I say, He which soweth sparingly shall reap also sparingly; and he which soweth bountifully shall reap also bountifully. ...And God is able to make all grace abound toward you; that ye, always having all sufficiency in all things, may abound to every good work. ...Now he that ministereth seed to the sower both minister bread for your eating, and multiply your seed sown, and increase the fruits of your righteousness* (2 Corinthians 9:6-10).

Paul directly applies agricultural language to financial giving. The amount and attitude of your sowing determines the amount of your reaping. God multiplies what you plant, not what you keep.

THE PHILIPPIAN PROMISE

Paul writes to the Philippians with gratitude for their consistent financial support and then makes a promise that extends beyond them to anyone who gives into legitimate Kingdom work: *"But my God shall supply all your need according to his riches in glory by Christ Jesus"* (Philippians 4:19).

This promise is directly connected to their giving. It's not a blanket statement for all believers regardless of their generosity. It's a promise specifically tied to those who sow into the gospel. Those who give to support Kingdom work access a supply line from God's riches in glory, not just earthly resources but heavenly abundance.

THE GALATIANS WARNING: DON'T MOCK GOD

There's one more passage we need to examine, and it may be the most direct of all. In Galatians 6, Paul writes:

> *Let him that is taught in the word communicate unto him that teacheth in all good things. Be not deceived; God is not mocked: for whatsoever a man soweth, that shall he also reap. For he that soweth to his flesh shall of the flesh reap corruption; but he that soweth to the Spirit shall of the Spirit reap life everlasting. And let us not be weary in well doing: for in due season we shall reap if we faint not* (Galatians 6:6-9).

Look at the context carefully. Galatians 6:6 is about financial giving. The word *communicate* means to share, to give, to financially support. Paul is instructing believers to support those who teach them the Word. Then, immediately, he launches into the sowing and reaping principle: *"Whatsoever a man soweth, that shall he also reap."*

Paul is clearly connecting financial giving directly to the law of seedtime and harvest. And then he issues a warning that should stop every skeptic in their tracks: *"God is not mocked."*

What does it mean to mock God in this context? It means to treat His law as if it doesn't work. It means to sow and then deny that a harvest is coming. It means to put seed in the ground and act as if nothing will grow.

When you sow a financial seed and refuse to expect a return, you are essentially saying, "God's law doesn't apply to me" or "God won't do what He said He would do."

That's mockery. You may not intend it as mockery, but that's what it is. You're treating the eternal, covenant law of seedtime and harvest as if it were optional or unreliable.

And then Paul adds the encouragement that so many need to hear: *"Let us not be weary in* ***well doing****: for in due season we shall reap, if we faint not."*

The *"well doing"* in this context is the giving he just described. He is telling them not to get tired of sowing. Not to give up because the harvest hasn't come yet. Due season is coming. The reaping is certain.

But you have to stay in the game. You have to keep sowing, keep believing, keep expecting. If you faint, if you quit, if you plow under your crop because you are discouraged, you'll miss the harvest that was on its way.

To sow and not expect a harvest is to mock the God who established the law. But to sow and keep believing through the waiting season is to honor Him and position yourself for the reaping that is guaranteed to come.

THE PATTERN IS UNDENIABLE

Spanning from the first family in Genesis to the churches in the New Testament, the pattern is consistent. It covers every era of biblical history. It involves men and women, rich and poor, Jews and Gentiles, kings and widows.

The pattern is consistent: give, and it shall be given. Sow, and you will reap. Plant, and harvest will come.

This isn't a manipulation technique:

- It's a biblical principle established by God.
- It's been demonstrated throughout Scripture.
- It is available to every believer who will embrace it.

EXPECT A RETURN?

There are even more verses throughout Scripture where God not only commanded His people to give but explicitly promised them blessing if they obeyed. We could spend an entire book cataloging them all. But the question worth asking is: why?

Why did God establish this pattern in the first place? Why does He consistently tie giving to receiving, sowing to reaping, releasing to multiplying?

The answer is simple but profound: He wants you to expect great things from Him.

Not from your job. Not from your government. Not from your own strength, your own cleverness, or your own hustle. He wants your expectation fixed on Him as your Source.

When you sow a seed and look to God for the harvest, you're doing something that shifts your entire orientation. You stop seeing your employer as your provider and start seeing God as your Provider who happens to use your employer.

You stop trusting in political systems or economic conditions and start trusting in the Kingdom economy that operates independently of Wall Street or Washington. You *stop believing* that your future depends on your own ability to figure it out and *start believing* that your future depends on your faithful God who watches over His Word to perform it.

This is what pleases Him. Hebrews 11:6 says: "*But without faith it is impossible to please him: for he that cometh to God must believe that he is, and that he is a* ***rewarder*** *of them that diligently seek him.*"

Did you catch that? It's not enough to believe that God exists. You must also believe that He is a rewarder. You must come to Him expecting that He will respond to your faith, your obedience, your seeking.

Expectation isn't greed. Expectation is faith. And faith is what pleases God.

When you sow a seed and refuse to expect a harvest, you're not being humble, you're being faithless. But when you sow and lift your eyes to Heaven anticipating what your Father has prepared for you, when you wake up every morning watching for the blade, the ear, and the full corn, when you thank Him in advance for the return that is surely coming, you are operating in the kind of faith that makes God smile.

He established the pattern because He wants your heart turned toward Him:

- Every seed is an opportunity to trust.
- Every offering is an invitation to expect.
- Every harvest is a reminder that He is exactly who He said He is: the Rewarder of those who diligently seek Him.

26

THE HUNDREDFOLD RETURN

The following is one of the clearest, most direct promises Jesus ever made about financial return on Kingdom giving. And just because it's been abused doesn't mean we get to ignore it. We need to understand it. The passage is Mark 10:17-30. Let's walk through it carefully.

A young man came running to Jesus and knelt before Him. He asked the right question: *"Good Master, what shall I do that I may inherit eternal life?"* (Mark 10:17).

Jesus pointed him to the commandments, and the young man replied that he had kept them all from his youth. Then Mark records something remarkable: *"Jesus beholding him loved him…."* (Mark 10:21).

This wasn't a con man trying to trick Jesus. This was a sincere seeker, and Jesus loved him for it.

But Jesus also saw what was holding him back and said, *"One thing thou lackest: go thy way, sell whatsoever thou hast, and give to the poor, and thou shalt have treasure in heaven: and come, take up the cross, and follow me"* (Mark 10:21).

The young man went away grieved because he had great possessions. He couldn't *release* what he had in order to *obtain* what Jesus offered. His wealth owned him more than he owned it.

Sadly, like many Christians, he didn't stick around to hear Jesus' promise.

After the young man left, Jesus told His disciples how hard it is for the rich to enter the Kingdom. The disciples were astonished, and Peter spoke up: *"Lo, we have left all, and have followed thee"* (Mark 10:28).

Peter wasn't bragging. He was asking a legitimate question. The rich young ruler was invited to give up everything and follow Jesus, but he refused to do it. Peter and the disciples had actually done it. They left their businesses, their homes, their families, and their security to follow an itinerant Rabbi with no guaranteed income.

Yet, even after giving everything up, they were still being blessed everywhere they went. Now you can understand Peter's concern. But Jesus wasn't talking about riches in and of themselves. He was talking about *trusting* in riches (Mark 10:24). Jesus answered him directly.

> *Verily I say unto you, There is no man that hath left house, or brethren, or sisters, or father, or mother, or wife, or children, or lands, for my sake, and the gospel's, but he shall receive an hundredfold now in this time, houses, and brethren, and sisters, and mothers, and children, and lands, with persecutions; and in the world to come eternal life* (Mark 10:29-30).

Read that again slowly. Jesus promised a hundredfold return. Not tenfold. Not double. He promises a hundred times what was given up. And notice the timing: *"now in this time."* Not just in Heaven. Not just in the sweet by and by. Now. In this present life. On this side of eternity.

He even listed specific categories of things that might be sacrificed for His sake and the gospel's: houses, family relationships, and lands. These represent the major areas of earthly security and wealth. Then He promised that anyone who releases these things for Kingdom purposes will receive a hundredfold return in the same categories.

Houses for houses. Lands for lands. Family for family (spiritual family in the body of Christ and restoration of natural family). The return corresponds to the sacrifice. The multiplication applies to what was released.

And Jesus added two important qualifiers. First, *"with persecutions"* (Mark 10:30). As we've discussed, the hundredfold return doesn't mean a trouble-free life. In fact, increased blessing attracts increased opposition. The enemy doesn't bother attacking people who aren't a threat to his kingdom. If you're walking in hundredfold blessing, expect spiritual resistance.

Second, *"and in the world to come eternal life"* (Mark 10:30). The hundredfold in this life is not the end of the story. There's more coming. This is the promise of an eternal life filled with eternal rewards. But that future promise doesn't negate the present one. Both are true.

A HUNDREDFOLD *NOW* IN *THIS* LIFE

When exactly does the hundredfold return manifest? Is it immediate? Does it take years? How do you know when it's coming? The answer is rooted in understanding how seedtime and harvest works. You don't receive the harvest the moment you plant the seed. There's a process, a season, a period of growth. But here's what you need to understand: from God's perspective, the harvest is determined the moment the seed goes into the ground.

When a farmer plants corn, he doesn't say, "I hope I get corn." He says, "I planted corn; therefore corn is coming."

The harvest is settled at the moment of planting. The only question is *when* it will manifest, not *whether* it will manifest.

The same is true for your financial seed. The moment you sow in faith, the return is established. You may not see it yet. It may still be underground, germinating, pushing up through the soil.

But it's as certain as if it were already in your barn. The moment you sow, you can say with confidence, "My harvest is coming. The hundredfold is on its way. I know it because I planted it."

This is why faith matters so much. Faith isn't pretending the harvest is already here when it isn't. Faith is knowing the harvest is certain because the seed has been sown. You're not hoping or wishing. You're standing on the law of seedtime and harvest that God Himself established and declared would never cease.

THE HUNDREDFOLD IS REAL

The hundredfold return is not a metaphor. It's not spiritual language for feeling good about your giving. It's not code for "you'll get treasure in Heaven someday." Jesus said it plainly: houses, lands, family—now in this time.

The multiplication often comes in various forms: opportunities, connections, ideas, favor, provision from unexpected sources, and needs met in supernatural ways.

God is creative in how He delivers the harvest. But the principle is real, the multiplication is real, and the promise stands.

The hundredfold return is available to every believer who will embrace the principle, sow in faith, guard against the enemies of their harvest, and stay faithful through the process. It's not reserved for special people. It's not limited to those with certain gifts. It's a promise from Jesus to anyone who gives for His sake and the gospel's.

PLANTING VERSUS BURYING

Once you see this, you can't unsee it—there's a difference between planting and burying. Both planting and burying require digging a hole and putting something in the ground. The physical actions look almost identical. An observer watching from a distance couldn't tell the difference. But the outcomes are completely opposite.

What's the difference? Expectation.

The Burial Mindset

When you bury something, you're putting it in the ground with no intention of seeing it again. Burial is final. It's an ending, not a beginning. You cover it with dirt, you walk away, and you don't come back expecting anything to emerge.

If you do return to a burial site, it's only to remember what was. You bring flowers to honor the past. You reflect on what you've lost. You might grieve, you might reminisce, but you never show up expecting resurrection. The thing you buried is gone. That's the whole point of burial.

This is exactly how many Christians approach their giving. They put money into the offering. They write a check to a ministry. They give to someone in need. And in their hearts, that money is dead to them. Gone. Buried. They have no expectation of ever seeing it again, no anticipation of return, no faith for multiplication. They might feel good about being generous. They might even believe they've done something spiritual. But in terms of expectation, they just conducted a funeral for their finances. And then they wonder why nothing grows.

The Planting Mindset

Planting looks the same on the surface. You dig a hole. You put something in the ground. You cover it with dirt. But everything about your posture is different.

When you plant, you're not saying goodbye. You're saying, "See you soon." That seed going into the ground isn't a loss, it's an investment. It's not dead, it's about to come alive in ways that multiply far beyond its original form.

When you plant, you come back. You don't visit a planting site to mourn. You visit to check on progress. You're looking for the blade. You're watching for the ear. You're anticipating the full corn. Every day you return with expectation, scanning the soil for evidence that life is emerging.

The farmer who plants corn doesn't weep over the seed he put in the ground. He doesn't hold a memorial service for his kernels. He goes to bed expecting growth. He wakes up expecting progress. He tends his field with confidence because he knows that what he planted is working beneath the surface even when he can't see it. This is how Kingdom giving is supposed to work.

Two believers can put the same amount in the same offering bucket at the same church on the same Sunday. One walks away having planted. The other walks away having buried. The amounts are identical. The recipient is identical. But the outcomes will be completely different.

The one who *planted* will be watching for harvest. She'll notice the unexpected check, the surprise opportunity, the door that opens out of nowhere. She'll recognize these as fruit from her seed. She'll thank God for the return and sow again with even greater confidence.

The one who *buried* may see the same unexpected check but attribute it to coincidence. He'll encounter the same opportunity but assume it came from his own networking. The harvest will pass right by him because he wasn't looking for it. He had no expectation, so he had no eyes to see what God was doing.

Expectation doesn't make the seed work. The law of seedtime and harvest makes the seed work. But expectation positions you to recognize, receive, and reinvest the harvest when it comes.

JESUS DESCRIBED THE PROCESS

In Mark 4:26-28, Jesus says:

> *...So is the kingdom of God, as if a man should cast seed into the ground; and should sleep, and rise night and day, and the seed should spring and grow up, he knoweth not how. For the earth*

> *bringeth forth fruit of herself; first the blade, then the ear, after that the full corn in the ear.*

Notice the farmer's rhythm: he sleeps and rises, night and day. This isn't the pattern of someone who buried and forgot. This is the pattern of someone who planted and is waiting with expectation. He goes to bed thinking about his crop. He wakes up thinking about his crop. His life rhythms are oriented around the field where his seed is growing.

When you give with a planting mindset, you start looking for blades. You notice small signs of increase. You recognize doors opening that weren't open before. You see God moving in your finances in incremental ways. And instead of being frustrated that the full harvest hasn't arrived, you're encouraged that the seed is working.

But when you give with a burial mindset, you don't even notice the blade. You're not watching for it. You've already written off what you gave. So the early signs of harvest go unrecognized, and you miss the opportunity to tend what's growing.

We've been taught that to give and expect a return is selfish—but what if it's just the opposite? What if *not* expecting a return makes you a selfish steward of the seed you were given by God?

Let me ask you a direct question: when you give, what happens in your heart? Do you feel a sense of loss? Do you tighten up inside, wondering how you'll make it without that money? Do you give grudgingly—out of obligation—because you're supposed to? Do you drop your offering in the bucket and immediately move on to thinking about something else? If so, you've been burying instead of planting. And buried seed doesn't produce a harvest.

But there's good news: you can change your posture starting today.

The next time you give, do it differently. Before you release the money, take a moment to acknowledge what you're doing. Say it aloud if you need to: *"This is not a burial. This is a planting. I am sowing seed into the Kingdom of God, and I am expecting a harvest."*

After you give, don't walk away and forget about it. Instead, start watching. Pay attention to what God does in the following days and weeks. Look for the blade. When something good happens in your finances, don't dismiss it as coincidence. Ask yourself: *Is this connected to what I planted?* Then give God praise.

And through the process, maintain your expectation. Don't let time erode your faith. Don't assume that because the full corn hasn't appeared yet, the seed must have failed. Stay in the posture of a farmer checking on his field, not a mourner visiting a grave.

THE PARABLE OF THE TALENTS REVISITED

Remember the parable of the talents in Matthew 25? Three servants received money from their master. Two of them invested and multiplied what they were given. But one servant did something different: *"But he that had received one went and digged in the earth, and hid his lord's money"* (Matthew 25:18).

He buried it.

When the master returned, the two who invested received praise and greater responsibility. But the one who buried received condemnation: *"Thou wicked and slothful servant…thou oughtest to have put my money to the exchangers, and then at my coming I should have received mine own with usury"* (Matthew 25:26-27).

This servant's problem wasn't that he did something evil with the money. He didn't steal it or waste it. His problem was that he buried it instead of planting it. He operated in fear instead of faith. He expected nothing, so he received nothing. And the master was not pleased. He was designated as *unfaithful* because he didn't expect multiplication.

God is not pleased when we bury what He gives us. He's not honored by offerings given with no expectation. He's not glorified by generosity rooted in a funeral mindset. He wants us to plant with faith, tend with prayer, and expect with confidence. That's what pleases Him.

Your seed, financial or otherwise, has resurrection power. It goes into the ground looking like loss, but it comes back up looking like harvest. It goes in as one thing and emerges as 30, 60, 100 times more than what was planted.

But you have to plant it expecting resurrection. You have to release it with faith that what goes down will come back up. You have to approach your giving not as a burial of dead money but as a planting of living seed that carries within it the power of multiplication.

DON'T EAT YOUR SEED

There will be moments when you're tempted to consume what you should be planting. The pressure will tell you that you can't afford to give right now, that you need every dollar for bills, that you'll start sowing again when things settle down.

That's a trap. The widow of Zarephath was down to her last meal, and God asked for seed even then. Your seed is never more powerful than when giving it requires faith. Don't eat what God is asking you to plant.

The hundredfold comes from God, not from the ministry you gave to, not from the person you blessed, not from the ground where you planted. Those are *channels*, not *sources*.

Keep your expectation fixed on God Himself. When the harvest comes through unexpected means, recognize His hand. When it comes through people, thank Him for using them. Never confuse the delivery method with the origin. God is your Source. Everyone and everything else is just a vehicle that He uses.

WHAT HAVE WE LEARNED?

Seed faith is not a modern invention or a manipulation technique. It's a biblical principle woven throughout Scripture from Genesis to the Epistles. Jesus taught it. Paul explained it. You've seen that many examples across thousands of years of biblical history confirm it.

Money has seed power, just like faith, the Kingdom, Christians, and Jesus Himself. When you release finances into Kingdom purposes, you're not losing something. You're planting something. As long as the earth remains, it will not cease. It's as reliable as the sunrise, as certain as the seasons. You can count on it because God established it and declared it would endure.

The hundredfold return is real. Jesus promised it plainly: houses, lands, family, now in this time. Not just in Heaven. Not just someday. Now. The return is established the moment the seed goes into the ground. The only question is whether you'll tend it faithfully until the harvest manifests.

Now speak this over your life:

> *I am a sower, not a thrower. Every seed I plant has purpose, and I tend it with prayer and expectation.*
>
> *I expect a harvest because God promised one. To expect anything less would be to mock the One who established the law.*
>
> *I am positioning myself for the wealth transfer. I am faithful in little, and I will be faithful in much.*
>
> *The hundredfold is mine. Not because I deserve it, but because Jesus promised it, now in this time. Houses and lands. With persecutions, yes, but also with abundance.*
>
> *I plant with faith. I wait with patience. I receive with gratitude.*
>
> *And I will not be weary in well doing, for in due season I will reap if I faint not.*

27

WAS JESUS POOR?

We've addressed many lies, myths, and misconceptions about the subject of prosperity throughout this book. We've examined what Scripture actually says about debt, about giving, about seedtime and harvest. But no book on this topic would be complete without addressing one of the biggest deceptions satan ever pulled on the Church.

There's a doctrine that has crept into the Church and done more damage to believers' faith than almost any other. It's the idea that Jesus was poor. Not just humble. Not just simple. But broke, destitute, homeless, and barely scraping by.

This teaching has become so ingrained in Christian culture that many believers accept it without question. They picture Jesus as a wandering beggar—sleeping under trees, owning nothing but the clothes on His back. And because they believe this about their Savior, they conclude that poverty must be spiritual. That lack is somehow godly. That wanting more is carnal and greedy.

This is a lie. And it has crippled the body of Christ financially for generations.

If Jesus were poor, then poverty becomes the model for discipleship. If Jesus had nothing, then having something must mean you're doing Christianity wrong. If Jesus struggled to make ends meet, then abundance must be worldly and suspect.

Do you see how this works?

The enemy doesn't have to convince you that God can't bless you. He just has to convince you that God doesn't want to bless you.

And the easiest way to do that is to make you believe that Jesus Himself rejected wealth.

But what if that picture is completely wrong? What if the evidence in Scripture tells a very different story?

THE ONE VERSE THEY USE

When people argue that Jesus was poor, they almost always go to one verse. You've probably heard it quoted a hundred times:

> *And Jesus said to him, "Foxes have holes, and birds of the air have nests, but the Son of Man has nowhere to lay His head"* (Matthew 8:20; Luke 9:58 NKJV).

There it is. Case closed. Jesus was homeless. He didn't even have a place to sleep at night. The foxes had it better than He did. But is that really what this verse is saying? We're going to examine it carefully later in this chapter, and I think you'll be shocked at what we find.

Context matters. And when you rip this verse out of its context and use it to build a theology of poverty, you end up with a Jesus that the Scriptures don't actually describe.

THE ONE VERSE THAT MATTERS

There is, however, one verse that does speak directly to the poverty of Jesus. And unlike the *"foxes have holes"* passage, this one actually says what people think it says:

> *For you know the grace of our Lord Jesus Christ, that though He was rich, yet for your sakes He became poor, that you through His poverty might become rich* (2 Corinthians 8:9 NKJV).

Now we're getting somewhere. This verse explicitly says Jesus was rich. It explicitly says He *"became poor."* And it explicitly says He did it so that we might *"become rich."* But here are questions nobody seems to ask: WHEN did Jesus become poor? And WHY?

WAS JESUS POOR IN HIS PERSONAL LIFE?

Was Jesus poor His whole life? Was He poor during His ministry? Was He poor in the manger? Or did something specific happen at a specific time that constitutes His becoming poor?

The answers to these questions change everything. And we're going to answer it before this chapter is finished. But first, we need to examine the evidence. We need to look at what Scripture actually reveals about Jesus' financial situation during His earthly life. And I believe you're going to be stunned by what we find because the evidence doesn't point to a broke, homeless beggar.

Let's look at the evidence.

Did Jesus Have a House?

Did Jesus have a house? The assumption is *no*. The mental image we've inherited from centuries of religious tradition is of a wandering Rabbi with no fixed address, sleeping wherever He could find a spot, relying entirely on the hospitality of strangers. But is that what Scripture actually describes?

Let's look at an encounter that happened early in Jesus' ministry. In John chapter 1, two of John the Baptist's disciples began following Jesus. When Jesus noticed them, He asked them what they were seeking. Their response was another question: *"Rabbi, where dwellest thou?"* (John 1:38).

Now watch His answer carefully. If Jesus were homeless, if He had no place to stay, this would have been the perfect moment to say so. He could have said, "Nowhere. I wander from place to place." He could have given them the *"foxes have holes"* speech right there. But that's not what He said. Jesus answered, *"Come and see"* (John 1:39).

Come and see. That's not the response of a homeless man. The verse continues: *"They came and saw where he dwelt, and abode with him that day"* (John 1:39).

They came. They saw where He lived. And they stayed with Him. This implies a dwelling large enough to accommodate guests, a place where Jesus felt comfortable inviting people to spend time. This was not a bench in the town square or a spot under a tree. This was His residence.

The evidence doesn't stop there.

In Mark 2:1 (NKJV), we read: *"And again He entered into Capernaum after some days; and it was heard that He was in the house."*

The Greek phrase translated *"in the house"* is *en oiko.* It can also be translated "at home." Word spread through town that Jesus was home. Not that He was visiting someone else's home. Not that He was passing through. He was at home.

Matthew's Gospel confirms this. In Matthew 9:1, Capernaum is called *"his own city."* Jesus had relocated from Nazareth (where He was rejected) and established Capernaum as His home base for ministry. This was His city, His home. And the house was not small.

Mark 2:2 (NKJV) tells us that when people heard He was home: *"Immediately many gathered together, so that there was no longer room to receive them, not even near the door. And He preached the word to them."*

The crowd was so large they couldn't even fit outside the doorway. This was a substantial dwelling, large enough that crowds gathered hoping to get inside.

Waterfront Property?

Here's something that might surprise you. Capernaum was located on the northern shore of the Sea of Galilee. Archaeological excavations have uncovered the remains of the village, including a house that early Christians venerated as Peter's house (where Jesus likely stayed) but what if it were actually Jesus' house? This house was situated near the synagogue and close to the water.

Jesus' home base was lakefront property. Waterfront property has always been premium property. Whether a lake, a river, or the ocean, property on the water commands a higher price than property inland. It was true in the first century, and it's true today.

Jesus didn't set up His ministry headquarters in the slums of Galilee. He based His operations in a lakefront community, in a house large enough to host His disciples and attract standing-room-only crowds. This is not the picture of a destitute, homeless beggar. This is the picture of someone with resources and a place to call home.

What About Peter's House?

Some will argue that Jesus was merely staying in Peter's house, that it wasn't really His. But consider this: even if the house originally belonged to Peter, Jesus lived there. He made it His home. Mark 2:1 doesn't say "it was heard that He was at Peter's house." It says He was at home.

And here's another thought. Peter and Andrew were fishermen with a successful business. They had boats and hired servants (Mark 1:20 mentions that James and John left their father Zebedee *"in the ship with the hired servants"*). These weren't impoverished subsistence fishermen. They ran a commercial fishing operation. Peter's house would have reflected that level of success.

When Jesus moved in, He wasn't sleeping on the floor of a shack. He was living in the home of a prosperous businessman, in a waterfront community, in a dwelling large enough to accommodate multiple disciples and host crowds of people.

The evidence is clear: Jesus had a house.

What "Foxes Have Holes" Means

Now let's deal with the verse that has been used more than any other to paint Jesus as a homeless wanderer. If you've ever heard someone argue that Jesus was poor, this is the verse they almost certainly quoted:

> *Foxes have holes, and birds of the air have nests; but the Son of man hath not where to lay his head* (Matthew 8:20; Luke 9:58).

On the surface, it sounds definitive. Jesus is comparing Himself unfavorably to animals. Even foxes have homes. Even birds have nests. But the Son of Man? He has nothing. But context changes everything. And the context of this verse has nothing to do with Jesus' financial status.

Luke's account gives us the fuller picture. In Luke 9:51, we read that Jesus *"steadfastly set his face to go to Jerusalem."* He knew what awaited Him there. He knew the Cross was coming. And He began the journey.

On the way, He sent messengers ahead to prepare a Samaritan village for His arrival. But verse 53 tells us: *"And they did not receive him, because his face was as though he would go to Jerusalem."*

The village rejected Him. They refused to give Him lodging. They turned Him away. It was in this context, immediately after being refused hospitality, that a man approached Jesus and said: *"Lord, I will follow thee whithersoever thou goest"* (Luke 9:57).

And Jesus responded with the famous words about foxes and birds.

Do you see what's happening? Jesus wasn't making a general statement about His poverty. He was responding to a man who just witnessed a village slam its doors in Jesus' face. The man said, "I'll follow You anywhere!"

And Jesus essentially replied, "Do you understand what that means? Right now, even foxes have more security than I do. Birds have somewhere to rest tonight. But I was just rejected, and I have nowhere to lay My head."

This was about persecution, not poverty. It was about opposition, not ownership. It was about the cost of following a controversial Messiah, not about Jesus' bank account. It didn't matter how much money Jesus had, they weren't going to give Him a place to stay that night.

The Life of an Itinerant Preacher

Here's what we need to understand. During His public ministry, Jesus was constantly on the move. He traveled from village to village—preaching, teaching, and healing. This was an itinerant lifestyle by design, not by destitution.

When you're on the road, you don't have access to your home. That's true for anyone. A businessman traveling for work doesn't have his bed with him. A soldier deployed overseas doesn't have his living room. That doesn't make them homeless. It makes them away from home.

Jesus had a home, but when He was traveling through Samaria and getting rejected by villages, He didn't have access to that home. At that moment, on that night, He had nowhere to lay His head. The verse is about the hardship of ministry, not the absence of resources. It's about being willing to face rejection for the sake of the gospel. It's a warning to would-be followers that this road is difficult—not a statement that Jesus owned nothing.

Here's the danger. When you take one verse out of context and build an entire theology on it, you end up with a distorted picture. The *"foxes have holes"* verse, ripped from its setting and treated as a summary statement about Jesus' life, creates a Jesus who never existed. The Jesus of Scripture had a home base. He wore quality clothing. He had a treasurer. He received expensive gifts. He gave money to the poor. None of that fits the image of a destitute, homeless man.

So the next time someone quotes *"foxes have holes"* to prove Jesus was poor, ask them a simple question: Have you read the verses before and after it? Because context tells a very different story.

The Gifts of the Magi

Let's go back to the very beginning of Jesus' life. Before He ever preached a sermon or performed a miracle, before He called a single disciple or set foot in Capernaum, something happened that set the financial trajectory of His entire earthly existence. Wealthy men from the East came looking for Him. And they didn't come empty-handed.

First, let's correct the picture that most of us grew up with. The traditional nativity scene shows three men in robes carrying small decorative boxes. It's a sweet image for a Christmas card, but it has almost nothing to do with what actually happened.

Scripture never says there were three wise men. We assume three because three gifts are mentioned, but the text simply says wise men (plural) came from the East. There could have been a dozen. There could have been dozens.

The term *magi* refers to an elite priestly class from Persia or Arabia. They were scholars, astronomers, and advisors to kings. In their culture, they held positions of power, influence, and immense wealth. When magi traveled, they didn't travel alone. They moved with caravans, armed guards, servants, and pack animals loaded with provisions and treasures.

Think about this: their arrival troubled King Herod and *"all Jerusalem with him"* (see Matthew 2:3). A few poor wanderers showing up wouldn't trouble anyone. But a royal delegation from a foreign nation, arriving with an entourage large enough to make the political establishment nervous? That's a different story entirely.

The Value of Their Gifts

Matthew 2:11 tells us they opened their treasures and presented Jesus with gifts of gold, frankincense, and myrrh. Let's consider what this actually means.

Gold needs no explanation. It was and is the universal symbol of wealth. But here's what you may not know: frankincense and myrrh were often *more* valuable than gold in the ancient world. These aromatic resins had to be harvested from trees that only grew in remote regions of Arabia and Africa. The process was labor intensive, the yield was small, and the demand was enormous. Frankincense was essential for temple worship. Myrrh was used in royal anointing oils and burial preparations.

Historical records indicate that 20 talents of gold were considered an appropriate gift for a lower-level king. But Jesus was not recognized as a lower-level king. The magi called Him *"King of the Jews"* and came specifically to worship Him. They would have brought gifts befitting the greatest king ever born.

We're not talking about trinket boxes. We're talking about treasure chests. Camel loads of wealth. Some scholars have estimated that the combined value of these gifts, in modern terms, could have been worth millions of dollars.

What Happened to These Gifts?

Here's a question worth asking: if Joseph and Mary received a fortune at Jesus' birth, why did Joseph continue working as a carpenter?

The answer might be simpler than you think. Perhaps he enjoyed his trade. Perhaps the gifts funded the family's flight to Egypt and their years living as refugees in a foreign land. I like to think that the gifts were invested or saved for Jesus' future ministry.

What we know for certain is that Jesus did not start His life in poverty. He started His life with the wealthiest people of the East seeking

Him out and presenting Him with treasures fit for royalty. From His earliest days, abundance followed Him.

WAS JESUS POOR IN HIS MINISTRY LIFE?

The magi set a pattern that would continue throughout Jesus' ministry. Wealthy supporters, costly gifts, and supernatural provision marked His life from the manger to the Cross.

Wealthy Supporters

The gifts of the magi were not an isolated incident. Throughout Jesus' ministry, wealthy supporters surrounded Him, gave to Him, and funded His work. This wasn't charity for a poor man. This was honor for a King.

Luke 8:1-3 gives us a behind-the-scenes look at how Jesus' ministry operated financially:

> *And it came to pass afterward, that he went throughout every city and village, preaching and shewing the glad tidings of the kingdom of God: and the twelve were with him, and certain women, which had been healed of evil spirits and infirmities, Mary called Magdalene, out of whom went seven devils, and Joanna the wife of Chuza Herod's steward, and Susanna, and many others, which* ***ministered unto him of their substance****.*

Read that last phrase carefully: they *"ministered unto him of their substance."* The Greek word for *substance* refers to possessions, property, means, and resources. These women didn't just pray for Jesus—they funded Him.

And notice who these women were. Joanna was the wife of Chuza, who was Herod's steward. That's not a low-level position. Herod's steward managed the royal household. Joanna was essentially a government official's wife, part of the upper class of Jewish society. She and the other women gave from their abundance, not their poverty. This wasn't a ragtag group of homeless followers pooling their pennies. This was a ministry supported by people of substantial means.

Mary's Costly Gift

Perhaps the most striking example of wealth flowing toward Jesus comes from John 12:1-3:

> *Then Jesus six days before the passover came to Bethany, where Lazarus was which had been dead, whom he raised from the dead. There they made him a supper; and Martha served: but Lazarus was one of them that sat at the table with him. Then took Mary a pound of ointment of spikenard, very costly, and anointed the feet of Jesus, and wiped his feet with her hair: and the house was filled with the odour of the ointment.*

The text tells us this ointment was "very costly." How costly? Judas provides the answer in verse 5: "Why was not this ointment sold for three hundred pence, and given to the poor?"

Three hundred denarii (the word *pence* often used in the New Testament to translate *denarii*) was nearly a full year's wages for a common laborer. In today's terms, we're talking about tens of thousands of dollars poured out on Jesus' feet in a single act of worship.

Jesus didn't refuse it. He didn't say, "No, I can't accept such extravagance. I'm a poor man." He received it. He honored Mary for it. He said her act would be remembered wherever the gospel was preached (Matthew 26:13).

Mary gave this gift because she recognized who Jesus was. And Jesus accepted it because it was fitting for who He was.

Everywhere Jesus went, people gave to Him and His ministry. Zacchaeus, the wealthy tax collector, hosted Him for dinner. Joseph of Arimathea, a rich man and secret disciple, provided an expensive tomb for His burial. Nicodemus brought 75 pounds of myrrh and aloes for His body. This is the pattern you see around someone recognized as worthy of honor, investment, and costly sacrifice.

Quality Clothing

Here's a detail from the crucifixion that many people might read right past without considering its implications. When Jesus was nailed to the Cross, the Roman soldiers did what soldiers always did: they divided up the victim's possessions among themselves. John 19:23-24 describes what happened at Jesus' crucifixion:

> *Then the soldiers, when they had crucified Jesus, took his garments, and made four parts, to every soldier a part; and also his coat: now the coat was without seam, woven from the top throughout. They said therefore among themselves, Let us not rend it, but cast lots for it, whose it shall be....*

Four soldiers divided His outer garments into four parts, one part for each of them. But when they got to His inner garment—His tunic—they stopped. They refused to tear it. Instead, they gambled for it. Why?

The text tells us the tunic was *"without seam, woven from the top throughout."* This was a seamless garment, woven in one continuous piece from top to bottom. This type of garment was significantly more expensive and time-consuming to produce than ordinary clothing made from pieces sewn together.

Historical records indicate that seamless garments were associated with quality and status. In fact, this was the same type of construction used for the garments worn by the high priest in the temple. It was a mark of distinction, not poverty. The soldiers recognized its value immediately. Tearing it into four pieces would destroy it, leaving them with worthless scraps. So they gambled because this garment was worth winning whole.

Think about this from a practical standpoint. Roman soldiers crucified criminals regularly. They had seen every kind of clothing pass through their hands. They knew the difference between worthless rags and something valuable. Nobody gambles for garbage. Nobody stops the division of spoils to cast lots unless the item is worth the trouble. These hardened soldiers looked at Jesus' tunic and recognized that it was too valuable to destroy.

If Jesus had been dressed in the threadbare clothing of a beggar, the soldiers would have torn it apart without a second thought. But they didn't. They treated His garment as a prize worth competing for.

A Treasurer and a Thief

Here's a piece of evidence that should settle the question once and for all: Jesus had an accountant.

John 12:6 (NKJV) reveals this detail while exposing Judas' character: *"This he said, not that he cared for the poor, but because he was a thief, and had the money box* [bag]; *and he used to take what was put in it."*

Judas had the money box, or *"the bag"* as the King James cites. He was the keeper of the money, the treasurer of Jesus' ministry. He managed the finances, handled the funds, and kept track of what came in and what went out.

Now ask yourself a simple question: Why would anyone need a treasurer if there were no money to manage?

You don't appoint someone to manage an empty account. You don't assign a treasurer to oversee nothing. The very existence of a money bag presupposes that there was money in the bag. And this wasn't pocket change.

The Greek word used for the *bag* is *glossokomon* and referred to a container used to carry money or valuables. It was substantial enough to require someone dedicated to its management. Jesus didn't just have a few coins jingling in His pocket. He had a treasury.

The disciples regularly put money into this common fund. Supporters contributed to it. And from it, the ministry's expenses were paid, and gifts were given to the poor.

Judas Was Stealing and Nobody Noticed

We all know now that Judas was stealing from the bag—but here's the remarkable thing: nobody noticed! Think about that. If you only have a few dollars and someone steals from you, you know immediately. The money is gone and there's nothing left. But if someone is skimming from abundance, small amounts could disappear without anyone noticing.

Judas was able to steal regularly from the ministry funds without raising suspicion. That tells us something crucial about the amount of money involved. There was enough in the treasury that Judas could pilfer without the shortfall being obvious.

This is not the financial picture of a broke, struggling ministry barely scraping by. This is a ministry with enough resources that embezzlement went undetected.

The most revealing moment comes on the night Jesus was betrayed. At the Last Supper, Jesus told Judas, *"What you do, do quickly"* (John 13:27 NKJV). Judas got up and left. What did the other disciples assume was happening? John 13:29 (NKJV) tells us:

> *For some thought, because Judas had the money box, that Jesus had said to him, "Buy those things we need for the feast," or that he should give something to the poor.*

Do you see what this reveals? The disciples' first thought was that Judas was either going to make a purchase or give money to the poor. These were normal activities for their ministry. This was business as usual.

Jesus regularly sent Judas out to buy provisions. Jesus regularly gave money to the poor. This was so common, so routine, that when Judas left suddenly during the Passover meal, the disciples assumed it was just another errand to give away money.

A broke ministry doesn't send people out to buy things. A poor man doesn't have such a strong reputation for giving to the poor that it's the first explanation his followers think of.

JESUS THE PHILANTHROPIST

This detail alone demolishes the myth of a poor Jesus. He gave to the poor so consistently that His disciples expected it even at the most sacred meal of the Jewish calendar. Generosity wasn't occasional for Jesus. It was characteristic. It was expected. It was who He was. And you cannot give what you do not have.

We've established that Jesus had a treasury and regularly gave money to the poor. But Scripture goes even further. It describes Jesus' ministry with a word that leaves no doubt about His financial activity.

Acts 10:38 (NKJV) records Peter's summary of Jesus' life and ministry:

> *God anointed Jesus of Nazareth with the Holy Spirit and with power, who went about doing good and healing all who were oppressed by the devil, for God was with Him.*

People might read that phrase *"doing good"* and think of it in general terms. He was kind. He was helpful. He did nice things. But the Greek word used here tells a much more specific story.

The phrase *"doing good"* is translated from the Greek word *euergeteo*. This is not a generic word for being nice. It carries the specific meaning being a benefactor, being philanthropic, and doing good.

This is where we get our English word *philanthropy*. A philanthropist is not just someone who wishes others well. A philanthropist is someone who uses their financial resources to help people. In the ancient world, this word was specifically used to describe wealthy individuals who provided food, clothing, shelter, or other material assistance to those in need.

When Peter described Jesus' ministry, he chose this word. Jesus didn't just heal people. He didn't just preach to them. He met their physical and material needs. He was a philanthropist. He gave money away.

A philanthropist, by definition, is someone who has resources to give. You cannot financially support charitable works if you have no finances. You cannot meet the material needs of disadvantaged people if you have no material means.

Peter's description of Jesus as one who went about *"doing good"* in the philanthropic sense only makes sense if Jesus had money to distribute. And we already know that He did. He had a treasury. He had a treasurer. He sent Judas out to give to the poor so regularly that the disciples assumed that's what He was doing even at Passover.

Jesus was not poor. Jesus was a Giver. And there's a massive difference between the two.

Put it all together. Jesus had a money bag managed by a treasurer. He received costly gifts from wealthy supporters. He wore quality clothing. He had a home base in a lakefront community. He regularly distributed funds to the poor with such consistency that it was the expected activity of His ministry. This is not poverty.

You can only give from what you have. A poor man cannot be a philanthropist. A broke ministry cannot regularly give to the poor. The very fact that Jesus' giving was so characteristic, so expected, so routine, tells us that supply was never the issue.

Jesus modeled something the Church desperately needs to understand. He didn't hoard. He didn't store up treasure for Himself. But He did have resources, and He used them to bless others. True prosperity is not about accumulation; it's about circulation. It's about having enough that you can continuously give to every good work.

Jesus had that. And He demonstrated it throughout His entire ministry.

WERE THE DISCIPLES POOR?

We've looked at Jesus' financial situation throughout His ministry. But what about those who walked with Him? What about the 12 men who left everything to follow a wandering Rabbi? Surely they experienced poverty, right?

Jesus Himself asked them this very question. And their answer should shock anyone who believes that following Jesus means embracing lack.

In Luke 22:35 (NKJV), on the night before His crucifixion, Jesus turned to His disciples and asked: *"'When I sent you without money bag, knapsack, and sandals, did you lack anything?' So they said, 'Nothing.'"*

Let's set the scene. Jesus had sent the disciples out on ministry assignments with specific instructions. They were told not to take money, not to bring an extra bag, not to pack extra sandals. They went out with nothing but the clothes on their backs and the message in their mouths. By every natural calculation, they should have starved. They should have gone without. They should have come back gaunt, exhausted, and desperate. They had no resources, no provisions, no backup plan.

So Jesus asked them directly: "Did you lack anything?"

Their answer: "Nothing."

Nothing. Not one thing. Not a single need went unmet.

They went out empty-handed and lacked nothing. They traveled without money and still had everything they needed. Food appeared. Lodging was provided. Every necessity was covered. This is the testimony of the men who walked with Jesus daily for three years. These were eyewitnesses giving a firsthand account. When asked point-blank if they had ever lacked anything, their answer was absolute: Nothing.

This changes everything. Following Jesus didn't mean embracing poverty. It meant accessing supernatural provision. The disciples weren't poor. They were provided for. There's a critical difference. A poor man lacks what he needs. The disciples never lacked what they needed. Everything was supplied—every door opened; every meal appeared.

This is the economy of the Kingdom. When you're aligned with Jesus' purpose, provision follows. You don't have to worry. You don't have to scheme. You don't have to hoard. The Father knows what you need, and He provides it. *Fish come first!*

THE PATTERN FOR MINISTRY

Jesus sent His disciples out with nothing to prove a point. He wanted them to learn that their provision didn't come from their own resources. It came from the Father working through Kingdom connections and supernatural supply.

And it worked. Not once did they go hungry. Not once did they sleep in the streets. Not once did they lack anything necessary for the assignment.

This is the model for ministry. Not poverty. Not lack. Not barely scraping by. Just abundant provision flowing from Heaven to meet every need according to God's riches in glory. The disciples' testimony stands as proof. Those closest to Jesus, those who walked with Him through every season of ministry, could look back and say with absolute confidence—we lacked nothing.

If following Jesus meant embracing poverty, the disciples would have been the first to experience it—but they didn't. They experienced the opposite. They experienced provision without explanation and abundance without effort. That's the Kingdom of God in operation.

WHEN WAS JESUS POOR?

We've examined the evidence. Jesus had a house. He wore quality clothing. He had a treasury with a treasurer. He received costly gifts from the wealthy. He gave money to the poor so regularly that it was expected. His disciples testified that they lacked nothing during the years they walked with Him. Acts 10:38 describes Him as a philanthropist who went about meeting the material needs of disadvantaged people.

None of this is poverty.

So what do we do with 2 Corinthians 8:9? The verse clearly says He became poor. It clearly says He was rich. It clearly says His poverty was for our sake so that we might become rich. The verse is true. But we've been reading it wrong. The question isn't *whether* Jesus became poor; the question is *when.*

If Jesus were poor throughout His earthly life, we would expect to see evidence of it. We would expect empty pockets, hungry nights, and constant lack. We would expect His disciples to testify of hardship and scarcity. But we don't find that. We find the opposite.

Jesus lived well during His ministry. He had what He needed and more. He had enough to give away. He had enough that someone could steal from the treasury without anyone noticing. So His *"becoming poor"* cannot refer to His daily life. It must refer to something specific. Something targeted. Something substitutionary.

THE POVERTY OF THE CROSS

Look at the context of 2 Corinthians 8:9. Paul is urging the Corinthians to give sacrificially to meet the needs of suffering believers in Jerusalem. His argument is simple: look at what Jesus gave for you. Follow His example. And then he writes: *"Though he was rich, yet for your sakes he became poor, that ye through his poverty might become rich."*

This is substitutionary language. Jesus did something *for your sake* that transferred His condition to you. His poverty produced your wealth. His loss became your gain. Where else do we see this pattern in Scripture? Isaiah 53:5 says:

> *He was wounded for our transgressions, he was bruised for our iniquities: the chastisement of our peace was upon him; and with his stripes we are healed.*

His wounds. Our healing. His punishment. Our peace. His suffering. Our deliverance. This is the language of substitution. And it points to one place—the Cross.

There was nothing substitutionary about Jesus eating dinner in Capernaum. There was nothing redemptive about Him walking the roads of Galilee. His daily life was not the payment for our sin.

The payment happened in a specific window of time. It began in Gethsemane and culminated at Calvary. It was in those final hours when Jesus took upon Himself everything that belonged to us so that we could receive everything that belonged to Him.

In Gethsemane, Jesus sweat drops of blood as He faced what was coming. The weight of the world's sin began pressing down on Him. An innocent man was about to become guilty on our behalf.

At His arrest, He was bound like a criminal. The One who had set captives free was Himself taken captive. He who had healed the sick was dragged before corrupt courts. He who had spoken only truth was accused by liars.

At His scourging, His back was torn open by a Roman whip embedded with bone and metal. Isaiah 53:5 says, *"with his stripes we are healed."* Every lash that ripped His flesh was purchasing our healing. Every wound was absorbing our sickness. This was substitution. He took our infirmity so we could walk in health.

THE CROWN OF THORNS: THE CURSE OF POVERTY

And then came the crown. Matthew 27:29 tells us: "*And when they had platted a crown of thorns, they put it upon his head....*"

The soldiers meant it as mockery. They were ridiculing His claim to be a king. They twisted together thorns from a local bush and jammed them onto His skull, driving the spikes into His scalp, drawing blood from His brow. But God was doing something far deeper than the soldiers understood.

Go back to Genesis 3. After Adam sinned, God pronounced a curse. And in that curse, we find these words:

> *...cursed is the ground for thy sake; in sorrow shalt thou eat of it all the days of thy life; thorns also and thistles shall it bring forth to thee; and in the sweat of thy face shalt thou eat bread, till thou return unto the ground...* (Genesis 3:17-19).

Thorns and thistles. The sweat of your face. Toil, struggle, lack, and frustration. The ground that once cooperated with man now resisted him. The abundance of Eden gave way to the scarcity of a cursed earth. Thorns became the symbol of the curse. They represented everything that came with the fall: poverty, lack, exhausting labor, and fruitless effort. When you see thorns in Scripture, you see the curse of poverty.

And what did they press onto Jesus' head? A crown of thorns.

Where sweat ran down Adam's brow as he tried to coax provision from a cursed ground, blood ran down Jesus' brow, as He took the curse of poverty upon Himself. The crown of thorns was a divine transaction.

The thorns that had plagued humanity since Eden were pressed into the skull of the only Man who had never deserved them. He wore the symbol of the curse so that we wouldn't have to live under it.

This is when Jesus became poor. Not in Bethlehem. Not in Nazareth. Not in Capernaum. At Calvary.

The poverty of Jesus reached its fullness at the Cross. He was stripped of His clothing. He was stripped of His dignity. He was stripped of His disciples, who fled. He was stripped of His Father's presence, crying out: *"My God, my God, why hast thou forsaken me?"* (Matthew 27:46).

In those hours, Jesus had nothing. The One who owned the cattle on a thousand hills hung naked and alone. The One through whom all things were made had not even a place to rest His head on a wooden beam. This was poverty. Complete, total, absolute poverty.

And it was for a purpose.

> *Though he was rich, yet for your sakes he became poor, that ye through his poverty might become rich.*

He wore the thorns so you wouldn't have to. He took the curse so you could walk in blessing. He embraced total *poverty* in that moment so that you could access total *provision* for the rest of your life.

This is the great exchange. His poverty purchased your prosperity. His lack secured your abundance. His suffering at Calvary unlocked the storehouse of Heaven for everyone who would believe.

JESUS' POVERTY PURCHASED YOUR PROSPERITY

Don't waste it. What a shame it would be to waste what Jesus so graciously provided.

Jesus suffered for it. Gethsemane. The arrest. The mockery. The scourging. The thorns. The nails. The Cross. The separation from His Father. The weight of every sin ever committed crushing down on the only innocent Man who ever lived.

Jesus bled for it. Blood from His brow where the thorns pierced His skull. Blood from His back where the whip tore His flesh. Blood from His hands and feet where the spikes held Him to the wood. Blood and water from His side where the spear confirmed His death.

Jesus died for it. The Son of God breathed His last. The Creator of the universe hung lifeless on a Roman cross. The One who spoke worlds into existence fell silent in a borrowed tomb.

And Jesus rose for it. Three days later, the grave couldn't hold Him. Death couldn't keep Him. The curse was broken, the penalty was paid, and Jesus walked out of that tomb with all authority in Heaven and earth in His hands.

He did all of this so that you may be forgiven, saved, healed, and made rich. These riches far exceed the lesser form of wealth we call money, but it also includes it.

Now here's my question: What are you going to do with it?

Jesus wore the crown of thorns so you wouldn't have to live under the curse of poverty. He took the symbol of lack and struggle and frustration upon His own head. He bled where Adam sweated. He purchased your freedom from financial bondage.

What a shame it would be to ignore what was purchased for you. What a tragedy to keep living as if the curse were still in effect. What a waste of His suffering to embrace poverty as though it were godly. What an insult to His sacrifice to believe that lack is your portion when He bled to give you abundance.

He didn't wear those thorns for nothing. He didn't hang on that Cross so you could remain broke, defeated, and barely surviving. He endured the poverty so you wouldn't have to. He took the curse so you could walk in blessing.

Galatians 3:13-14 says:

> *Christ hath redeemed us from the curse of the law, being made a curse for us: for it is written, Cursed is every one that hangeth on a tree. That the blessing of Abraham might come on the Gentiles through Jesus Christ; that we might receive the promise of the Spirit through faith.*

Why did Jesus have to die on a cross? Why not a guillotine or a hanging? The entire purpose of the cross was to connect you to the blessing of Abraham!

Jesus became a curse. He absorbed it. He exhausted it. He defeated it.

And the curse included poverty. Read Deuteronomy 28. The blessings for obedience include abundance, overflow, lending and not borrowing, being the head and not the tail. The curses for disobedience include lack, scarcity, debt, and being consumed by enemies.

Jesus redeemed you from that curse. He paid the price. The transaction is complete.

You don't have to earn it. You can't earn it—He already paid for it. Your job is simply to receive it by faith and walk in it.

STOP APOLOGIZING FOR THE BLESSING

Was Jesus poor? Only in one moment, and it was for a purpose. At the Cross, He became poor. He took the curse. He wore the thorns. He was stripped of everything. And He did it all for you.

So stop apologizing for expecting God to bless you. Stop feeling guilty for wanting more than just enough. Stop treating poverty like a virtue and abundance like a vice. Jesus didn't suffer so you could remain under a curse He already broke.

Honor what He paid for. Receive it. Walk in it. Let the blessing flow through you to bless others. That's what He died for. That's what He rose for.

They may have lied to you about prosperity. But now you know the truth and the truth has made you free. Walk in it.

The lies end here, and the blessing begins now!

NOTES

1. "Report on the Economic Well-Being of U.S. Households," *Board of Governors of the Federal Reserve System*, 2023; https://www.federalreserve.gov/publications/2024-economic-well-being-of-us-households-in-2023-executive-summary.htm.
2. "Stress in America 2023," *American Psychological Association;* www.apa.org/news/press/releases/stress/2023/collective-trauma-recovery.
3. H6743, ṣālēaḥ, *Strong's Hebrew Lexicon (KJV);* www.blueletterbible.org/lexicon/h6743/kjv/wlc/0-1/.
4. H7919, śāḵal, *Strong's Hebrew Lexicon (KJV);* www.blueletterbible.org/lexicon/h7919/kjv/wlc/0-1/.
5. H7962, šalvâ, *Strong's Hebrew Lexicon (KJV);* www.blueletterbible.org/lexicon/h7962/kjv/wlc/0-1/.
6. G2137, euodoō, *Strongs Greek Lexicon;* https://www.blueletterbible.org/lexicon/g2137/web/tr/0-1/.
7. G4052, perisseuō, *Strong's Greek Lexicon (NKJV);* https://www.blueletterbible.org/lexicon/g4052/nkjv/tr/0-1/.
8. G841, autarkeia, *Strong's Greek Lexicon (KJV);* https://www.blueletterbible.org/lexicon/g841/kjv/lxx/0-1/.
9. G4149, ploutos, *Strong's Greek Lexicon (NIV);* https://www.blueletterbible.org/lexicon/g4149/niv/mgnt/0-1/.
10. H3519, kāḇôḏ, *Strong's Hebrew Lexicon(KJV);* https://www.blueletterbible.org/lexicon/h3519/kjv/wlc/0-1/.

11. Ibid.
12. Ibid.
13. "Poverty," *The World Bank;* https://www.worldbank.org/en/topic/poverty/overview.
14. "Working Poverty," *International Labour Organization;* https://www.ilo.org/global/topics/working-poverty/lang-en/index.htm.
15. "Global Multidimensional Poverty Index 2023," *United Nations Development Programme;* https://hdr.undp.org/content/2023-global-multidimensional-poverty-index-mpi.
16. "Looking to the Future, Public Sees an America in Decline on Many Fronts," *Pew Research Center,* March 2019; www.pewresearch.org/social-trends/2019/03/02/views-of-the-economic-system-and-social-safety-net.
17. "The State of Personal Finance in America Q3 2025," *Ramsey Research,* November 2025; www.ramseysolutions.com/company/newsroom.
18. "Research Statistic on Financial Windfalls and Bankruptcy," *National Endowment for Financial Education,* January 2018; www.nefe.org.
19. "No Longer A Coin Toss: Less Than Half Of Marriages Predicted To End In Divorce," *Institute for Family Studies,* July 2025; https://ifstudies.org.
20. "Fewer Churches Face Limited Cash Reserves," *Lifeway Research,* March 2023; www.christianitytoday.com.
21. "Global Wealth Report 2025," *UBS Media,* June 2025; www.ubs.com.
22. Ibid.
23. "The World's Billionaires List," *Forbes,* March 2025; www.forbes.com/billionaires.
24. "Giving USA 2023: The Annual Report on Philanthropy," *Giving USA Foundation,* 2023; https://givingusa.org.

25. "World Economic Outlook Database," *International Monetary Fund,* 2023; https://www.imf.org.
26. Richard Cavendish, "Latimer and Ridley Burned at the Stake," *History Today,* Vol 55, Issue 10, October 2005; https://www.historytoday.com/archive/months-past/latimer-and-ridley-burned-stake.
27. "Thomas Cranmer," *Wikipedia,* October 11, 2025, January 2 2026.
28. Mark Brooks, "What Happens If You Fail To Preach On Money," *Sermon Central,* June 26, 2021; https://sermoncentral.com/pastors-preaching-articles/mark-brooks-what-happens-if-you-fail-to-preach-on-money-1664.
29. "Pastors, Your People Need You to Preach on Money," *Christian Stewardship Network,* September 2024; https://www.christianstewardshipnetwork.com/blog/2020/9/24/mo3uqeieh02i5yope1mxv92fy2e928.
30. Ibid.
31. G627, apologia, *Strong's Greek Lexicon (KJV), Blue Letter Bible;* https://www.blueletterbible.org/lexicon/g627/kjv/tr/0-1/.
32. "Logical Fallacies: Definition, Types, List & Examples," *Scribbr,* October 9, 2023. https://www.scribbr.com/fallacies/logical-fallacy/.
33. "Informal Fallacy," *Wikipedia,* November 9, 2025.
34. Bradley Dowden, "Fallacies," *Internet Encyclopedia of Philosophy,* December 30, 2025; https://iep.utm.edu/fallacy/.
35. Ibid.
36. Lindsey Kramer, "15 Logical Fallacies to Know, With Definitions and Examples," *Grammarly,* April 10, 2023; www.grammarly.com/blog/rhetorical-devices/logical-fallacies/.
37. "Informal Fallacy," Wikipedia.
38. Lindsey Kramer, "15 Logical Fallacies to Know, With Definitions and Examples," *Grammarly.*
39. "Logical Fallacies," *Purdue Owl,* December 30, 2025; https://owl.purdue.edu/owl/general_writing/academic_writing/logic_in_argumentative_writing/fallacies.html.

40. "Logical Fallacies: Definition, Types, List & Examples," *Scribbr,* October 9, 2023.
41. "Logical Fallacies," *Purdue Owl,* December 30, 2025.
42. "Informal Fallacy," *Wikipedia,* November 9, 2025.
43. "Logical Fallacies," *Philosophical Society.com,* December 30, 2025; www.philosophicalsociety.com/HTML/LogicalFallacies.html.
44. "Sola scriptura," *Wikipedia,* December 27, 2025.
45. "Logical Fallacies," *Purdue Owl,* December 30, 2025.
46. "On the Jews and Their Lies," *Wikipedia,* November 7, 2025.
47. Martin Luther, "On the Jews and Their Lies" (1543) *Luther's Works, Vol. 47* (Fortress Press, 1971), 137.
48. Eric W. Gritsch, "Was Luther anti-Semitic?" *Christian History Institute,* December 30 2025; https://christianhistoryinstitute.org/magazine/article/was-luther-anti-semitic.
49. Noam Marans, "On Luther and His Lies," *American Jewish Committee,* October 3, 2019; www.ajc.org/news/on-luther-and-his-lies.
50. Ibid.
51. Emily Paras, "The Darker Side of Martin Luther," *Constructing the Past,* Vol. 9: Issue 1, Article 4, 2008, p. 8; https://digitalcommons.iwu.edu/constructing/vol9/iss1/4.
52. "On the Jews and Their Lies," *Wikipedia,* November 7, 2025.
53. "Luther's Canon," *Wikipedia,* November 17, 2025.
54. Martin Luther, "Luther's Antilegomena," in *Luther's Works, Vol. 35.* (Concordia, 1963), 395-399; www.bible-researcher.com/antilegomena.html.
55. Ibid.
56. Ibid.
57. Ibid.
58. "Luther's Canon," *Wikipedia,* November 17, 2025.
59. Ibid.

60. Mark Talbot, "The Servetus Affair: The Story of Calvin and His Critics," *Desiring God,* September 26, 2009; https://www.desiringgod.org/articles/the-servetus-affair.
61. "Michael Servetus," *Wikipedia,* December 24, 2025.
62. Mark Talbot, "The Servetus Affair: The Story of Calvin and His Critics" *Desiring God.*
63. Philip Schaff, *History of the Christian Church,* citing Galiffe; Beggars All Reformation & Apologetics, June 19, 2019; https://beggarsallreformation.blogspot.com/2019/06/john-calvin-had-58-people-executed-in.html.
64. Ibid.
65. Michael Frost, "7 Broken Men: John Calvin," *mikefrost.net,* November 3, 2016; https://mikefrost.net/7-broken-men-john-calvin/
66. Jim McClarty, "Was John Calvin a Murderer?" *Salvation By Grace,* December 3, 2014; https://salvationbygrace.org/current-qa/john-calvin-a-murderer/.
67. "Geneva Witch Trials," *Wikipedia,* November 25, 2025.
68. "List of fallacies," Wikipedia, December 26, 2025.
69. "Logical Fallacies," *Philosophical Society.com,* December 30, 2025; https://www.philosophicalsociety.com/HTML/LogicalFallacies.html.
70. Ibid.
71. "Logical Fallacies," *Purdue Owl,* December 30, 2025.
72. Ibid.
73. "Logical Fallacies," Philosophical Society.com.
74. "Giving USA 2024: The Annual Report on Philanthropy for the Year 2023," *Giving USA Foundation,* 2024.
75. "Who Gives Most to Charity?" *The Philanthropy Roundtable,* December 30, 2025; www.philanthropyroundtable.org.
76. Caleb Maglaya Galaraga, "Lausanne Report: Most Missionaries Are Reaching the Reached," *Christianity Today,* September 25, 2024.

77. Anup Malani and Tomas J. Philipson, "The Regulation of Medical Products," *University of Chicago Law School,* 2012.
78. Kevin Gardner and Kinch, Michael, "The Astounding U.S. University Impact on Drug Innovation" *STAT-News,* June 6, 2025; https://www.statnews.com/2025/06/06/us-universities-fda-approved-drugs-research-patents-orange-book/.
79. Karl Marx and Friedrich Engels, *The Communist Manifesto*, 1848.
80. Gustavo Gutiérrez, A Theology of Liberation: History, Politics, and Salvation (Orbis Books, 1971, 1973, 1988. (Original Spanish: Teología de la liberación: Perspectivas, 1971.)
81. Ion Mihai Pacepa, "Russian Footprints: What does Moscow have to do with the new endeavor to transform America into a socialist country?" *National Review*, August 24, 2009.
82. "The 'Demonarchization' of the Ecclesiastical Authorities," *Nobility.com,* May 5, 2022.
83. Gustavo Gutiérrez, *A Theology of Liberation: History, Politics, and Salvation.*
84. Congregation for the Doctrine of the Faith (Cardinal Joseph Ratzinger, Prefect), "Instruction on Certain Aspects of the Theology of Liberation," *Vatican City,* August 6, 1984.
85. Ducksters, "Middle Ages: Feudal System and Feudalism," *Technological Solutions, Inc.;* www.ducksters.com/history/middle_ages_feudal_system.php.
86. "Medieval Abusive Wealth: Power, Exploitation, and Corruption," *Brewminate,* July 7, 2025; https://brewminate.com/medieval-abusive-wealth-the-role-of-power-exploitation-and-corruption/
87. "Middle Ages: Feudal System and Feudalism," *Technological Solutions, Inc.*
88. Elaine Graham-Leigh, "The Catholic Church Has Always Been a Worldly Institution," *Jocobin,* https://jacobin.com/2025/05/catholic-church-feudalism-class-exploitation.

89. Gene Edward Veith, "How the Protestant Reformation Renewed the Church, Our Work, and Society," *Institute for Faith, Work & Economics,* October 24, 2017; https://tifwe.org/how-the-protestant-reformation-renewed-the-church-our-work-and-society/.
90. Max Weber, *The Protestant Ethic and the Spirit of Capitalism* (Originally published 1905. Revised edition: Oxford University Press, 2011).
91. Roger B. Hill, *History of Work Ethic: Protestantism and the Protestant Ethic* (University of Georgia, College of Education, 1992, 1996); http://workethic.coe.uga.edu/hpro.html.
92. Alister McGrath, "Calvin and the Christian Calling," *First Things,* June 1, 1999; https://www.firstthings.com/article/1999/06/calvin-and-the-christian-calling.
93. Roger Schultz,"Direction for Life: Calvin's Concept of Calling," *Chalcedon Foundation,* January 1, 2004; https://chalcedon.edu/resources/articles/direction-for-life-calvins-concept-of-calling.
94. Jesse Wisnewski, "The Protestant Work Ethic: How a 500-Year-Old Idea Still Shapes Our World"; www.jessewisnewski.co/article/protestant-work-ethic.
95. Benjamin Hart, *Faith and Freedom: The Christian Roots of American Liberty* (Lewis and Stanley, 1988).
96. Leonard E. Read, "I, Pencil: My Family Tree as Told to Leonard E. Read," *Foundation for Economic Education,* December 1958; https://fee.org/resources/i-pencil/.
97. "The Constitution of the United States: A Transcription," *National Archives,* Article I, Section 8, Clause 8; US National Archives and Records Administration, December 31 2025; www.archives.gov/founding-docs/constitution-transcript.
98. Bao Tran, "US Patent Statistics: Key Trends and Insights," *PatentPC,* January 27, 2026; https://patentpc.com/blog/us-patent-statistics-key-trends-and-insights.

99. Robert Kneller, "The Importance of New Companies for Drug Discovery: Origins of a Decade of New Drugs," *Nature Reviews Drug Discovery* 9 (2010), 867-882.

100. Kevin Gardner and Michael Finch, "The Astounding U.S. University Impact On Drug Innovation," *STAT News,* June 6, 2025; https://www.statnews.com/2025/06/06/us-universities-fda-approved-drugs-research-patents-orange-book/.

101. "United States: #4 in the 2020 World Index of Healthcare Innovation," *Foundation for Research on Equal Opportunity*, September 4, 2020; https://freopp.org/united-states-health-system-profile-4-in-the-world-index-of-healthcare-innovation/.

102. Thomas Sowell, *Controversial Essays* (Hoover Institution Press, 2002).

103. Thomas Sowell, "Thomas Sowell on 'The Real Public Service,'" *AEI,* June 1, 2010; accessed December 30, 2025.

104. Thomas Sowell, "Sowell: The Welfare State Is Doing Its Beneficiaries No Favors," *The Columbian,* June 7, 2016.

105. Thomas Sowell, "Barbarians Inside the Gates and Other Controversial Essays," *Hoover Institution Press,* January 1, 1999.

106. Milton Friedman, *Capitalism and Freedom* (University of Chicago Press, 1962, 2002).

107. "Norman Borlaug," Wikipedia, November 30, 2025.

108. "Happy Birthday Thomas Sowell - Top 11 Sowell Quotes for Conservative Activists," *Young America's Foundation,* September 8, 2023; https://yaf.org/news/happy-birthday-thomas-sowell-top-11-sowell-quotes-for-conservative-activists/.

109. "The Historic Choice," *Margaret Thatcher Foundation,* Speech to Conservative Central Council, March 20, 1976; www.margaretthatcher.org/document/102990.

110. Caleb Maglaya Galaraga, "Lausanne Report: Most Missionaries Are Reaching the Reached," *Christianity Today,* September 25, 2024.

111. "Giving USA 2024: The Annual Report on Philanthropy for the Year 2023," *Giving USA Foundation,* 2024.
112. "Missions Statistics: Money and Missions," *The Traveling Team;* https://www.thetravelingteam.org/stats.
113. Bob Ditmer, "America's Economy (and social programs): Fueled by Faith," *Church Leaders,* July 25, 2018.
114. "2024 Charitable Giving Statistics, Trends & Data," *Nonprofits Source,* July 23, 2024; https://nonprofitssource.com/online-giving-statistics/
115. "What Is A UPG?" *Global Frontier Missions,* December 30, 2025; https://www.globalfrontiermissions.org/missions-101/the-unreached-peoples-and-their-role-in-the-great-commission.
116. "2025 Christian Missionary Statistics," *Nations Outreach,* April 12, 2025; https://nationsoutreach.org/blog/christian-missionary-statistics/.
117. Rakesh Kochhar and Stella Sechopolous, "How the American Middle Class Has Changed in the Past Five Decades," *Pew Research Center,* April 20, 2022; https://www.pewresearch.org/short-reads/2022/04/20/how-the-american-middle-class-has-changed-in-the-past-five-decades/.
118. Ibid.
119. Ibid.

ABOUT ALAN DIDIO

Pastor Alan DiDio is the host of *Revival Nation* and the founder of Revival Nation Church. In more than two decades of ministry, he has traveled internationally working with the persecuted Church around the world and directed an international prayer center where he prayed one-on-one with more than 100,000 people. This unique experience comes out in his writings and ministry as he seeks to ignite the fire of God in the hearts of humanity and equip end-time believers for the next great awakening.

Alan DiDio was an avowed atheist—that is until he had a transforming, radical encounter with the living God at age 17. After giving his life to Christ, Pastor Alan attended a Christian college and began working with an international ministry, where he gained experience in every possible area of ministry from running a prayer center to traveling across the country spreading the gospel.

He has since launched Encounter Ministries with the new emphasis and branding of Revival Nation.

To connect with Pastor Alan, visit: www.RevivalNation.com